D1002877

Descartes's *Meditations on First Philosophy*, published in Latin in 1641, is one of the most widely studied philosophical texts of all time, and inaugurates many of the key themes that have remained central to philosophy ever since. In his original Latin text Descartes expresses himself with great lucidity and elegance, and there is enormous interest, even for those who are not fluent in Latin, in seeing how the famous concepts and arguments of his great masterpiece unfold in the original language. John Cottingham's acclaimed English translation of the work is presented here in a facing-page edition alongside the original Latin text. Students of classical philosophy have long had the benefit of dual-language editions, and the availability of such a resource for the canonical works of the early-modern period is long overdue. This volume now makes available, in an invaluable dual-language format, one of the most seminal texts of Western philosophy.

JOHN COTTINGHAM is Professor Emeritus of Philosophy at the University of Reading, Professorial Research Fellow at Heythrop College, University of London, and an Honorary Fellow of St John's College, Oxford. He is co-editor and translator of the standard English edition of the *Philosophical Writings of Descartes* (1991), and editor of the *Cambridge Companion to Descartes* (1992), and his own books in this area include *Descartes* (1986), *The Rationalists* (1997), and *Cartesian Reflections* (2008). He has also published extensively in the fields of moral philosophy and philosophy of religion.

RENÉ DESCARTES

MEDITATIONS ON FIRST PHILOSOPHY

With Selections from the Objections and Replies

A LATIN–ENGLISH EDITION

EDITED AND TRANSLATED
WITH TEXTUAL AND PHILOSOPHICAL INTRODUCTIONS
BY
JOHN COTTINGHAM

CAMBRIDGE
UNIVERSITY PRESS

CAMBRIDGE
UNIVERSITY PRESS

University Printing House, Cambridge CB2 8BS, United Kingdom

Cambridge University Press is part of the University of Cambridge.

It furthers the University's mission by disseminating knowledge in the pursuit of education, learning and research at the highest international levels of excellence.

www.cambridge.org
Information on this title: www.cambridge.org/9781107576353

© John Cottingham 2013

This publication is in copyright. Subject to statutory exception and to the provisions of relevant collective licensing agreements, no reproduction of any part may take place without the written permission of Cambridge University Press.

First published 2013
First paperback edition 2015

A catalogue record for this publication is available from the British Library

Library of Congress Cataloguing in Publication data
Descartes, René, 1596–1650.
Meditations on first philosophy : with selections from the objections and replies :
a Latin-English edition / René Descartes ; edited and translated with textual and philosophical
introductions by John Cottingham.
pages cm
Includes index.
ISBN 978-0-521-19138-8 (hardback)
1. First philosophy.   2. God – Proof, Ontological.   3. Methodology.   4. Knowledge, Theory of.
I. Cottingham, John, 1943–   II. Descartes, René, 1596–1650. Meditationes de prima philosophia.
III. Descartes, René, 1596–1650. Meditationes de prima philosophia. English.   IV. Title.
B1853.E5C68   2012
194 – dc23   2012049256

ISBN 978-0-521-19138-8 Hardback
ISBN 978-1-107-57635-3 Paperback

Cambridge University Press has no responsibility for the persistence or accuracy of URLs for external or third-party internet websites referred to in this publication, and does not guarantee that any content on such websites is, or will remain, accurate or appropriate.

Contents

v

Philosophical introduction
The Meditations *and Cartesian philosophy*

Descartes's *Meditations on First Philosophy*[1] is, indisputably, one of the greatest philosophical classics of all time. The challenge it offers is in many ways definitive of the philosophical enterprise: to leave behind the comfortable world of inherited prejudice and preconceived opinion; to take nothing for granted in the determination to achieve secure and reliable knowledge. Descartes talks of 'demolish[ing] everything completely and start[ing] again right from the foundations',[2] and for this purpose he famously uses doubt, stretched to its limits, as an instrument which self-destructs, impelling him forwards on the journey towards certainty and truth. These central themes are today part of every introductory course in the philosophy of knowledge: Descartes's masterpiece has achieved canonical status in that part of the philosophy syllabus we now call 'epistemology'. Yet for Descartes himself these epistemic concerns were but one part of a much wider project: the construction of a grand, all-embracing system of philosophy which would encompass metaphysics, natural science, psychology and morals, connecting all the objects within the scope of human understanding. In the words of the famous metaphor which he deployed some six years after the publication of the *Meditations*, 'the whole of philosophy is like a tree. The roots are metaphysics, the trunk is physics, and the branches . . . all the other sciences.'[3]

---

[1] The present introduction to the work, and the English translation of the *Meditations* and *Objections and Replies* that follows, are based, with modifications and additions, on those found in René Descartes, *Meditations on First Philosophy with Selections from the Objections and Replies*, trans. and ed. J. Cottingham (Cambridge: Cambridge University Press, rev. edn, 1996).

[2] See the opening paragraph of the First Meditation, pp. 22–3 below.

[3] *Principles of Philosophy*, Preface to the French Edition of 1647 (AT IXB 14: CSM I 186). Throughout the present volume, 'AT' refers to the standard Franco-Latin edition of Descartes by C. Adam and P. Tannery, *Œuvres de Descartes*, rev. edn (12 vols., Paris: Vrin/CNRS, 1964–76); 'CSM' refers to the English translation by J. Cottingham, R. Stoothoff and D. Murdoch, *The Philosophical Writings of Descartes*, vols. I and II (Cambridge: Cambridge University Press,

Descartes spent much of his career occupied with what we would nowadays call theoretical physics: he devised a radical new theory of the nature of matter, defined simply as extension in three dimensions, and formulated a number of mathematical laws describing the results of collisions of moving particles of matter. He then proposed to apply these principles to a wide variety of subjects, from cosmology and astronomy to physiology and medicine; and towards the end of his life he planned to include a science of man, which would develop prescriptions for how to understand and control the workings of our bodies, and how to live fulfilled and worthwhile lives. Examining the course of Descartes's life, and the context in which the *Meditations* was written, helps us deepen our understanding of the metaphysical and epistemological themes of his most famous book by seeing how they fit into the broader philosophical system which he devoted his life to creating.

THE SHAPING OF A PHILOSOPHER

René Descartes was born in France on 31 March 1596 in the small town of La Haye (now renamed 'Descartes'), some fifty kilometres south of Tours. Not a very great deal is known of his early life, but it seems likely that his childhood was not a particularly happy one. His health was poor, and he appears not to have got on very well with his father, Joachim, who was often away discharging his duties as Counsellor at the Parliament of Brittany. Relations between the two in later life were certainly strained, and when René sent his father a copy of his first published book the father's only reported reaction was that he was displeased to have a son 'idiotic enough to have himself bound in vellum'.[4] Descartes's mother died, in childbirth, a year after his own birth,[5] and he was looked after by his maternal grandmother until, at the age of ten, he was sent away as a boarding pupil to the recently founded Jesuit college of La Flèche in Anjou, where he remained for eight or nine years. During Descartes's time there the school was steadily building up a reputation for excellence (he later

1985) and 'CSMK' to vol. III, *The Correspondence*, by the same translators and A. Kenny (Cambridge: Cambridge University Press, 1991).

[4] Cf. AT XII 7, 8, and 433–4.

[5] Despite what the philosopher himself told a correspondent (letter to Elizabeth of May or June 1645, AT IV 220–1: CSMK 250–1), it was not René's own birth that cost his mother her life, but that of a younger brother (who lived only three days); see G. Rodis-Lewis, 'Descartes' Life and the Development of his Philosophy', in J. Cottingham (ed.), *The Cambridge Companion to Descartes* (Cambridge: Cambridge University Press, 1992), p. 23.

described it as 'one of the most famous schools in Europe');[6] pupils followed a comprehensive curriculum which included classical literature and traditional classics-based subjects such as history and rhetoric, as well as, in the senior years, higher mathematics and philosophy. The approach to philosophy taken by Descartes's teachers belonged to what we now know as the 'scholastic' tradition; that is to say, it was based on broadly Aristotelian principles, adapted in an attempt to make them consistent with the demands of Christian orthodoxy, and elaborated over many centuries by a host of learned commentators. Descartes's teachers at La Flèche would have been well versed in such commentaries, and would also have made use of compendious textbooks like the *Summa philosophiae quadripartita*, a four-part treatise by a noted contemporary Scholastic, Eustachius a Sancto Paulo, which provided a complete philosophical system, including logic, metaphysics, moral philosophy and 'natural philosophy' or physics.[7] Descartes was not impressed with the philosophy he learned at school, and later wrote that the subject, despite being 'cultivated for many centuries by the most excellent minds', contained no point which was not 'disputed and hence doubtful'. The 'shaky foundations' of the traditional system meant, in his view, that all the specific sciences built on them were equally suspect.[8]

In 1610, about halfway through Descartes's time at La Flèche, the College marked the death of its founder, Henry IV, with a series of grand observances, including the reciting of poems, one of which hailed the recent discovery by Galileo of the moons of Jupiter (which 'brightened the gloom of the King's death').[9] We do not know what part if any Descartes played in these ceremonies (though some have suggested that he was the author of the poem honouring Galileo); what is certain is that Galileo's discovery came in due course to be widely acknowledged as strong experimental support for the new Copernican cosmology, dethroning the earth from its privileged place at the centre of the universe – a shift which, more than any other, has subsequently come to be seen as central to the philosophical and scientific revolution of the early-modern period. Descartes himself was to become a convinced if cautious adherent of the new heliocentric model, and his own scientific career was to intertwine, at a crucial point, with that of Galileo.

---

[6] *Discourse on the Method*, Part One (AT VI 5: CSM I 113).
[7] The *Summa philosophiae quadripartita* was published in 1609. For more on Eustachius, and on some of the commentaries on Aristotle which Descartes may have read at La Flèche, see R. Ariew, 'Descartes and Scholasticism', in Cottingham, *Cambridge Companion to Descartes*, pp. 74ff.
[8] See *Discourse*, Part One (AT VI 8: CSM I 115).
[9] See Rodis-Lewis, 'Descartes' Life', p. 26, and AT XII 29.

By his late thirties Descartes had produced a comprehensive treatise on cosmology and physics, *Le Monde* ('The World' or 'The Universe'), which applied reductive mechanical principles to the explanation of a wide variety of celestial and terrestrial phenomena; in the course of the work (though carefully insisting that it was an account of how things *might* have evolved in an imaginary universe) he places the sun at the centre of the planetary system.[10] But on hearing of the condemnation of Galileo by the Inquisition for advocating the heliocentric hypothesis, Descartes decided to withdraw his own treatise from publication. 'I desire to live in peace', he wrote to his friend and chief correspondent, Marin Mersenne.[11]

The cautious and reclusive attitude which became typical of Descartes's middle years was in some respects at odds with the rather more active and outgoing life he pursued in his twenties. After taking a law degree at Poitiers, at the age of twenty-two Descartes went to Holland and enrolled in the army of Prince Maurice of Nassau; this was the prelude for a series of travels in Europe, inspired by the resolve, as Descartes later put it, 'to seek no knowledge other than that which could be found in myself or else in the great book of the world'.[12] The comment suggests that his motive for choosing the soldier's life was the prospect for travel it offered, though in later life he commented acidly that the chief attraction of a military career for the young was the opportunity it provided for 'idleness and debauchery'.[13] At all events, the most significant result of his initial journey to Holland was the friendship Descartes formed with the Dutch mathematician Isaac Beeckman, whom he met accidentally in 1618. Beeckman made Descartes party to a number of projects on which he was working in pure and applied mathematics, and was described by Descartes in terms reminiscent of those later used by Immanuel Kant when he acknowledged Hume as the one who had roused him from his 'dogmatic slumbers'. 'You alone', Descartes wrote to Beeckman in 1619, 'roused me from my state of indolence'; in another letter, he spoke of the 'gigantic task' which, inspired by Beeckman's ideas, he had set himself: that of devising a method which would provide 'a general solution of all possible equations involving any sort of quantity'.[14] Descartes continued to work on arithmetic, algebra and geometry (and the relationship between them) for much of the following decade, and it was to become a central theme of his later philosophy that mathematics possessed the kind of precision

---

[10] See *Le Monde*, ch. 10 (AT XI 69–70).   [11] Letter of April 1634 (AT I 285–6: CSMK 43).
[12] *Discourse*, Part One (AT VI 9: CSM I 115).
[13] Letter to Pollot of 1648 (AT V 557: CSMK 359).
[14] Letters of 23 April and 26 March 1619 (AT X 163, 157–8: CSMK 4, 2–3).

and certainty which the traditional philosophy he had learnt at school conspicuously lacked. Mathematics was a paradigm of what Descartes came to call *scientia* – genuine and systematic knowledge based on reliable principles.

Descartes's earliest work, the *Compendium musicae*, written in 1618 and dedicated to Beeckman, applied quantitative principles to the study of musical harmony and dissonance. But the wider significance which mathematical reasoning later came to have for Descartes consisted in its being a model for all human understanding: 'Those long chains composed of very simple and easy reasonings, which geometers customarily use to arrive at their most difficult demonstrations, had given me occasion to suppose that all the things which fall within the scope of human knowledge are interconnected in the same way.'[15] This ambitious vision of a new model for the sciences was probably shaped and nurtured over a number of years, but according to Descartes himself it took root in his mind after an extraordinary experience which occurred during his European travels.

On 10 November 1619 Descartes found himself closeted in a 'stove-heated room' (*poêle*) in a town in southern Germany, where, after a day of intense meditation, he fell asleep and had a series of three strikingly vivid dreams. In the first, he was assailed by phantoms and a violent whirlwind, took refuge in a college, where he tried to reach the chapel, and was greeted by a friend who gave him a present which he took to be 'melon brought from a foreign country'. As he woke up he felt a sharp pain in his side which made him fear that an 'evil demon was trying to deceive' him; such was the sense of dread produced by the dream that he lay awake for several hours. In the second dream he heard a terrible noise like a thunderclap, and saw a shower of bright sparks, whereupon he awoke at once, still in a state of terror. The last and most complex dream involved the appearance and disappearance of various books on a table: first an encyclopaedia, which he thought might be 'very useful' to him; then an anthology of poetry containing the Pythagorean motto for truth and falsity, *Est et non*, and an ode of Ausonius beginning *Quod vitae sectabor iter?* ('What road in life shall I follow?'); and finally (after a long dialogue with a stranger about the contents of the books) the encyclopaedia again, this time incomplete. As he began to wake up, he immediately started interpreting the dream, the most significant feature being the encyclopaedia, which he took for a symbol of 'how the sciences are linked together'. The upshot of this

---

[15] *Discourse*, Part Two (AT VI 19: CSM I 120).

night of troubled visions was that Descartes became convinced that his own life's journey should be devoted to completing the 'encyclopaedia': his mission was to found a new and comprehensive philosophical and scientific system.[16]

THE DEVELOPMENT OF DESCARTES'S METHODOLOGY

Returning to Paris after his travels, Descartes began work on a treatise in Latin entitled *Regulae ad directionem ingenii*, the *Rules for the Direction of our Native Intelligence*. Though never completed (and never published during his lifetime), the *Regulae* inaugurates the project, glimpsed in Descartes's dream, of founding a universal scientific system. The inspiration, as with so much of his work (particularly so during this early period), is mathematical, and much of the book is concerned with devising of 'rules' or methods for the solution of problems in arithmetic and geometry. But Descartes pointedly observes that he 'would not value these Rules so highly if they were good only for solving those pointless problems with which arithmeticians and geometers are inclined to while away their time'. He goes on to speak of a general discipline that contains the 'rudiments of human reason' and can 'extend to the discovery of truths in any field whatever': 'there must be a general science which explains all the points that can be raised concerning order and measure irrespective of the subject-matter'.[17] The tool for the discovery of such truths would not be a study of traditional methods and authorities, but, instead, the ordinary 'native intelligence' of each individual: the simple and clear perceptions of the intellect, uncluttered by considerations of 'what other people have thought or what we ourselves conjecture'.[18]

This vision of how to proceed in philosophy remained Descartes's guiding principle when he came to write the *Meditations*, over ten years later. In the *Regulae*, Descartes uses the term 'intuition' (in Latin *intuitus*) for the kind of reliable cognition he is seeking – a word which suggests looking directly at something, a kind of straightforward inspection or vision (though of a purely intellectual, not an ocular, kind):

---

[16] The dreams are described in some detail by A. Baillet (*La Vie de Monsieur Des-Cartes*, Paris: Horthemels, 1691; photographic reprint Hildesheim: Olms, 1972, vol. I, pp. 81ff.), but some of his embellishments are almost certainly apocryphal; see Rodis-Lewis, 'Descartes' Life' (pp. 30–2). Fragments which have survived from Descartes's own early notebooks provide more reliable, if somewhat sparse, information. See CSM I 2ff.

[17] *Regulae*, Rule Four (AT X 374, 378: CSM I 17, 19).

[18] Ibid., Rule Three (AT X 366: CSM I 13).

By 'intuition' I do not mean the fluctuating testimony of the senses or the deceptive judgement of the imagination as it botches things together, but the conception of a clear and attentive mind, which is so easy and distinct that there can be no room for doubt about what we are understanding. Alternatively, and this comes to the same thing, intuition is the indubitable conception of a clear and attentive mind which proceeds solely from the light of reason.[19]

The 'light of reason' (*lux rationis*) which is invoked in this passage (and which reappears in the *Meditations* and elsewhere as the 'natural light') has a long ancestry. Plato, in the *Republic* (*c.* 380 BC), had used the simile of the sun to describe the Form of the Good which makes manifest the objects of abstract intellectual cognition (just as the sun sheds light on ordinary visible objects). In St John's Gospel (*c.* AD 100), the *Logos*, the 'Word' or divine creative intelligence, is identified with 'the Light that lighteth every man coming into the world' (1:9). And Augustine, in the *De Trinitate* (*c.* 410), welding together Platonic and Christian ideas, asserts that 'the mind, when directed to intelligible things in the natural order, according to the disposition of the Creator, sees them in a certain incorporeal light which has a nature all of its own, just as the body's eye sees nearby objects in the ordinary light'.[20] Descartes certainly shares with Platonic and Augustinian 'rationalism' a distrust of the 'fluctuating testimony' of the senses, and a belief in the pure inner light of the intellect as a vastly more reliable source of knowledge than anything which is received from the external world via the sensory organs.[21] This rationalist perspective remains strikingly present in the way the argument of the *Meditations* was later developed. And beyond this there is the deeper theological dimension (though this aspect tends to be played down by many modern commentators): Descartes's faith in the reliability of the intellectual light comes to be closely linked, in his later metaphysics, with the fact that it is bestowed on us by God, the source of all truth. Our own route to secure knowledge is, ultimately, illuminated by the 'immense light' proceeding from the perfect divine nature, and shining, albeit with diminished scope, in each individual mind.[22]

Back in the late 1620s, however, the relationship between the divine nature and the attainment of reliable human knowledge was an issue that

---

[19] Ibid. (AT X 368: CSM I 14).   [20] *De Trinitate* XII xv 24. Cf. Plato, *Republic* 514–18.

[21] Though he is very much *not* the caricature 'rationalist' who holds that there is no role whatever for the senses in the development of science: see *Discourse*, Part Six (AT VI 65: CSM I 144).

[22] For the immensity of the divine light, see the resounding final paragraph of the Third Meditation, pp. 72–3. For the limited scope of the natural light within the individual soul, see the Fourth Meditation, pp. 83–5.

Descartes had probably not examined in any detail. Despite the underlying theological implications of the notion of the 'light of reason', his early work in the *Rules for the Direction of our Native Intelligence* contains little if any metaphysical argument, and tends instead to proceed as if epistemology and methodology are relatively self-standing and self-contained disciplines capable of providing an autonomous route to 'certain and evident cognition'.[23] We know, however, that Descartes had at least begun to work on metaphysics around this time, since a letter to Marin Mersenne mentions a 'little treatise' started in 1629, soon after he had decided to leave France to take up permanent residence in Holland. The 'little treatise' (now lost) aimed to prove 'the existence of God and of our souls when they are separate from the body';[24] but the work was laid aside, and Descartes did not come back to a full treatment of these issues until the late 1630s.

The reasons for Descartes's self-imposed exile from his native land have been much disputed. He certainly complained of the 'innumerable distractions' of Paris,[25] but though many of his residences in Holland were in secluded country locations, he was not wholly averse to town life (soon after arriving he took lodgings in the bustling city of Amsterdam). It has been suggested that he hoped the Netherlands would provide a more tolerant and free-thinking atmosphere for the reception of his 'modern' views on physics and cosmology; but in the event his philosophical views provoked as much controversy and hostility from Protestant Dutch academics as any he might have expected from Catholic scholars in France. Most likely, Descartes experienced (at least at first) that sense of freedom and release which many expatriates discover on moving away from the culture in which they were born and brought up; the 'masked man', as Descartes had earlier called himself, spoke in his first (anonymously) published work of his pleasure at living amidst a mass of busy people 'more concerned with their own affairs than curious about those of others'.[26]

The main preoccupations of Descartes during the early and middle 1630s were scientific. His treatise on physics, *Le Monde* (already mentioned above), was completed by 1633. It contained a complete description of the origins and workings of the physical universe in accordance with the 'laws

---

[23] AT X 362: CSM I 10.   [24] AT I 182: CSMK 29.
[25] Letter to Mersenne of 27 May 1638 (AT II 151–2).
[26] *Discourse*, Part Three (AT VI 31: CSM I 126). The image of the 'masked man' (*larvatus*) occurs in one of Descartes's early notebooks probably composed during his travels in Europe during the years 1619–22: 'Actors, taught not to let any embarrassment show on their faces, put on a mask. I will do the same. So far, I have been a spectator in this theatre which is the world; but I am now about to mount the stage, and I come forward masked' (AT X 213: CSM I 2).

of mechanics', and a concluding section, known as the *Traité de l'homme* (*Treatise on Man*), supplied an account of human physiology employing the self-same mechanical principles. Descartes had a keen interest in physiology (which stayed with him all his life), and when he lived in Kalverstraat ('Calf Street') in Amsterdam he made a habit of collecting carcases from the butcher for dissection. His approach to the processes and functions of the living human body was strongly reductionistic: the body was essentially a 'machine', which, like 'clocks, artificial fountains and mills', has the power to operate purely in accordance with its own internal principles, depending 'solely on the disposition of our organs'.[27] Cartesian physiology and biology entirely dispenses with the traditional Scholastic apparatus that had tried to explain such functions as movement, digestion and sensation by appeal to the operation of the so-called locomotive, nutritive and sensory 'souls'. In Descartes's programme for science, mechanism replaces psychism, and the workings of the animal, and indeed human, organism become no different, in principle, from the workings of any other material structure in the universe; all is to be explained purely in terms of size, shape and motion of the component parts. Only in the case of *thought* does Descartes find it necessary to have recourse to a 'rational soul' (*âme raisonable*), specially created by God and 'united' to the complex machinery of the human body.[28]

By 1637, Descartes was ready to publish three 'specimen essays' illustrating his new scientific method. The first was the *Optics* (*La Dioptrique*), which applied mathematical and mechanical principles to the explanation of 'refraction and the manufacture of lenses, . . . of the eye, of light, of vision, and of everything belonging to catoptrics and optics'.[29] The achievement was a considerable one: in the course of the work, Descartes accurately sets out, in precise mathematical terms, a version of what is now known as Snell's law of refraction. The second essay, the *Meteorology* (*Les Météores*), applies the reductionistic mechanical approach to a wide variety of phenomena including 'vapours and exhalations, salt, winds, clouds, snow, rain and hail, storms and lightning, and the rainbow'.[30] The guiding principle here is one that remains dominant throughout Cartesian science:

---

[27] *Treatise on Man* (AT XI 120: CSM I 99).   [28] Ibid., AT XI 143: CSM I 102.
[29] Letter to Mersenne of March 1636 (AT I 339–40: CSMK 51). The scope of Descartes's essay was thus wider than its original French title *La Dioptrique* (literally 'Dioptrics') suggests. ('Dioptrics' was the traditional name given to the study of refracted light; 'catoptrics' to reflected light.)
[30] AT VI 231 ff.: CSM I 175.

differences in the size, shape and motion of constituent particles are suffi-cient to explain all the phenomena we observe in the world around us and the sky above us, without the need to posit any of the traditional 'substantial forms', or indeed any qualitative differences between supposedly different 'kinds' of matter. 'I regard [these particles] as all being composed of one single kind of matter,' Descartes observes in the *Meteorology*, 'and believe that each of them could be divided repeatedly in infinitely many ways, and that there is no more difference between them than there is between stones of various different shapes cut from the same rock'.[31] Finally, in the published trio of specimen essays, comes the *Geometry* (*La Géométrie*), an accomplished work, reflecting Descartes's long-standing interest in pure mathematics, which laid down the foundations for what we now know as coordinate geometry.

THE CORE OF DESCARTES'S PHILOSOPHY

Prefaced to the three essays just mentioned was an extended introduction in six parts, the *Discourse on the Method of rightly conducting one's reason and seeking the truth in the sciences* (*Discours de la Méthode pour bien conduire sa raison, et chercher la vérité dans les sciences*). The whole volume consisting of the *Discourse* and *Essays* was published anonymously in Leiden in June 1637; in an earlier letter to Mersenne, Descartes had compared himself to the painter who wished to 'hide behind the picture in order to hear what people will say about it'.[32] The *Discourse*, which next to the *Meditations* is nowadays Descartes's best known and most widely read work, provides a remarkably clear and accessible overview of his philosophical and scien-tific ideas, though it is very different both in tone and content from the *Meditations*, published four years later. The latter work was composed in Latin, the international language of scholarship in the seventeenth century, whereas Descartes chose to write the *Discourse* in French, precisely in order to present his views more informally, and to a wider audience. Though the author's name did not appear on the title page, the *Discourse* is an intensely personal work, a kind of intellectual autobiography which describes (in Part One) the influences on Descartes's early development and his dissatis-faction with the traditional philosophical curriculum, and (in Part Two) his determination to establish a new, clear and orderly method, modelled on the reasoning found in mathematics: 'provided we refrain from accepting anything as true which is not, and always keep to the order required for

---

[31] AT VI 239: CSM II 173, n. 2.   [32] Letter of 8 October 1629 (AT I 23: CSMK 6).

deducing one thing from another, there can be nothing too remote to be reached in the end or too well hidden to be discovered'.[33] The project is nothing less than the construction of a new system of knowledge, starting from scratch – a complete 'rebuilding of the house' as Descartes puts it.[34]

Part Three of the *Discourse* then goes on to set out a 'provisional moral code',[35] which will provide a reliable practical shelter while the edifice of knowledge is being reconstructed; and Part Four (to be discussed below) gives a compelling account of how the metaphysical foundations of the new edifice are to be laid down. Part Five provides a discussion of some of Descartes's scientific work, and is by way of being a summary of the cosmology, physics and physiology covered in the earlier suppressed treatise on the universe and man (*Le Monde* and the *Traité de l'homme*). It includes a detailed account of the circulation of the blood,[36] as well as a series of arguments designed to show that the mechanistic schema which suffices to explain all observed functions in animals totally breaks down when it comes to explaining the capacity for thought and language in human beings. 'It is not conceivable', Descartes argues, that 'a machine should produce different arrangements of words so as to give an appropriately meaningful answer to whatever is said in its presence, as the dullest of men can do'. This leads to the idea of a radical difference between animals and men. The former are simply mechanical automata – natural machines (albeit highly complex ones) made, 'by the hand of God', out of the same material ingredients which compose the rest of the physical universe. But human beings, whose conceptual and linguistic abilities cannot be explained in this way, must possess a rational soul which 'cannot be derived in any way from the potentiality of matter, but must be specially created'.[37] Finally, in Part Six of the *Discourse*, Descartes says something of his plans for future research, and underlines the need for empirical observation to establish which hypotheses, of the several alternatives consistent with the general principles of his science, are in fact correct:

the power of nature is so ample and so vast, and these principles so simple and so general, that I notice hardly any particular effect of which I do not know at once that it can be deduced from the principles in many different ways; and my greatest

---

[33] AT VI 19: CSM I 120.   [34] *Discourse*, Part Three (AT VI 22: CSM I 122).   [35] Ibid.

[36] In supporting the idea of the circulation of the blood, Descartes praises the 'English physician, who . . . [broke] the ice on this subject', referring to William Harvey, whose *De motu cordis* was published in 1628. But Descartes takes the cause of circulation to be expansion caused by the 'heat of the heart', a view which led him to insist that the blood gushes from heart to arteries during the diastole phase, not (as Harvey had correctly maintained) during the systole (contraction) phase (AT VI 50, 52: CSM I 136, 137).

[37] AT VI 55–9: CSM I 139–41.

difficulty is usually to discover in which of these ways it depends on them. I know no other means to discover this than by seeking further observations whose outcomes vary according to which of these ways provides the correct explanation.[38]

Interesting though these scientific and methodological issues are, it is Part Four of the *Discourse*, the metaphysical core of the work, which has called forth the greatest discussion and commentary. For students of the *Meditations* it is of particular interest, since, in the space of eight paragraphs, it anticipates, if only in outline, many of the more complex and extended arguments of the later work. Descartes begins Part Four of the *Discourse* by stressing the need to make sure the foundations of his new science are sufficiently firm and secure. The way to achieve this is to 'reject as if absolutely false everything in which I could imagine the least doubt, in order to see if I was left believing anything that was entirely indubitable'. He continues:

Thus, because our senses sometimes deceive us, I decided to suppose that nothing was such as they led us to imagine. And since there are people who make mistakes in reasoning, committing logical fallacies concerning the simplest questions in geometry, and because I judged that I was as prone to error as anyone else, I rejected as unsound all the arguments I had previously taken as demonstrative proofs. Lastly, considering that the very thoughts we have while awake may also occur while we sleep without any of them being at that time true, I resolved to pretend that all the things that had ever entered my mind were no more true than the illusions of my dreams. But immediately I noticed that even while I was endeavouring in this way to think that everything was false, it was necessary that I, who was thinking this, was something. And observing that this truth *I am thinking, therefore I exist* was so firm and sure that all the most extravagant suppositions of the sceptics were incapable of shaking it, I decided that I could accept it without scruple as the first principle of the philosophy I was seeking.[39]

Here we have the same technique for systematically 'leading the mind away from the senses' which is later found in the First Meditation (below, p. 25). The unreliability of the senses is underscored by appeal to the fact that they 'sometimes deceive us'; the celebrated dreaming argument is deployed, first to cast doubt on our ability to distinguish between waking and sleeping experience, and then to raise more radical doubts about the existence of anything external to the mind. The possibility of error even with regard to the simple propositions of geometry is also raised, though without the appeal, found in the *Meditations*, to the possible existence of an all-powerful God who might bring it about that 'I . . . go wrong every time

---

[38] AT VI 64–5: CSM I 144.   [39] AT VI 32: CSM I 127.

I . . . count the sides of a square' (p. 27).[40] And finally, the successive waves of doubt collapse on an immovable rock of certainty, as the doubter arrives at the indubitable awareness of his own existence: 'I am thinking, therefore I exist.' The original French phrase in the *Discourse* is *je pense donc je suis*, but the argument has come to be known as 'the Cogito' (from the Latin version *Cogito ergo sum* found in Descartes's later work, the *Principles of Philosophy*, as well as in the subsequent Latin edition of the *Discourse*). It is notable that the celebrated phrase does not appear in the *Meditations*, although there is a closely similar argument: despite the most extravagant doubts that can be raised, '*I am, I exist*, is necessarily true whenever it is put forward by me or conceived in my mind' (p. 35).

The argument of the *Discourse* now proceeds to a new phase. The narrator, having achieved certainty of his own existence, turns next to examining what *kind* of being he is. And here the methodical doubts just canvassed are taken to yield a remarkable result:

I saw that while I could pretend that I had no body and that there was no world and no place for me to be in, I could not for all that pretend that I did not exist . . . From this I knew I was a substance whose whole essence or nature is only to think, and which does not require any place, or depend on any material thing, in order to exist. Accordingly this 'I' – that is, the soul by which I am what I am – is entirely distinct from the body, and indeed is easier to know than the body, and would not fail to be whatever it is, even if the body did not exist.[41]

Descartes is thus led to propound one of his most controversial theses, that the thinking self is essentially incorporeal. What makes me *me* is, by nature, entirely independent of the body and could exist without it. Though consistent with Descartes's earlier arguments in the *Treatise on Man*, that humans consist of a mechanical body plus an immaterial 'rational soul', it is a thesis that is harshly out of tune with the dominant approach to the philosophy of mind in our own time; the majority of modern philosophers have entirely rejected what has scathingly been called the Cartesian doctrine of the 'ghost in the machine'.[42] But even among Descartes's contemporaries there was serious criticism of the argument he offered in the *Discourse*. From

---

[40] The 'deceiving God' argument in the First Meditation takes the form of a dilemma: either God exists, in which case he has the power to make me go astray in the manner suggested, or there is no God, in which case I owe my origins to some less perfect cause, with the result that I have even less reason to suppose myself free of error in these matters. Neither this argument, nor the later scenario of a 'malicious demon of the utmost power and cunning' who 'employ[s] all his energies in order to deceive me' (p. 29) makes any appearance in the *Discourse*.

[41] Part Four (AT VI 31–3: CSM I 127).

[42] The phrase is Gilbert Ryle's (*The Concept of Mind*, London: Hutchinson, 1949).

what looks like a purely epistemological point, that I can doubt my body's existence, or that I am less certain of it than I am of my own thinking, how is it supposed to follow that the essential 'me' is, in reality, distinct from and independent of the body? How can we move so swiftly from epistemology to ontology, from questions about what we are capable of knowing, doubting or imagining to answers about the real and essential truth of things? Readers of the *Discourse* were quick to fasten on this difficulty, and when Descartes came to write the *Meditations*, although he refused to abandon the reasoning (it reappears in more elaborate form in the Second Meditation, pp. 35–7), he did undertake to clarify his position and to strengthen his arguments. The clarification is offered in the Preface to the *Meditations* (p. 11), and the strengthening is offered in the Sixth Meditation (pp. 109, 119). It is for the reader to judge the merits of what appears in these passages, together with Descartes's attempts to defend his view against the powerful criticisms offered by the author of the Fourth Objections, Antoine Arnauld (below, pp. 221ff.). What is unmistakably clear is that Descartes continues to insist on the independence of the mind, *qua* 'thinking thing', from anything bodily: 'if a foot or arm or any other part of the body is cut off, nothing has thereby been taken away from the mind' (p. 119). The claim is revealed in its full starkness, and (to most philosophers nowadays) its overwhelming implausibility, when we remember that the *brain*, being a purely bodily organ, must, for Descartes, be as inessential to the mind's continued functioning as foot or arm.

The remainder of Part Four of the *Discourse* is concerned with the celebrated Cartesian 'truth rule' ('Whatever is very clearly and distinctly conceived is true'),[43] and with the proofs of the existence of a perfect God, which enable us to be sure that 'our ideas or notions, being real things and coming from God, cannot be anything but true, in every respect in which they are clear and distinct'.[44] This opens the gateway to the construction of a reliable science, based not on the deliverances of the senses, but on the divinely implanted truths of mathematics which give us clear and distinct knowledge of the material world. Making the transition from metaphysics to science at the start of Part Five of the *Discourse*, Descartes resoundingly

---

[43] Cf. AT VI 33: CSM I 127. The invoking of God as the guarantor of the reliability of our clear and distinct ideas, which is even more prominent in the *Meditations*, gives rise to the notorious problem of the 'Cartesian Circle': if we can be sure of the reliability of such ideas only after we have proved the existence of a perfect God who created us, how can we, without circularity, rely on the ideas which we need to prove his existence in the first place? For more on this, see the detailed exchange between Descartes and his contemporary critics (below, pp. 211–19).

[44] AT VI 38: CSM I 130.

declares: 'I have noticed certain laws which God has so established in nature, and of which he has implanted such notions in our minds, that after adequate reflection we cannot doubt that they are exactly observed in everything which exists or occurs in the world.'[45]

When Descartes came to write the *Meditations*, which he began to compose not long after the publication of the *Discourse*, his aim was to provide a richer and more detailed elaboration of these metaphysical themes, and thus ensure a firm and unshakable base for his new philosophical system. We have already drawn attention to a number of themes in the *Meditations* which had been prefigured in his earlier writings. The 'rationalistic' move away from the senses towards the inner light of the intellect – a movement which is steadily developed from the barrage of doubt which opens the First Meditation, through to the articulation of the mind's innate ideas in the Third – had been anticipated in the *Discourse*, and, much earlier, if less explicitly, in the *Regulae*. The Cogito argument set out in the *Discourse* provides the bones for the fuller and more sophisticated treatment in the Second Meditation. The notion of the thinking self as essentially incorporeal, tentatively explored in the Second Meditation, and defended at length in the Sixth, was also a development of earlier reflections in the *Discourse*. And the central role of God as guarantor of the possibility of knowledge, a thread that runs right through the *Meditations*, has its roots in the doctrine of the 'light of reason' appearing in the *Regulae*, and the more direct appeal, in the *Discourse*, to divine perfection as the source of all truth in our ideas.

The theocentric character of Descartes's thinking here is underlined by the language of the *Meditations*, which, especially in the original Latin, is often strongly reminiscent of the patristic and medieval world that shaped the intellectual culture Descartes inherited. We often read the *Meditations* nowadays as a work of epistemology, as if Descartes's sole aim was to refute scepticism. But Descartes observes in the Preface to the *Meditations* that his aim is not to prove 'that there really is a world, and that human beings have bodies and so on – *since no sane person has ever seriously doubted these things*' (below, p. 21, emphasis added). The Cartesian quest did not spring into existence as a set of intellectual puzzles or diversions, but fits into a long tradition (going back to Augustine and beyond), which sees the philosopher as using doubt and self-discovery as the first step in the search for objective truth. The point of his arguments establishing the external world, says Descartes, is that 'in considering [them] we come to realize that

[45] AT VI 41: CSM I 131.

they are not as solid or as transparent as the arguments which lead us to knowledge of our own minds and of God' (ibid.). For Descartes himself the primary significance of the self-awareness he achieves is that it is the first step on the road to awareness of God.

Descartes's conception of himself as a thinking being immediately leads him to reflect on his finitude and imperfection; and this in turn leads him directly forward to contemplate the 'immense light' of the Godhead, the infinite incorporeal being whose image is reflected, albeit dimly, in the finite created intellect of the meditator.[46] Like Bonaventure before him, whose own *Itinerarium mentis in Deum* (*The Journey of the Mind towards God*) was profoundly conditioned by the contemplative and immaterialist tradition of Plato and Augustine, Descartes has a conception of ultimate truth that required an *aversio* – a turning of the mind away from the world of the senses – in order to prepare it for glimpsing the reality that lies beyond the phenomenal world. Both Bonaventure and Descartes, following Augustine's famous slogan *In interiore homine habitat veritas* ('The truth dwells within the inner man'),[47] undertake an interior journey. 'Go back into yourself', says Augustine; 'let us return to ourselves, into our mind', says Bonaventure, that we may search for the *lux veritatis in facie nostrae mentis* – 'the light of truth shining in our minds, as through a glass, in which the image of the Blessed Trinity shines forth'.[48] 'I turn my mind's eye upon myself', says Descartes, and find the idea of God stamped there, like the 'mark the craftsman has set on his work'.[49]

There is a paradox here which lies at the heart of Descartes's philosophy. On the one hand, it is clearly motivated by the desire of the independent-mind researcher to shake off the shackles of preconceived opinion and stride forward in search of the truth: this is the image of Descartes as inaugurator of the modern scientific age, and the champion of human autonomy and independence. But on the other hand, the path to truth is conditioned, in Descartes's conception, by the traditional religious idea of

---

[46] Third Meditation, below, p. 73.
[47] 'Noli foras ire, in teipsum redi; in interiore homine habitat veritas' ('Go not outside, but return within thyself; in the inward man dwelleth the truth'). Augustine, *De vera religione* [391] XXXIX 72.
[48] 'Ad nos reintraremus, in mentem scilicet nostram, in qua divina relucet imago; hinc . . . conari debemus per speculum videre Deum, ubi ad modum candelabri relucet lux veritatis in facie nostrae mentis, in qua scilicet resplendet imago beatissimae Trinitatis.' Bonaventure, *Itinerarium mentis in Deum* [1259] III 1. For more on the theocentric character of Descartes's philosophy, see J. Cottingham, *Cartesian Reflections* (Oxford: Oxford University Press, 2008), chs. 13 and 14.
[49] Third Meditation below, p. 73.

our creatureliness – the idea that we are sustained at every moment of our existence by a creative power who is the source of all truth and goodness, and without whom we would remain adrift in the darkness, bereft of that 'light of reason' which, for Descartes, is the divine gift to each human soul.

The tension between independence and creatureliness pervades the entire structure of the *Meditations*. 'I am here quite alone', the meditator announces in the opening paragraph (p. 23). There follows, in vividly dramatic detail, a compelling account of the journey of discovery taken by the isolated thinker as he[50] searches for secure foundations for knowledge. A series of progressively more radical and extreme doubts are employed to question all preconceived opinions (First Meditation), but (soon after the start of the Second) an 'Archimedean point' of unshakable certainty is reached with the meditator's indubitable awareness of his own existence (pp. 33–5). The meditator then reflects on his essence or nature as a 'thinking thing', and reasons that the mind is better known than the body (pp. 35–47). The Third Meditation begins by laying down the rule that 'whatever I perceive very clearly and distinctly is true' (p. 49); but there remain doubts about the reliability of the mind that can only be allayed by establishing 'whether there is a God, and, if there is, whether he can be a deceiver' (p. 51). The meditator proceeds to reflect on the innate ideas he finds within himself, and reasons that the representational content (or 'objective reality')[51] of one of these ideas, that of a supremely perfect being, is so great that it cannot have been constructed from the resources of the meditator's own finite mind; the conclusion is that God must really exist, and that 'in creating me, [he] . . . placed this idea in me to be, as it were, the mark of the craftsman stamped on his work' (p. 73). The Fourth Meditation tackles the problem of truth and falsity, and argues that the way for humans to avoid error is to restrain their (infinite) will, so as to make judgements only when the perceptions of the (finite) intellect are clear and distinct. The intellect, though limited, is created by a perfect God, and what it *does* clearly perceive can therefore be guaranteed to be true.[52] The

---

[50] A genderless pronoun would be more appropriate here, since the meditator is identified purely as a 'thinking thing'; the existence of the body is at this stage still in doubt, and the subject is considered entirely in abstraction from the bodily attributes that make one male or female. Modern writers often use the plural 'they' and 'their' when a neutral pronoun is required, but unfortunately this useful convention would be highly misleading in the present context, since it is a crucial part of Descartes's argument that the meditator is a *singular* isolated individual (at this stage I cannot know whether anyone else exists apart from myself).

[51] For the meaning of this technical term, see pp. 57, n. 1, and 173–5.

[52] The problem of the 'Cartesian Circle' is never far beneath the surface here and in many other crucial stages of the argument of the *Meditations*. See n. 43, above.

effect of the argument is to provide a kind of Cartesian theodicy, which parallels traditional attempts to vindicate the goodness of God notwithstanding the existence of evil; in this case, Descartes aims to show that error is not to be laid at God's door, but is the result of an improper use of the gift of free will (by assenting to what is not clearly perceived). The Fifth Meditation prepares the way for Cartesian science by establishing the nature of matter as something extended and divisible, which can be accurately and correctly described in mathematical language (pp. 89, 99). We are also offered a second proof for God's existence, namely that the concept of a supremely perfect being (one who is the sum of all perfections) implies that such a being cannot lack the perfection of existence, and hence that such a being must, by its very nature, exist (pp. 91–5).[53] Lastly, in the Sixth Meditation, the actual existence of the external world (called into doubt in the First Meditation) is finally re-established (p. 111), and we are offered a series of arguments which purport to demonstrate the 'real' distinction between mind and body: they are mutually independent substances, each of which can exist without the other. But having used philosophical reason to establish the distinction, the Sixth Meditation closes by invoking our everyday experience of the sensations 'of hunger, thirst, pain and so on' as showing that mind and body, though distinct, are closely 'intermingled' or 'united' (p. 113). The final paragraphs return to the problem of truth and error, and continue the theodicy of the Fourth Meditation, arguing that 'notwithstanding the immense goodness of God, the nature of man as a combination of mind and body is such that it is bound to mislead him from time to time' (p. 123).[54] Descartes himself provided a tolerably informative *Synopsis* of the argument which is not only worth consulting as a summary, but also contains some interesting additional reflections by the author on his work (pp. 17–21). For detailed discussion of some of the chief philosophical difficulties arising from the argument of the *Meditations*, an invaluable starting point is the published *Objections* of Descartes's

---

[53] This is Descartes's version of the so-called 'ontological' argument, first invented by St Anselm of Canterbury. Descartes was at pains to distinguish it from the *causal* argument of the Third Meditation, which proceeds from effect (the idea of God found in the meditator's mind) to cause (the God who placed it there, like a trademark). The Fifth Meditation argument, by contrast, is purely a priori, and depends merely on reflecting on the defining *essence* of a supremely perfect being. For criticism of the argument, and Descartes's replies, see pp. 195ff.

[54] The naturally ordained patterns of psycho-physical response in human beings (for example, a sensation of dryness when the nerves in the tongue and throat are in a certain state) are such as to conduce in general to the health of the mind–body composite. But because nature's laws are constant, there are bound to be occasions when such correlations will produce a desire to drink even in those rare and exceptional morbid conditions where fluid intake is not beneficial; see below, p. 123.

distinguished contemporaries, and the author's own *Replies* (extracts from some of the most important of these exchanges are provided in the present volume, pp. 127ff.).[55]

Descartes hoped that the arguments of the *Meditations*, in particular those purporting to demonstrate the existence of God and the 'real distinction' between soul and body, would find favour with the theologians, and he prefixed to the work a dedicatory letter to the members of the Theology Faculty at the Sorbonne, asking for their approval in his battle for the cause of religion against the atheists (pp. 3–9). The approbation of the Sorbonne was not, however, forthcoming, and the years following the publication of the *Meditations* saw Descartes embroiled in a series of bitter debates with a variety of theological and philosophical critics.[56] One may see some of these debates prefigured in some of the extracts from the *Objections and Replies* included in the present volume, which give an idea of the sensitivity of the questions about God and the soul tackled by Descartes in the *Meditations*, lying as they do at the very interface between philosophy and theology.

THE CARTESIAN SYSTEM AND THE HUMAN BEING

Notwithstanding the controversies and disputes that plagued him, Descartes's reputation continued to grow, particularly after the publication, in 1644, of the *Principia philosophiae*, a grand exposition of the Cartesian system in four parts. Unlike Descartes's earlier writings, the *Principles of Philosophy* was explicitly planned as a university textbook, and like the traditional handbooks it was divided up into a series of small sections or 'articles' (there are 504 in all). Part One ('The Principles of Human Knowledge') covers much the same metaphysical ground as the *Meditations*, though the exposition is much more formal and impersonal; Part Two ('The Principles of Material Things') presents a complete account of Cartesian physics and the laws of matter in motion; Part Three ('The Visible Universe') describes the structure and workings of the solar system; and Part Four ('The Earth') offers explanations of a wide variety of terrestrial phenomena, as well as giving a brief account, in the closing articles, of Descartes's plans for future work on animals and man, with special

---

[55] For publication details relating to the *Meditations* and *Objections and Replies*, and information about the authors of the *Objections*, see Editorial Introduction, p. xxxi below.

[56] Particularly savage were the attacks of the Dutch theologian Gisbertus Voetius, which led to the publication by Descartes of a lengthy defence of his views, the *Epistola ad Voetium* (1643). (Cf. AT VIIIB 25: CSMK 220.)

reference to the explanation of sense perception and sensory awareness. A French version of the original Latin text was issued three years later, in 1647, by which time the Cartesian philosophy, despite strong opposition from many parts of the academic establishment, was beginning to gain widespread support.

Descartes's programme for establishing a fully comprehensive philosophical system was, however, still incomplete in at least one important respect: he had as yet provided little indication of how his philosophy would deal with the psychological and ethical realms. In the preface to the 1647 French edition of the *Principles of Philosophy* he referred to the project of constructing a 'perfect morality' – *la plus parfaite morale* – which was to be the crowning achievement of his philosophical endeavours. The traditional goal of moral philosophy was to articulate 'the good for humankind';[57] but the concept of a *human being*, an embodied creature of flesh and blood, had been left rather in limbo by the results of the *Meditations*. His metaphysical arguments, as we have seen, had led Descartes to the conclusion that the thinking subject was an essentially incorporeal entity whose nature was utterly distinct and alien from the body. And the implication of this was that a human being was an amalgam of seemingly incompatible elements, an immaterial spirit and a mechanical assemblage of bodily organs. Taking his cue from this, Descartes's zealous disciple Regius had insistently proclaimed that the Cartesian doctrine was that man was nothing more than an 'accidental entity' – in the jargon, an *ens per accidens*, as opposed to an *ens per se* (a genuine entity in its own right). Descartes, in correspondence, had angrily dissociated himself from this interpretation, insisting that his view was that 'the mind is united in a real and substantial manner to the body'.[58] But although the Sixth Meditation had called attention to how mind and body were 'very closely joined and, as it were, intermingled' (below, p. 113), it must have left most readers puzzled as to how such intermingling of incommensurable elements could come about.

One of those who were puzzled was the young Princess Elizabeth of Bohemia, only twenty-four years of age when, in 1643, she began a long and fruitful correspondence with Descartes, largely devoted to the topic of the mind–body union. Her initial question to the philosopher was about the possibility of interaction between 'thinking' and 'extended' substances: how can the soul, or thinking substance, causally influence the behaviour of the body to bring about voluntary actions? In his reply, Descartes acknowledged

---

[57] The phrase is Aristotle's (*Nicomachean Ethics*, Book 1, ch. 7).
[58] Letter to Regius of January 1642 (AT III 493: CSMK 206).

that this question was 'the one which can most properly be put to me in view of my published writings'. He went on to introduce a distinction between three 'primitive notions', which are 'the patterns on the basis of which we form all our other conceptions':

> . . . as regards body we have only the notion of extension, which entails the notions of shape and motion. As regards the soul on its own, we have only the notion of thought, which includes the perceptions of the intellect and the inclinations of the will. Lastly, as regards the soul and body together, we have only the notion of their union, on which depend our notions of the soul's power to move the body, and the body's power to act on the soul and cause its sensations and passions.[59]

This third 'primitive notion' comprises, in effect, whatever is attributable to an embodied human being. The *Meditations* had mentioned 'pain, hunger, thirst' in this connection, while the *Principles of Philosophy* had provided a rather fuller list: 'first, appetites like hunger and thirst; secondly, the emotions or passions of the mind which do not consist of thought alone, such as the emotions of anger, joy, sadness and love; and finally, all the sensations, such as those of pain, pleasure, light, colours, sounds, smells, tastes, heat, hardness and the other tactile qualities'.[60]

Our life on this earth, as Descartes came increasingly to underline, involves far more than the intellectual and volitional activities that belong to our essence as immaterial 'thinking things'. If we were like angels (pure thinking beings), Descartes once observed, our existence would be entirely devoid of sensation;[61] we would lack the manifold and varied sensory awareness that is an inescapable part of our everyday human experience. And it is this sensory and affective dimension, with all the vivid phenomenal quality of the various feelings involved, that gives colour and richness to our lives as human beings. Of particular importance here is the category of the passions, which in his last work, *Les Passions de l'âme* (*The Passions of the Soul*, 1649), Descartes grouped under six basic kinds: wonder, love, hatred, desire, joy and sadness. Dissociating himself from earlier intellectualist approaches to ethics which had often attempted to suppress the passions as inimical to the good life, Descartes declared: 'The philosophy I cultivate is not so savage or grim as to outlaw the operation of the passions; on the contrary, it is here, in my view, that the entire sweetness and joy of life is to be found'.[62] Descartes's final project was to ground his ethics, his recipe for how humans could achieve fulfilling and worthwhile lives,

---

[59] Letter of 21 May 1643 (AT III 664, 665: CSMK 217, 218); cf. AT III 660.
[60] Part One, article 48 (AT VIIIA 23: CSM I 209).
[61] Letter to Regius of January 1642 (AT III 493: CSMK 206).
[62] Letter to Silhon, March or April 1648 (AT V 135).

in a systematic understanding of the operation of the passions, both on a physiological and on a psychological level. Here he hoped that his new method for science would yield a rich harvest. A detailed grasp of the bodily mechanisms which give rise to our emotional responses would, he envisaged, enable us to modify those responses where appropriate, and thus channel our feelings and emotions in such a way as to generate a harmonious human life, lived in accordance with our best perceptions of the good for mankind. Cartesian science, pressed into the service of ethics, would allow us to fulfil the dream first announced in the *Discourse on the Method* and reiterated in the *Principles of Philosophy*: instead of the abstract speculative philosophy of the past, we would have at our disposal a new and genuinely practical philosophy, one that would make us the 'lords and masters of nature', and bring us closer to achieving 'perfection and felicity of life'.[63]

THE CARTESIAN LEGACY

Descartes's ambitious programme was cut short by his own untimely death, in Stockholm, where, after much hesitation, he had taken up residence at the invitation of Queen Christina of Sweden in 1649. His vitality sapped by the rigours of the Swedish winter, and the need to rise early in the morning to give philosophy tutorials to the queen, he succumbed to pneumonia and died on 11 February 1650, just under two months short of his fifty-fourth birthday. But although he died leaving his philosophical system not fully complete, the remarkably wide range of what he had achieved, and the clarity and precision of its execution, meant that Cartesian ideas dominated the scientific and philosophical thinking of Europe for a long time to come.[64] The writings of the philosophical giants of the early-modern period, Spinoza, Malebranche and Leibniz, on the Continent, and Locke, Berkeley and Hume, in the British Isles, all, in different ways, bear the unmistakable imprint of Descartes's thought concerning the structure of human knowledge, the nature of the mind and the relationship between mind and matter. It is impossible to examine the arguments and conceptual apparatus of any of the canonical philosophers of the late seventeenth and early eighteenth century without seeing the irresistible aptness of

---

[63] *Discourse*, Part Six (AT VI 62: CSM I 142–3); Preface to the French edition of the *Principles of Philosophy* (AT IXB 20: CSM I 190).

[64] Cartesian physics, however, was by the end of the century to come under increasing pressure from the vastly more sophisticated (and accurate) Newtonian system.

the traditional accolade which is so often bestowed on Descartes: he is, indubitably, the true 'father of modern philosophy'.

The story in our own era has been very different. Much twentieth-century philosophy has developed along tracks that diverge sharply from those which Descartes laid down. In the theory of knowledge, what has come to be known as 'foundationalism' – the Cartesian project of trying to build a reliable belief system from scratch, starting from a supposedly self-standing and indubitably certain base – has come to be seen as radically misguided. In the philosophy of mind, Descartes's notion of an immaterial thinking substance has been derided as an explanatory dead-end, powerless to account in any illuminating way for the phenomenon of consciousness and its relationship to the physical world. And, perhaps most devastating of all, the very starting point of Cartesian metaphysics, with its focus on the private reflections of the isolated thinker, has been attacked as incoherent: in the aftermath of Wittgenstein, it has become a ruling orthodoxy that thought and language are inescapably public, socially mediated phenomena, and hence that there is something deeply wrong with the very idea of 'Cartesian privacy' – of solitary, introspective access to the truth. But for all that, the enduring influence of Descartes's ideas remains. It is of the nature of philosophy that its advances are always achieved by means of a continuing dialogue with the great thinkers of the past. The very fact that so much contemporary philosophy defines its goals and methods in stark opposition to Cartesian paradigms itself bears witness to the powerful pressures which Descartes's approach to philosophy still continues to exert. What is called 'common sense' in any age frequently turns out to be the half-digested remains of earlier philosophical theories. Many people's supposedly 'pre-philosophical' intuitions about knowledge, the mind and the nature of certainty, the very intuitions which the philosophers of the twentieth century have struggled to dismantle, have been conditioned by the long-standing dominance of ways of thinking which Descartes helped create.

But there is a final point to be made. Though philosophers sometimes like to think of themselves as belonging to a quasi-scientific, progressive discipline, with steady 'advances' in research, the actual history of the subject shows that it does not, and cannot, proceed in this rectilinear way. Rather, it is a matter of currents and counter-currents, of theses conquered by antitheses which themselves then fall victim to newer and reinvigorated incarnations of earlier rejected ideas. For this reason alone, it is plausible to think that the anti-Cartesian thrust of contemporary philosophizing is destined, in some areas at least, to overreach itself. As far as Descartes's

general conception of philosophy is concerned, philosophers nowadays live in a cautiously specialized world which is wary of grand systems; but just as the dominant Scholasticism prior to Descartes ran out of energy, so it is conceivable that today's compartmentalized approach to philosophy may lose its appeal, and give way to a faintly recognizable successor to the Cartesian vision of a comprehensive philosophy that strives to integrate the disparate areas of human cognition.[65] Such speculations aside, one thing is certain, that over three and a half centuries after they were written, the *Meditations* have lost none of their power to fascinate. The vividly dramatic narrative in which Descartes presents the metaphysical core of his philosophy still exerts an extraordinary spell, whether as a specimen of a splendid but doomed enterprise, or as an inspiring exemplar of what the individual intellect can achieve when it casts off the bonds of authority and convention and sets out on the long search for security and truth. In his Preface to the first edition, Descartes observed that he did not expect his *Meditations* to attract 'any great crowd of readers' (p. 13). History has proved him wrong, and will surely continue to do so for a very long time to come.

---

[65] For more on this, see 'Descartes the Synoptic Philosopher', in Cottingham, *Cartesian Reflections*.

Editorial introduction
The text and its translation

Descartes's *Meditations on First Philosophy* is perhaps the most widely studied philosophy text in the English-speaking world. It is used in hundreds of Introduction to Philosophy courses, and is one of the most important of the great canonical texts of Western philosophy. It inaugurates many of the key themes that have remained central to philosophy ever since.

The original Latin text (published in 1641, with a second edition the following year) displays Descartes not just as a philosophical genius but as a writer of great lucidity and elegance, and there is great profit to be had, even for those who are not fluent in Latin, in seeing how the famous concepts and arguments of his great masterpiece are expressed in the author's own words. Students of classical philosophy have long had the benefit of facing-page dual-language editions, and the availability of such a resource for those working in the early-modern period is long overdue. Following the pattern established in the celebrated Loeb Classical Library, the original text is here presented on the left hand (verso) page, with the translation on the right hand (recto) side. The pagination is arranged so that the texts run parallel throughout the work.

Descartes's most celebrated philosophical work was written in Latin during the period 1638–40, when the philosopher was living for the most part at Santpoort. This 'corner of north Holland', he wrote to his friend and editor Marin Mersenne on 27 May 1638, was much more suitable for his work than the 'air of Paris' with its 'vast number of inevitable distractions'.[1] The work was completed by April 1640, and was first published in Paris in 1641 by Michel Soly under the title *Meditationes de prima philosophia* ('Meditations on first philosophy'); the subtitle adds 'in which is demonstrated the existence of God and the immortality of the soul'. In earlier correspondence Descartes had referred to his work as the *Metaphysics*, but he eventually decided that 'the most suitable title is *Meditations on First*

[1] AT II 152.

Philosophy, because the discussion is not confined to God and the soul but treats in general of all the first things to be discovered by philosophizing'.[2]

Descartes was not entirely satisfied with Soly as a publisher, and he arranged for a second edition of the *Meditations* to be brought out in Holland, by the house of Elzevir of Amsterdam. This second edition appeared in 1642, with a new and more appropriate subtitle, viz. 'in which are demonstrated the existence of God and the distinction between the human soul and the body'. The second edition contains a number of minor corrections to the text (though in practice the sense is seldom affected), and except where indicated it is the text of this superior 1642 edition that is reproduced in the present volume (with silent correction of a few small typographical slips).[3] Where the wording of the earlier (1641) edition is significantly different, the earlier version of the relevant passage is given in a footnote.[4]

Students of classical Latin and Greek works will be familiar with the complexities of establishing a definitive text, and the elaborate *apparatus criticus* of variant readings that has to be supplied at the foot of each page. The problems for a seventeenth-century work, where the author himself could review the printed edition and bring out a second version the following year, are, by comparison, minimal, and in the case of this particular text there is generally very little difficulty determining the authentic Latin text composed by Descartes. A further bonus for Descartes scholars is the availability of the magisterial twelve-volume Adam and Tannery edition of Descartes's works (known as 'AT'), which has been invaluable in preparing the present volume.[5] 'AT' references have become the standard way of referring to all Descartes's work, and in the present edition running references to the relevant page numbers of AT volume VII (the volume containing the

---

[2] Letter to Mersenne of 11 November 1640 (AT III 235: CSMK 157).

[3] I have also silently made some minor typographical changes in order to produce a cleaner and more legible Latin text than the seventeenth-century original, for example by dropping the fussy, unlatinate (and redundant) accents over certain vowels, by substituting the modern 's' for the now obsolete medial letterform, by restoring the Latin word *et* in place of the ampersand symbol (&), and by emending some degenerate Latin forms (e.g. *infoeliciter* for *infeliciter*, *omneis* for *omnes*) occurring in the text of the Fifth Objections.

[4] For a full discussion of the differences between the 1641 and 1642 editions, see AT vol. VII, *Avertissement*, pp. xi–xvii.

[5] See 'Philosophical introduction', n. 3 (p. vii, above). There is also an excellent Latin text of the *Meditations* in the invaluable three-volume edition of Ferdinand Alquié, *Descartes: Œuvres philosophiques* (Paris: Garnier, 1967), vol. II, pp. 177ff. Alquié takes issue with Adam on a few points relating to the superiority of the 1642 edition, and notes some small slips in Adam's editing, but his own text does not diverge from Adam's on any point that substantially affects its meaning or philosophical significance.

Meditations and *Objections and Replies*) are supplied in the margins both of the Latin text and the English translation, in order to assist the reader.

The English translation presented alongside the Latin is based on the version which I originally prepared for the two (later three) volume Cambridge edition of the *Philosophical Writings of* Descartes,[6] which was subsequently published with minor changes in my one-volume edition of the *Meditations with Selections from the Objections and Replies*, and later reprinted, with revisions, in the *Cambridge Texts in the History of Philosophy* series.[7] I have taken the opportunity of the present edition to make a few further minor corrections.

Translating a writer whose style is as compelling as that of Descartes presents some fascinating challenges. Descartes's Latin in the *Meditations* is beautifully written, and its ease and elegance testifies to the author's complete mastery of the language. As a schoolboy at the Jesuit college of La Flèche ('one of the most famous schools in Europe', as he was later to describe it),[8] he would have become a fluent Latinist at a very early age. But his polished Latin was no mere scholastic achievement – of the kind familiar until comparatively recently among those educated in the classical tradition in, say, England or Germany. In addition, Latin was of course the language of Descartes's Church (he remained a devout Roman Catholic all his life); but more than that, it was in the seventeenth century the language of international communication, filling much of the role that English does nowadays. We know from Descartes's voluminous correspondence that it was as natural and automatic for him to use Latin when addressing a foreign correspondent or publishing for an international audience as it is today for a Dutch or Swedish writer to use English. Even that comparison does not quite do justice to the situation in which Descartes found himself; for

---

[6] J. Cottingham, R. Stoothoff and D. Murdoch, *The Philosophical Writings of Descartes*, vols. I and II (Cambridge: Cambridge University Press, 1985) and vol. III, *The Correspondence*, by the same translators and A. Kenny (Cambridge: Cambridge University Press, 1991). In the division of labour adopted for the first two volumes of CSM, it fell to me to translate the *Meditations* and the *Objections and Replies*. I should like, however, to take the present opportunity to underline once again the very considerable debt I owe to my friends and colleagues Bob Stoothoff and Dugald Murdoch, who scrutinized my work at every stage, and made numerous corrections and suggestions for improvement. I also owe thanks to Dr Hilary Gaskin of Cambridge University Press for her encouragement in the planning of the present dual-language edition, and to Iveta Adams for her thoughtful and judicious copy-editing. I am also deeply grateful to Marcos and Modesto Gómez Alonso for kindly scrutinizing the Latin text and saving me from many errors.

[7] René Descartes, *Meditations on First Philosophy with Selections from the Objections and Replies*, trans. and ed. J. Cottingham (Cambridge: Cambridge University Press, 1986; 2nd edn with new Introduction 1996).

[8] *Discourse*, Part One (AT VI 5: CSM I 113).

the impressive linguistic skills of the educated modern Dutchman, say, are seldom so perfect that he will not occasionally betray by some slight error or nuance of phrasing that English is not his mother tongue. Descartes's fluency in Latin, by contrast, was mastery not of some 'foreign' language, but rather a kind of complete immersion in a classical language whose timeless and (by the seventeenth century) formalized modes of thought had become second nature to him. There is a real sense in which Descartes is a Latin writer, as much as he is a French writer.

All this raises formidable problems for the translator. Seeing the author's original Latin words right there on the facing page invites the reader to match up the two texts, and when, as will be inevitable, they don't seem to mirror each other word for word, a certain type of critic may be inclined to shout 'Hey! But that's not exactly what the Latin says!' The only reply to this must be: 'Of course it isn't!' Translating is not about word-for-word correspondence, but about rendering the *meaning* of a text in a way that is (or should aspire to be) as lucid and engaging as the original, while sticking as close to the original structure and phrasing as is consistent with writing decent modern English. Trying to force things into an ever closer match may initially look 'scholarly', but all too often the result will be an ugly or even unreadable translation, which is probably not going to be much use to anyone except those who can mentally translate it back into the original. (For all their scholarly virtues, this seems to have been the fate of some of the recent English modern translations of Aristotle, which are full of grotesque phrases like *the that for the sake of which*, unintelligible to any but those who already know classical Greek and so don't really need the translation in the first place.) It was and remains my guiding aim in offering this English version of the *Meditations* to provide a text that is as clear and readable as the original, and which is also as philosophically sensitive (for translating a thinker such as Descartes is as much a philosophical as a purely linguistic enterprise). I am all too keenly aware of the imperfections that no doubt remain even after several revisions; but I venture to hope that what follows may at least serve to convey something of the linguistic fluency and philosophical power of Descartes's masterpiece.

Descartes himself was no stranger to the problem of translation, and many of his French works appeared in his lifetime in Latin versions, and vice versa. A French edition of the *Meditations* by Louis-Charles d'Albert, Duc de Luynes (1620–90) was published six years after the original Latin edition, in 1647. This is a tolerably accurate version which was printed with Descartes's approval; Adrien Baillet, in his biography of Descartes,

goes so far as to claim that the philosopher took advantage of the French edition to 'retouch his original work'.[9] In fact, however, the French version generally stays fairly close to the Latin. There are a number of places where phrases in the original are paraphrased or expanded somewhat, but it is impossible to say which of these modifications, if any, were directly initiated by Descartes (some are certainly too clumsy to be his work). There is thus no good case for giving the French version greater authority than the Latin text, which we know that Descartes himself composed. There are however a number of places where the French version provides expansions or modifications which offer useful glosses on, or additions to, the original; and for the benefit of readers who wish to consult the French version it seemed helpful to give some indication of passages where this may profitably be done. In my English translation, I have therefore from time to time inserted a translation of this later French material, but always within diamond brackets, or in footnotes, to avoid confusion.

As soon as he had completed the *Meditations*, Descartes began to circulate them among his friends, asking for comments and criticisms. He also sent the manuscript to Friar Marin Mersenne (1588–1648), his friend and principal correspondent, asking him to obtain further criticisms. He wrote to Mersenne in a letter of 28 January 1641: 'I will be very glad if people put to me many objections, the strongest they can find, for I hope that the truth will stand out all the better.'[10] The resulting six sets of Objections (the first set collected by Descartes himself, the remainder by Mersenne) were published in Latin, together with Descartes's Replies, in the same volume as the first (1641) edition of the *Meditations*. The second edition of the *Meditations* (1642) contained in addition the Seventh Set of Objections together with Descartes's Replies, and also the Letter to Dinet (all in Latin). The terms 'Objections' and 'Replies' were suggested by Descartes himself, who asked that his own comments should be called 'Replies' rather than 'Solutions' in order to leave the reader to judge whether his replies contained solutions to the difficulties offered.[11]

The volume containing the French translation of the *Meditations* (by de Luynes), which appeared in 1647, also contained a French version of the first six sets of *Objections and Replies* by Descartes's disciple Claude

[9] *La Vie de Monsieur Des-Cartes* (Paris: Horthemels, 1691; photographic reprint Hildesheim: Olms, 1972), vol. XI, p. 172.

[10] AT III 297: CSMK 172.

[11] Letters to Mersenne of 30 September 1640 and 18 March 1641 (AT III 184, 340: CSMK 153, 177).

Clerselier (1614–84). Although it is frequently said that Descartes saw and approved of this translation, there is, as with the *Meditations* proper, no good case for preferring the French version to the original Latin which Descartes himself composed. It should also be remembered that all the objectors wrote in Latin, and had before them only the Latin text of the *Meditations* when they wrote. The present extracts from the *Objections and Replies* are therefore based entirely on the original Latin.

The First Set of Objections is by a Catholic theologian from Holland, Johannes Caterus (Johan de Kater), who was priest in charge of the church of St Laurens at Alkmaar from 1632 to 1656. Caterus had been asked to comment on the *Meditations* by two fellow priests who were friends of Descartes, Bannius and Bloemaert; and it is to these two intermediaries that both Caterus' Objections and Descartes's Replies are addressed. Descartes wrote to Mersenne on 24 December 1640 that Caterus himself wished to remain anonymous.[12]

The Second Set of Objections is simply attributed to 'theologians and philosophers' in the index to the first edition, but the French version of 1647 announces that they were 'collected by the Reverend Father Mersenne'. In fact they are largely the work of Mersenne himself.

The Third Set of Objections ('by a celebrated English philosopher', says the 1647 edition) is by Thomas Hobbes (1588–1679), who had fled to France, for political reasons, in 1640. Although many of Hobbes's points are of considerable philosophical interest, Descartes's comments are mostly curt and dismissive in the extreme.

The Fourth Set of Objections is by the French theologian and logician Antoine Arnauld (1612–94), who became Doctor of Theology at the Sorbonne in 1641. Both the Objections and Replies are addressed to Mersenne as intermediary, and the tone of both authors is courteous and respectful throughout.

The Fifth Set of Objections is by the philosopher Pierre Gassendi (1592–1655). His comments are very lengthy and come near to being a paragraph-by-paragraph commentary on the *Meditations*. Gassendi's tone is often acerbic, and Descartes frequently reacts with bristly defensiveness.

The Sixth Set of Objections was printed with no indication of the author in the first and second editions, and is described in the 1647 French edition as being 'by various theologians and philosophers'. The compiler, as in the case of the Second Objections, is Mersenne.

---

[12] AT III 265: CSMK 163.

The Seventh Set of Objections is by the Jesuit Pierre Bourdin (1595–1653). Descartes had been eager to obtain the support of the Jesuits for his philosophy, but he was very disappointed with what he called 'the quibbles of Father Bourdin'; he wrote to Mersenne, 'I have treated him as courteously as possible, but I have never seen a paper so full of faults.'[13]

The choice of extracts from the Objections and from Descartes's Replies follows that made in my earlier one-volume edition of the *Meditations on First Philosophy with Selections from the Objections and Replies*,[14] but with the inclusion of one additional extract, and some minor additional modifications. The reader should note that the extracts are not necessarily arranged in the order in which they appeared in Descartes's original volume. Instead, the material is here arranged thematically, so as to indicate the main points of criticism that occurred to Descartes's contemporaries as they read through the *Meditations*, and to show how Descartes clarified and developed his arguments in response to those criticisms. In condensing the massive text of the *Objections and Replies* (around 320 pages) down to some fifty-five pages of extracts, I inevitably had to be ruthlessly selective. The aim is to assist the reader in coming to terms with the complex and subtle reasoning of the *Meditations* by focusing attention on some of the principal philosophical difficulties which arise out of Descartes's deceptively lucid masterpiece. Often the points raised by critics hinge on the precise meaning of a Latin term used by Descartes, and for this reason, amongst others, I hope it will be particularly useful for readers to be able to look across to the Latin text of the relevant extract (and indeed, where appropriate, to cross-refer to the relevant Latin passage in the *Meditations* which gave rise to the query). Before each extract, or group of extracts, I have inserted, in the English version, a short heading indicating the topic dealt with; and at the end of each extract the reader will find a note of the set of Objections or Replies to which it belongs, together with a page reference to volume II of CSM, where the unabridged English text may be found. Marginal references to the pages of Adam and Tannery volume VII are in any case supplied throughout for both the Latin and the English texts, enabling the reader to identify each passage using the 'AT' numbering that has now become standard for all editions and translations of Descartes.[15]

---

[13] Letter of March 1642 (AT III 543: CSMK 211).   [14] See above, p. xxxiii, n. 7.

[15] Where a marginal reference appears in parentheses (thus (481)), this indicates that the extract in question begins part way down an AT page, rather than at the start of that page.

Meditationes de prima philosophia
Meditations on First Philosophy

[Epistola dedicatoria]

SAPIENTISSIMIS CLARISSIMISQUE VIRIS
SACRAE FACULTATIS THEOLOGIAE PARISIENSIS
DECANO ET DOCTORIBUS
RENATUS DES CARTES S. D.

Tam justa causa me impellit ad hoc scriptum vobis offerendum, et tam justam etiam vos habituros esse confido ad ejus defensionem suscipiendam, postquam instituti mei rationem intelligetis, ut nulla re melius illud hic possim commendare, quam si quid in eo sequutus sim paucis dicam.

Semper existimavi duas quaestiones, de Deo et de Anima, praecipuas esse ex iis quae Philosophiae potius quam Theologiae ope sunt demonstrandae: nam quamvis nobis fidelibus animam humanam cum corpore non interire, Deumque existere, fide credere sufficiat, certe infidelibus nulla religio, nec fere etiam ulla moralis virtus, videtur posse persuaderi, nisi prius illis ista duo ratione naturali probentur: cumque saepe in hac vita majora vitiis quam virtutibus praemia proponantur, pauci rectum utili praeferrent, si nec Deum timerent, nec aliam vitam expectarent. Et quamvis omnino verum sit, Dei existentiam credendam esse, quoniam in sacris scripturis docetur, et vice versa credendas sacras scripturas, quoniam habentur a Deo; quia nempe, cum fides sit donum Dei, ille idem qui dat gratiam ad reliqua credenda, potest etiam dare, ut ipsum existere credamus; non tamen hoc infidelibus proponi potest, quia circulum esse judicarent. Et quidem animadverti non modo vos omnes aliosque Theologos affirmare Dei existentiam naturali ratione posse probari, sed et ex sacra Scriptura inferri, ejus cognitionem multis, quae de rebus creatis habentur, esse faciliorem, atque omnino esse tam facilem, ut qui illam non habent sint culpandi. Patet enim Sap. 13 ex his verbis: *Nec his debet ignosci. Si enim tantum potuerunt scire, ut possent aestimare saeculum, quomodo hujus dominum non facilius invenerunt?* Et ad Rom. cap. I, dicitur

[Dedicatory letter to the Sorbonne]

To those most learned and distinguished men,
the Dean and Doctors
of the sacred Faculty of Theology at Paris,
from René Descartes

I have a very good reason for offering this book to you, and I am confident that you will have an equally good reason for giving it your protection once you understand the principle behind my undertaking; so much so, that my best way of commending it to you will be to tell you briefly of the goal which I have aimed at in the book.

I have always thought that two topics – namely God and the soul – are prime examples of subjects where demonstrative proofs ought to be given with the aid of philosophy rather than theology. For us who are believers, it is enough to accept on faith that the human soul does not die with the body, and that God exists; but in the case of unbelievers, it 2 seems that there is no religion, and practically no moral virtue, that they can be persuaded to adopt until these two truths are proved to them by natural reason. And since in this life the rewards offered to vice are often greater than the rewards of virtue, few people would prefer what is right to what is expedient if they did not fear God or have the expectation of an afterlife. It is of course quite true that we must believe in the existence of God because it is a doctrine of Holy Scripture, and conversely, that we must believe Holy Scripture because it comes from God; for since faith is the gift of God, he who gives us grace to believe other things can also give us grace to believe that he exists. But this argument cannot be put to unbelievers because they would judge it to be circular. Moreover, I have noticed both that you and all other theologians assert that the existence of God is capable of proof by natural reason, and also that the inference from Holy Scripture is that the knowledge of God is easier to acquire than the knowledge we have of many created things – so easy, indeed, that those who do not acquire it are at fault. This is clear from a passage in the Book of Wisdom, Chapter 13: 'Howbeit they are not to be excused; for if their knowledge was so great that they could value this world, why did they not rather find out the Lord thereof?' And in Romans, Chapter 1 it is said

illos esse *inexcusabiles*. Atque ibidem etiam per haec verba: *Quod notum est Dei, manifestum est in illis,* videmur admoneri ea omnia quae de Deo sciri possunt, rationibus non aliunde petitis quam ab ipsamet nostra mente posse ostendi. Quod idcirco quomodo fiat, et qua via Deus facilius et certius quam res saeculi cognoscatur, non putavi a me esse alienum inquirere.

Atque quantum ad animam, etsi multi ejus naturam
3 non facile investigari posse judicarint, et nonnulli etiam dicere ausi sint rationes humanas persuadere illam simul cum corpore interire, solaque fide contrarium teneri, quia tamen hos condemnat Concilium Lateranense sub Leone 10 habitum, sessione 8, et expresse mandat Christianis Philosophis ut eorum argumenta dissolvant, et veritatem pro viribus probent, hoc etiam aggredi non dubitavi.

Praeterea, quoniam scio plerosque impios non aliam ob causam nolle credere Deum esse, mentemque humanam a corpore distingui, quam quia dicunt haec duo a nemine hactenus potuisse demonstrari: etsi nullo modo iis assentiar, sed contra rationes fere omnes, quae pro his quaestionibus a magnis viris allatae sunt, cum satis intelliguntur, vim demonstrationis habere putem, vixque ullas dari posse mihi persuadeam, quae non prius ab aliquibus aliis fuerint inventae: nihil tamen utilius in Philosophia praestare posse existimo, quam si semel omnium optimae studiose quaerantur, tamque accurate et perspicue exponantur, ut apud omnes constet in posterum eas esse demonstrationes. Ac denique, quoniam nonnulli quibus notum est me quandam excoluisse Methodum ad quaslibet difficultates in scientiis resolvendas, non quidem novam, quia nihil est veritate antiquius, sed qua me saepe in aliis non infeliciter uti viderunt, hoc a me summopere flagitarunt: ideoque officii mei esse putavi nonnihil hac in re conari.

4 Quicquid autem praestare potui, totum in hoc Tractatu continetur. Non quod in eo diversas omnes rationes, quae ad eadem probanda afferri possent, colligere conatus sim, neque enim hoc videtur operae pretium esse, nisi ubi nulla habetur satis certa; sed primas tantum et praecipuas

that they are 'without excuse'. And in the same place, in the passage 'that which is known of God is manifest in them', we seem to be told that everything that may be known of God can be demonstrated by reasoning which has no other source but our own mind. Hence I thought it was quite proper for me to inquire how this may be, and how God may be more easily and more certainly known than the things of this world.

As regards the soul, many people have considered that it is not easy to 3 discover its nature, and some have even had the audacity to assert that, as far as human reasoning goes, there are persuasive grounds for holding that the soul dies along with the body and that the opposite view is based on faith alone. But in its eighth session the Lateran Council held under Leo X condemned those who take this position,[1] and expressly enjoined Christian philosophers to refute their arguments and use all their powers to establish the truth; so I have not hesitated to attempt this task as well.

In addition, I know that the only reason why many irreligious people are unwilling to believe that God exists and that the human mind is distinct from the body is the alleged fact that no one has hitherto been able to demonstrate these two points. Now I completely disagree with this: I think that when properly understood almost all the arguments that have been put forward on these issues by the great men have the force of demonstrations, and I am convinced that it is scarcely possible to provide any arguments which have not already been produced by someone else. Nevertheless, I think there can be no more useful service to be rendered in philosophy than to conduct a careful search, once and for all, for the best of these arguments, and to set them out so precisely and clearly as to produce for the future a general agreement that they amount to demonstrative proofs. And finally, I was strongly pressed to undertake this task by several people who knew that I had developed a method for resolving certain difficulties in the sciences – not a new method (for nothing is older than the truth), but one which they had seen me use with some success in other areas; and I therefore thought it my duty to make some attempt to apply it to the matter in hand.

The present treatise contains everything that I have been able to accom- 4 plish in this area. Not that I have attempted to collect here all the different arguments that could be put forward to establish the same results, for this does not seem worthwhile except in cases where no single argument is regarded as sufficiently reliable. What I have done is to take merely the

---

[1] The Lateran Council of 1513 condemned the Averroist heresy, which denied personal immortality.

ita prosecutus sum, ut jam pro certissimis et evidentissimis demonstrationibus illas ausim proponere. Addamque etiam tales esse, ut non putem ullam viam humano ingenio patere, per quam meliores inveniri unquam possint: cogit enim me causae necessitas, et gloria Dei, ad quam totum hoc refertur, ut hic aliquanto liberius de meis loquar quam mea fert consuetudo. Atqui quantumvis certas et evidentes illas putem, non tamen ideo mihi persuadeo ad omnium captum esse accommodatas: sed, quemadmodum in Geometria multae sunt ab Archimede, Apollonio, Pappo, aliisve scriptae, quae, etsi pro evidentibus etiam ac certis ab omnibus habeantur, quia nempe nihil plane continent quod seorsim spectatum non sit cognitu facillimum, nihilque in quo sequentia cum antecedentibus non accurate cohaereant, quia tamen longiusculae sunt, et valde attentum lectorem desiderant, non nisi ab admodum paucis intelliguntur: ita, quamvis eas quibus hic utor, certitudine et evidentia Geometricas aequare, vel etiam superare, existimem, vereor tamen ne a multis satis percipi non possint, tum quia etiam longiusculae sunt, et aliae ab aliis pendent, tum praecipue quia requirunt mentem a praejudiciis plane liberam, et quae se ipsam a sensuum consortio facile subducat. Nec certe plures in mundo Metaphysicis studiis quam Geometri-
5 cis apti reperiuntur. Ac praeterea in eo differentia est, quod in Geometria, cum omnibus sit persuasum nihil scribi solere, de quo certa demonstratio non habeatur, saepius in eo peccant imperiti, quod falsa approbent, dum ea videri volunt intelligere, quam quod vera refutent: contra vero in Philosophia, cum credatur nihil esse de quo non possit in utramque partem disputari, pauci veritatem investigant, et multo plures, ex eo quod ausint optima quaeque impugnare, famam ingenii aucupantur.

Atque ideo, qualescunque meae rationes esse possint, quia tamen ad Philosophiam spectant, non spero me illarum ope magnum operae pretium esse facturum, nisi me patrocinio vestro adjuvetis. Sed cum tanta inhaereat omnium mentibus de vestra Facultate opinio,

principal and most important arguments and develop them in such a way that I would now venture to put them forward as very certain and evident demonstrations. I will add that these proofs are of such a kind that I reckon they leave no room for the possibility that the human mind will ever discover better ones. The vital importance of the cause and the glory of God, to which the entire undertaking is directed, here compel me to speak somewhat more freely about my own achievements than is my custom. But although I regard the proofs as quite certain and evident, I cannot therefore persuade myself that they are suitable to be grasped by everyone. In geometry there are many writings left by Archimedes, Apollonius, Pappus and others which are accepted by everyone as evident and certain because they contain absolutely nothing that is not very easy to understand when considered on its own, and each step fits in precisely with what has gone before; yet because they are somewhat long, and demand a very attentive reader, it is only comparatively few people who understand them. In the same way, although the proofs I employ here are in my view as certain and evident as the proofs of geometry, if not more so, it will, I fear, be impossible for many people to achieve an adequate perception of them, both because they are rather long and some depend on others, and also, above all, because they require a mind which is completely free from preconceived opinions and which can easily detach itself from involvement with the senses. Moreover, people who have an aptitude for metaphysical studies are certainly not to be found in the world in any greater numbers than those who have an aptitude for geometry. What is 5 more, there is the difference that in geometry everyone has been taught to accept that as a rule no proposition is put forward in a book without there being a conclusive demonstration available; so inexperienced students make the mistake of accepting what is false, in their desire to appear to understand it, more often than they make the mistake of rejecting what is true. In philosophy, by contrast, the belief is that everything can be argued either way; so few people pursue the truth, while the great majority build up their reputation for ingenuity by boldly attacking whatever is most sound.

Hence, whatever the quality of my arguments may be, because they have to do with philosophy I do not expect they will enable me to achieve any very worthwhile results unless you come to my aid by granting me your patronage.[1] The reputation of your Faculty is so firmly fixed in the

---

[1] Although the title page of the first edition of the *Meditations* carries the words 'with the approval of the learned doctors', Descartes never in fact obtained the endorsement from the Sorbonne which he sought.

tantaeque sit authoritatis SORBONAE nomen, ut non modo in rebus fidei nulli unquam Societati post sacra Concilia tantum creditum sit quam vestrae, sed etiam in humana Philosophia nullibi major perspicacia et soliditas, nec ad ferenda judicia major integritas et sapientia esse existimetur; non dubito quin, si tantam hujus scripti curam suscipere dignemini, *primo* quidem, ut a vobis corrigatur: memor enim, non modo humanitatis, sed maxime etiam inscitiae meae, non affirmo nullos in eo esse errores; *deinde*, ut quae vel desunt, vel non satis absoluta sunt, vel majorem explicationem desiderant, addantur, perficiantur, illustrentur, aut a vobis ipsis, aut saltem a me, postquam a vobis ero admonitus; ac *denique*, ut postquam rationes in eo contentae, quibus Deum esse, mentemque a corpore aliam esse probatur, ad eam perspicuitatem erunt perductae, ad quam ipsas perduci posse confido, ita

6 nempe ut pro accuratissimis demonstrationibus habendae sint, hoc ipsum declarare et publice testari velitis: non dubito, inquam, quin, si hoc fiat, omnes errores, qui de his quaestionibus unquam fuerunt, brevi ex hominum mentibus deleantur. Veritas enim ipsa facile efficiet ut reliqui ingeniosi et docti vestro judicio subscribant; et authoritas, ut Athei, qui scioli magis quam ingeniosi aut docti esse solent, contradicendi animum deponant, atque etiam ut forte rationes, quas ab omnibus ingenio praeditis pro demonstrationibus haberi scient, ipsi propugnent, ne non intelligere videantur. Ac denique caeteri omnes tot testimoniis facile credent, nemoque amplius erit in mundo, qui vel Dei existentiam, vel realem humanae animae a corpore distinctionem ausit in dubium revocare. Cujus rei quanta esset utilitas, vos ipsi, pro vestra singulari sapientia, omnium optime aestimare potestis; nec deceret me vobis, qui maximum Ecclesiae Catholicae columen semper fuistis, Dei et Religionis causam pluribus hic commendare.

minds of all, and the name of the Sorbonne has such authority that, with the exception of the Sacred Councils, no institution carries more weight than yours in matters of faith; while as regards human philosophy, you are thought of as second to none, both for insight and soundness and also for the integrity and wisdom of your pronouncements. Because of this, the results of your careful attention to this book, if you deigned to give it, would be threefold. First, the errors in it would be corrected – for when I remember not only that I am a human being, but above all that I am an ignorant one, I cannot claim it is free of mistakes. Secondly, any passages which are defective, or insufficiently developed or requiring further explanation, would be supplemented, completed and clarified, either by yourselves or by me after you have given me your advice. And lastly, once the arguments in the book proving that God exists and that the mind is distinct from the body have been brought, as I am sure they can be, to such a pitch of clarity that they are fit to be regarded as very exact demonstrations, 6 you may be willing to declare as much, and make a public statement to that effect. If all this were to happen, I do not doubt that all the errors which have ever existed on these subjects would soon be eradicated from the minds of men. In the case of all those who share your intelligence and learning, the truth itself will readily ensure that they subscribe to your opinion. As for the atheists, who are generally posers rather than people of real intelligence or learning, your authority will induce them to lay aside the spirit of contradiction; and, since they know that the arguments are regarded as demonstrations by all who are intellectually gifted, they may even go so far as to defend them, rather than appear not to understand them. And finally, everyone else will confidently go along with so many declarations of assent, and there will be no one left in the world who will dare to call into doubt either the existence of God or the real distinction between the human soul and body. The great advantage that this would bring is something which you, in your singular wisdom, are in a better position to evaluate than anyone;[1] and it would ill become me to spend any more time commending the cause of God and religion to you, who have always been the greatest tower of strength to the Catholic Church.

[1] 'It is for you to judge the advantage that would come from establishing these beliefs firmly, since you see all the disorders which come from their being doubted' (French version).

Quaestiones de Deo et mente humana jam ante paucis attigi in *Dissertatione de Methodo recte regendae rationis et veritatis in scientiis investigandae*, gallice edita anno 1637, non quidem ut ipsas ibi accurate tractarem, sed tantum ut delibarem, et ex lectorum judiciis addiscerem qua ratione postea essent tractandae. Tanti enim momenti mihi visae sunt, ut plus una vice de ipsis agendum esse judicarem; viamque sequor ad eas explicandas tam parum tritam, atque ab usu communi tam remotam, ut non utile putarim ipsam in gallico et passim ab omnibus legendo scripto fusius docere, ne debiliora etiam ingenia credere possent eam sibi esse ingrediendam.

Cum autem ibi rogassem omnes quibus aliquid in meis scriptis reprehensione dignum occurreret, ut ejus me monere dignarentur, nulla in ea quae de his quaestionibus attigeram notatu digna objecta sunt, praeter duo, ad quae hic paucis, priusquam earumdem accuratiorem explicationem aggrediar, respondebo.

8   Primum est, ex eo quod mens humana in se conversa non percipiat aliud se esse quam rem cogitantem, non sequi ejus naturam sive *essentiam* in eo tantum consistere, quod sit res cogitans, ita ut vox *tantum* caetera omnia excludat quae forte etiam dici possent ad animae naturam pertinere. Cui objectioni respondeo me etiam ibi noluisse illa excludere in ordine ad ipsam rei veritatem (de qua scilicet tunc non agebam), sed dumtaxat in ordine ad meam perceptionem, adeo ut sensus esset me nihil plane cognoscere quod ad essentiam meam scirem pertinere, praeterquam quod essem res cogitans, sive res habens in se facultatem cogitandi. In sequentibus autem ostendam quo pacto, ex eo quod nihil aliud ad essentiam meam pertinere cognoscam, sequatur nihil etiam aliud revera ad illam pertinere.

Alterum est, ex eo quod ideam rei me perfectioris in me habeam, non sequi ipsam ideam esse me perfectiorem, et multo minus illud quod per istam ideam repraesentatur existere. Sed respondeo hic subesse aequivocationem in voce ideae: sumi

Preface to the reader[1]

I briefly touched on the topics of God and the human mind in my *Discourse on the method of rightly conducting reason and seeking the truth in the sciences*, which was published in French in 1637. My purpose there was not to provide a full treatment, but merely to offer a sample, and learn from the views of my readers how I should handle these topics at a later date. The issues seemed to me of such great importance that I considered they ought to be dealt with more than once; and the route which I follow in explaining them is so untrodden and so remote from the normal way, that I thought it would not be helpful to give a full account of it in a book written in French and designed to be read by all and sundry, in case weaker intellects might believe that they ought to set out on the same path.

In the *Discourse* I asked anyone who found anything worth criticizing in what I had written to be kind enough to point it out to me.[2] In the case of my remarks concerning God and the soul, only two objections worth mentioning were put to me, which I shall now briefly answer before embarking on a more precise elucidation of these topics.

The first objection is this. From the fact that the human mind, when 8 directed towards itself, does not perceive itself to be anything other than a thinking thing, it does not follow that its nature or essence consists only in its being a thinking thing, where the word 'only' excludes everything else that could be said to belong to the nature of the soul. My answer to this objection is that in that passage it was not my intention to make those exclusions in an order corresponding to the actual truth of the matter (which I was not dealing with at that stage) but merely in an order corresponding to my own perception. So the sense of the passage was that I was aware of nothing at all that I knew belonged to my essence, except that I was a thinking thing, or a thing possessing within itself the faculty of thinking.[3] I shall, however, show below how it follows, from the fact that I am aware of nothing else belonging to my essence, that nothing else does in fact belong to it.

The second objection is this. From the fact that I have within me an idea of a thing more perfect than myself, it does not follow that the idea itself is more perfect than me, still less that what is represented by the idea exists. My reply is that there is an ambiguity here in the word 'idea'. 'Idea'

---

[1] The French version of 1647 does not translate this preface, but substitutes a brief foreword, *Le Libraire au lecteur* (*The Publisher to the Reader*), which is probably not by Descartes.
[2] See *Discourse*, Part Six; AT VI 75: CSM I 149.
[3] See *Discourse*, Part Four; AT VI 32: CSM I 127.

enim potest vel materialiter, pro operatione intellectus, quo sensu me perfectior dici nequit, vel objective, pro re per istam operationem repraesentata, quae res, etsi non supponatur extra intellectum existere, potest tamen me esse perfectior ratione suae essentiae. Quomodo vero, ex hoc solo quod rei me perfectioris idea in me sit, sequatur illam rem revera existere, fuse in sequentibus exponetur.

Vidi quidem praeterea duo quaedam scripta satis longa, sed quibus non tam meae his de rebus rationes quam conclusiones argumen-
9 tis ex Atheorum locis communibus mutuatis impugnabantur. Et quoniam istiusmodi argumenta nullam vim habere possunt apud eos, qui rationes meas intelligent, adeoque praepostera et imbecillia sunt multorum judicia, ut magis a primum acceptis opinionibus, quantumvis falsis et a ratione alienis, persuadeantur, quam a vera et firma, sed posterius audita, ipsarum refutatione, nolo hic ad illa respondere, ne mihi sint prius referenda. Tantumque generaliter dicam ea omnia, quae vulgo jactantur ab Atheis ad existentiam Dei impugnandam, semper ex eo pendere, quod vel humani affectus Deo affingantur, vel mentibus nostris tanta vis et sapientia arrogetur, ut quidnam Deus facere possit ac debeat, determinare et comprehendere conemur; adeo ut, modo tantum memores simus mentes nostras considerandas esse ut finitas, Deum autem ut incomprehensibilem et infinitum, nullam ista difficultatem sint nobis paritura.

Jam vero, postquam hominum judicia semel utcunque sum expertus, iterum hic aggredior easdem de Deo et mente humana quaestiones, simulque totius primae Philosophiae initia tractare; sed ita ut nullum vulgi plausum, nullamque Lectorum frequentiam expectem: quin etiam nullis author sum ut haec legant, nisi tantum iis qui serio mecum meditari, mentemque a sensibus, simulque ab omnibus praejudiciis, abducere poterunt ac volent, quales non nisi admodum paucos reperiri satis scio. Quantum autem ad illos, qui, rationum mearum seriem et nexum comprehendere
10 non curantes, in singulas tantum clausulas, ut multis in more est, argutari studebunt, non magnum ex hujus scripti lectione fructum sunt percepturi; et quamvis forte in multis cavillandi occasionem

can be taken materially, as an operation of the intellect, in which case it cannot be said to be more perfect than me. Alternatively, it can be taken objectively, as the thing represented by that operation; and this thing, even if it is not regarded as existing outside the intellect, can still, in virtue of its essence, be more perfect than myself. As to how, from the mere fact that there is within me an idea of something more perfect than me, it follows that this thing really exists, this is something which will be fully explained below.

Apart from these objections, there are two fairly lengthy essays which I have looked at,[1] but these did not attack my reasoning on these matters so much as my conclusions, and employed arguments lifted from the standard sources of the atheists. But arguments of this sort can carry no weight with those who understand my reasoning. Moreover, the judgement of many people is so silly and weak that, once they have accepted a view, they continue to believe it, however false and irrational it may be, in preference to a true and well-grounded refutation which they hear subsequently. So I do not wish to reply to such arguments here, if only to avoid having to state them. I will only make the general point that all the objections commonly tossed around by atheists to attack the existence of God invariably depend either on attributing human feelings to God or on arrogantly supposing our own minds to be so powerful and wise that we can attempt to grasp and set limits to what God can or should perform. So, provided only that we remember that our minds must be regarded as finite, while God is infinite and beyond our comprehension, such objections will not cause us any difficulty.

But now that I have, after a fashion, taken an initial sample of people's opinions, I am again tackling the same questions concerning God and the human mind; and this time I am also going to deal with the foundations of First Philosophy in its entirety. But I do not expect any popular approval, or indeed any great crowd of readers. On the contrary, I would not urge anyone to read this book except those who are able and willing to meditate seriously with me, and to withdraw their minds from the senses and from all preconceived opinions. Such readers, as I well know, are few and far between. Those who do not bother to grasp the proper order of my arguments and the connection between them, but merely try to carp at individual sentences, as is the fashion, will not get much benefit from reading this book. They may well find an opportunity to quibble in many

---

[1] One of the critics referred to here is Petit: see letter to Mersenne of 27 May 1638 (AT II 144: CSMK 104). The other is unknown.

inveniant, non facile tamen aliquid quod urgeat aut responsione dignum sit objicient.

Quia vero nequidem etiam aliis spondeo me in omnibus prima fronte satisfacturum, nec tantum mihi arrogo ut confidam me omnia posse praevidere quae alicui difficilia videbuntur, primo quidem in Meditationibus illas ipsas cogitationes exponam, quarum ope ad certam et evidentem cognitionem veritatis mihi videor pervenisse, ut experiar an forte iisdem rationibus, quibus ego persuasus sum, alios etiam possim persuadere. Postea vero respondebo ad objectiones virorum aliquot ingenio et doctrina excellentium, ad quos hae Meditationes, antequam typis mandarentur, examinandae missae sunt. Satis enim multa et varia ab illis fuerunt objecta, ut ausim sperare non facile quicquam aliis, saltem alicujus momenti, venturum in mentem, quod ii nondum attigerint. Ideoque rogo etiam atque etiam Lectores, ut non prius de Meditationibus judicium ferant, quam objectiones istas earumque solutiones omnes perlegere dignati sint.

places, but it will not be easy for them to produce objections which are telling or worth replying to.

But I certainly do not promise to satisfy my other readers straightaway on all points, and I am not so presumptuous as to be sure that I am capable of foreseeing all the difficulties which anyone may find. So first of all, in the *Meditations*, I will set out the very thoughts which have enabled me, in my view, to arrive at a certain and evident knowledge of the truth, so that I can find out whether the same arguments which have convinced me will enable me to convince others. Next, I will reply to the objections of various men of outstanding intellect and scholarship who had these Meditations sent to them for scrutiny before they went to press. For the objections they raised were so many and so varied that I would venture to hope that it will be hard for anyone else to think of any point – at least of any importance – which these critics have not touched on. I therefore earnestly request my readers not to pass judgement on the *Meditations* until they have been kind enough to read through all these objections and my replies to them.

Synopsis
sex sequentium Meditationum

In prima, causae exponuntur propter quas de rebus omnibus, praesertim materialibus, possumus dubitare; quandiu scilicet non habemus alia scientiarum fundamenta, quam ea quae antehac habuimus. Etsi autem istius tantae dubitationis utilitas prima fronte non appareat, est tamen in eo maxima quod ab omnibus praejudiciis nos liberet, viamque facillimam sternat ad mentem a sensibus abducendam; ac denique efficiat, ut de iis, quae postea vera esse comperiemus, non amplius dubitare possimus.

In secunda, mens quae, propria libertate utens, supponit ea omnia non existere de quorum existentia vel minimum potest dubitare, animadvertit fieri non posse quin ipsa interim existat. Quod etiam summae est utilitatis, quoniam hoc pacto facile distinguit quaenam ad se, hoc est, ad naturam intellectualem, et quaenam ad corpus pertineant. Sed quia forte nonnulli rationes de animae immortali-
13 tate illo in loco expectabunt, eos hic monendos puto me conatum esse nihil scribere quod non accurate demonstrarem; ideoque non alium ordinem sequi potuisse, quam illum qui est apud Geometras usitatus, ut nempe omnia praemitterem ex quibus quaesita propositio dependet, antequam de ipsa quidquam concluderem. Primum autem et praecipuum quod praerequiritur ad cognoscendam animae immortalitatem, esse ut quam maxime perspicuum de ea conceptum, et ab omni conceptu corporis plane distinctum, formemus; quod ibi factum est. Praeterea vero requiri etiam ut sciamus ea omnia quae clare et distincte intelligimus, eo ipso modo quo illa intelligimus, esse vera: quod ante quartam Meditationem probari non potuit; et habendum esse distinctum naturae corporeae conceptum, qui partim in ipsa secunda, partim etiam in quinta et sexta formatur; atque ex his debere concludi ea omnia quae clare et distincte concipiuntur ut substantiae diversae, sicuti concipiuntur mens et corpus, esse revera substantias realiter a se mutuo distinctas; hocque in sexta concludi. Idemque etiam in ipsa confirmari ex eo quod nullum corpus nisi divisibile

Synopsis
of the following six Meditations

In the First Meditation reasons are provided which give us possible grounds for doubt about all things, especially material things, so long as we have no foundations for the sciences other than those which we have had up till now. Although the usefulness of such extensive doubt is not apparent at first sight, its greatest benefit lies in freeing us from all our preconceived opinions, and providing the easiest route by which the mind may be led away from the senses. The eventual result of this doubt is to make it impossible for us to have any further doubts about what we subsequently discover to be true.

In the Second Meditation, the mind uses its own freedom and supposes the non-existence of all the things about whose existence it can have even the slightest doubt; and in so doing the mind notices that it is impossible that it should not itself exist during this time. This exercise is also of the greatest benefit, since it enables the mind to distinguish without difficulty what belongs to itself, i.e. to an intellectual nature, from what belongs to the body. But since some people may perhaps expect arguments for the immortality of the soul in this section, I think they should be warned here and now that I have tried not to put down anything which I could not precisely demonstrate. Hence the only order which I could follow was that normally employed by geometers, namely to set out all the premises on which a desired proposition depends, before drawing any conclusions about it. Now the first and most important prerequisite for knowledge of the immortality of the soul is for us to form a concept of the soul which is as clear as possible and is also quite distinct from every concept of body; and that is just what has been done in this section. A further requirement is that we should know that everything that we clearly and distinctly understand is true in a way which corresponds exactly to our understanding of it; but it was not possible to prove this before the Fourth Meditation. In addition we need to have a distinct concept of corporeal nature, and this is developed partly in the Second Meditation itself, and partly in the Fifth and Sixth Meditations. The inference to be drawn from these results is that all the things that we clearly and distinctly conceive of as different substances (as we do in the case of mind and body) are in fact substances which are really distinct one from the other; and this conclusion is drawn in the Sixth Meditation. The conclusion is confirmed in the same Meditation by the fact that we cannot understand a body except as being

intelligamus, contra autem nullam mentem nisi indivisibilem: neque enim possumus ullius mentis mediam partem concipere, ut possumus cujuslibet quantamvis exigui corporis; adeo ut eorum naturae non modo diversae, sed etiam quodammodo contrariae agnoscantur. Non autem ulterius ea de re in hoc scripto me egisse; tum quia haec sufficiunt ad ostendendum ex corporis corruptione mentis interitum non sequi, atque sic ad alterius vitae spem mortalibus faciendam; tum etiam quia praemissae, ex quibus ipsa mentis immortalitas concludi

14 potest, ex totius Physicae explicatione dependent: primo ut sciatur omnes omnino substantias, sive res quae a Deo creari debent ut existant, ex natura sua esse incorruptibiles, nec posse unquam desinere esse, nisi ab eodem Deo concursum suum iis denegante ad nihilum reducantur; ac deinde ut advertatur corpus quidem in genere sumptum esse substantiam, ideoque nunquam etiam perire. Sed corpus humanum, quatenus a reliquis differt corporibus, non nisi ex certa membrorum configuratione aliisque ejusmodi accidentibus esse conflatum; mentem vero humanam non ita ex ullis accidentibus constare, sed puram esse substantiam: etsi enim omnia ejus accidentia mutentur, ut quod alias res intelligat, alias velit, alias sentiat, etc., non idcirco ipsa mens alia evadit; humanum autem corpus aliud fit ex hoc solo quod figura quarumdam ejus partium mutetur: ex quibus sequitur corpus quidem perfacile interire, mentem autem ex natura sua esse immortalem.

In tertia Meditatione, meum praecipuum argumentum ad probandum Dei existentiam satis fuse, ut mihi videtur, explicui. Verumtamen, quia, ut Lectorum animos quam maxime a sensibus abducerem, nullis ibi comparationibus a rebus corporeis petitis volui uti, multae fortasse obscuritates remanserunt, sed quae, ut spero, postea in responsionibus ad objectiones plane tollentur; ut, inter caeteras, quomodo idea entis summe perfecti, quae in nobis est, tantum habeat realitatis objectivae, ut non possit non esse a causa summe perfecta, quod ibi illustratur comparatione machinae valde perfectae, cujus idea est in mente alicujus artificis; ut enim artificium objectivum hujus ideae debet habere aliquam causam, nempe

divisible, while by contrast we cannot understand a mind except as being indivisible. For we cannot conceive of half of a mind, while we can always conceive of half of a body, however small; and this leads us to recognize that the natures of mind and body are not only different, but in some way opposite. But I have not pursued this topic any further in this book, first because these arguments are enough to show that the decay of the body does not imply the destruction of the mind, and are hence enough to give mortals the hope of an afterlife, and secondly because the premises which lead to the conclusion that the soul is immortal depend on an account of the whole of physics. This is required for two reasons. First, we need to   14 know that absolutely all substances, or things which must be created by God in order to exist, are by their nature incorruptible and cannot ever cease to exist unless they are reduced to nothingness by God's denying his concurrence[1] to them. Secondly, we need to recognize that body, taken in the general sense, is a substance, so that it too never perishes. But the human body, in so far as it differs from other bodies, is simply made up of a certain configuration of limbs and other accidents[2] of this sort; whereas the human mind is not made up of any accidents in this way, but is a pure substance. For even if all the accidents of the mind change, so that it has different objects of the understanding and different desires and sensations, it does not on that account become a different mind; whereas a human body loses its identity merely as a result of a change in the shape of some of its parts. And it follows from this that while the body can very easily perish, the mind[3] is immortal by its very nature.

In the Third Meditation I have explained quite fully enough, I think, my principal argument for proving the existence of God. But in order to draw my readers' minds away from the senses as far as possible, I was not willing to use any comparison taken from bodily things. So it may be that many obscurities remain; but I hope they will be completely removed later, in my Replies to the Objections. One such problem, among others, is how the idea of a supremely perfect being, which is in us, possesses so much objective[4] reality that it can come only from a cause which is supremely perfect. In the Replies this is illustrated by the comparison of a very perfect machine, the idea of which is in the mind of some engineer. Just as the objective intricacy belonging to the idea must have some cause, namely the

---

[1] The continuous divine action necessary to maintain things in existence.
[2] Descartes here uses this scholastic term to refer to those features of a thing which may alter, e.g. the particular size, shape etc. of a body, or the particular thoughts, desires etc. of a mind.
[3] '. . . or the soul of man, for I make no distinction between them' (added in French version).
[4] For Descartes's use of this term, see Med. III, pp. 57–9 below.

scientiam hujus artificis, vel alicujus alterius a quo illam accepit, ita
15 idea Dei, quae in nobis est, non potest non habere Deum ipsum pro
causa.

In quarta, probatur ea omnia quae clare et distincte percipimus,
esse vera, simulque in quo ratio falsitatis consistat explicatur: quae
necessario sciri debent tam ad praecedentia firmanda, quam ad reliqua
intelligenda. (Sed ibi interim est advertendum nullo modo agi de
peccato, vel errore qui committitur in persecutione boni et mali,
sed de eo tantum qui contingit in dijudicatione veri et falsi. Nec ea
spectari quae ad fidem pertinent, vel ad vitam agendam, sed tantum
speculativas et solius luminis naturalis ope cognitas veritates.)

In quinta, praeterquam quod natura corporea in genere sumpta
explicatur, nova etiam ratione Dei existentia demonstratur: sed in qua
rursus nonnullae forte occurrent difficultates, quae postea in responsione ad objectiones resolventur: ac denique ostenditur quo pacto
verum sit, ipsarum Geometricarum demonstrationum certitudinem a
cognitione Dei pendere.

In sexta denique, intellectio ab imaginatione secernitur; distinc-
tionum signa describuntur; mentem realiter a corpore distingui probatur; eandem nihilominus tam arcte illi esse conjunctam, ut unum
quid cum ipsa componat, ostenditur; omnes errores qui a sensibus
oriri solent recensentur; modi quibus vitari possint exponuntur; et
denique rationes omnes ex quibus rerum materialium existentia possit
concludi, afferuntur: non quod eas valde utiles esse putarim ad proban-
16 dum id ipsum quod probant, nempe revera esse aliquem mundum,
et homines habere corpora, et similia, de quibus nemo unquam sanae
mentis serio dubitavit; sed quia, illas considerando, agnoscitur non
esse tam firmas nec tam perspicuas quam sunt eae, per quas in mentis nostrae et Dei cognitionem devenimus; adeo ut hae sint omnium
certissimae et evidentissimae quae ab humano ingenio sciri possint.
Cujus unius rei probationem in his Meditationibus mihi pro scopo
proposui. Nec idcirco hic recenseo varias illas quaestiones de quibus
etiam in ipsis ex occasione tractatur.

scientific knowledge of the engineer, or of someone else who passed the idea on to him, so the idea of God which is in us must have God himself 15 as its cause.

In the Fourth Meditation it is proved that everything that we clearly and distinctly perceive is true, and I also explain what the nature of falsity consists in. These results need to be known both in order to confirm what has gone before and also to make intelligible what is to come later. (But it should be noted in passing that I do not here deal at all with sin, i.e. the error which is committed in pursuing good and evil, but only with the error that occurs in distinguishing truth from falsehood. And there is no discussion of matters pertaining to faith or the conduct of life, but simply of speculative truths which are known solely by means of the natural light.)[1]

In the Fifth Meditation, besides an account of corporeal nature taken in general, there is a new argument demonstrating the existence of God. Again, several difficulties may arise here, but these are resolved later in the Replies to the Objections. Finally I explain the sense in which it is true that the certainty even of geometrical demonstrations depends on the knowledge of God.

Lastly, in the Sixth Meditation, the intellect is distinguished from the imagination; the criteria for this distinction are explained; the mind is proved to be really distinct from the body, but is shown, notwithstanding, to be so closely joined to it that the mind and the body make up a kind of unit; there is a survey of all the errors which commonly come from the senses, and an explanation of how they may be avoided; and, lastly, there is a presentation of all the arguments which enable the existence of material things to be inferred. The great benefit of these arguments is not, in my view, that they prove what they establish – namely that there 16 really is a world, and that human beings have bodies and so on – since no sane person has ever seriously doubted these things. The point is that in considering these arguments we come to realize that they are not as solid or as transparent as the arguments which lead us to knowledge of our own minds and of God, so that the latter are the most certain and evident of all possible objects of knowledge for the human intellect. Indeed, this is the one thing that I set myself to prove in these Meditations. And for that reason I will not now go over the various other issues in the book which are dealt with as they come up.

---

[1] Descartes added this passage on the advice of Arnauld (cf. AT VII 215: CSM II 151). He told Mersenne, 'Put the words between brackets so that it can be seen that they have been added' (letter of 18 March 1641, AT III 335: CSMK 175).

MEDITATIONES
DE PRIMA PHILOSOPHIA

IN QUIBUS DEI EXISTENTIA
ET ANIMAE HUMANAE A CORPORE
DISTINCTIO DEMONSTRANTUR[1]

MEDITATIO PRIMA

17   *De iis quae in dubium revocari possunt*

Animadverti jam ante aliquot annos quam multa, ineunte aetate, falsa pro veris admiserim, et quam dubia sint quaecunque istis postea superextruxi, ac proinde funditus omnia semel in vita esse evertenda, atque a primis fundamentis denuo inchoandum, si quid aliquando firmum et mansurum cupiam in scientiis stabilire; sed ingens opus esse videbatur, eamque aetatem expectabam, quae foret tam matura, ut capessendis disciplinis aptior nulla sequeretur. Quare tamdiu cunctatus sum ut deinceps essem in culpa, si quod temporis superest ad agendum,
18 deliberando consumerem. Opportune igitur hodie mentem curis omnibus exsolvi, securum mihi otium procuravi, solus secedo, serio tandem et libere generali huic mearum opinionum eversioni vacabo.

Ad hoc autem non erit necesse, ut omnes esse falsas ostendam, quod nunquam fortassis assequi possem; sed quia jam ratio persuadet, non minus accurate ab iis quae non plane certa sunt atque indubitata, quam ab aperte falsis assensionem esse cohibendam, satis erit ad omnes rejiciendas, si aliquam rationem dubitandi in unaquaque reperero. Nec ideo etiam singulae erunt percurrendae, quod operis esset infiniti; sed quia, suffossis fundamentis, quidquid iis superaedificatum est sponte collabitur, aggrediar statim ipsa principia, quibus illud omne quod olim credidi nitebatur.

---

[1] From the 1642 title page. The 1641 title page has: 'In qua Dei existentia et animae immortalitas demonstratur'.

MEDITATIONS
ON FIRST PHILOSOPHY

IN WHICH ARE DEMONSTRATED THE EXISTENCE OF GOD AND THE DISTINCTION BETWEEN THE HUMAN SOUL AND THE BODY[1]

FIRST MEDITATION

What can be called into doubt

17

Some years ago I was struck by the large number of falsehoods that I had accepted as true in my childhood, and by the highly doubtful nature of the whole edifice that I had subsequently based on them. I realized that it was necessary, once in the course of my life, to demolish everything completely and start again right from the foundations if I wanted to establish anything at all in the sciences that was stable and likely to last. But the task looked an enormous one, and I began to wait until I should reach a mature enough age to ensure that no subsequent time of life would be more suitable for tackling such inquiries. This led me to put the project off for so long that I would now be to blame if by pondering over it any further I wasted the time still left for carrying it out. So today I have expressly rid my mind of all 18 worries and arranged for myself a clear stretch of free time. I am here quite alone, and at last I will devote myself sincerely and without reservation to the general demolition of my opinions.

But to accomplish this, it will not be necessary for me to show that all my opinions are false, which is something I could perhaps never manage. Reason now leads me to think that I should hold back my assent from opinions which are not completely certain and indubitable just as carefully as I do from those which are patently false. So, for the purpose of rejecting all my opinions, it will be enough if I find in each of them at least some reason for doubt. And to do this I will not need to run through them all individually, which would be an endless task. Once the foundations of a building are undermined, anything built on them collapses of its own accord; so I will go straight for the basic principles on which all my former beliefs rested.

---

[1] 'In which the existence of God and the immortality of the soul is [*sic*] demonstrated' (first edition).

23

Nempe quidquid hactenus ut maxime verum admisi, vel a sensibus, vel per sensus accepi; hos autem interdum fallere deprehendi, ac prudentiae est nunquam illis plane confidere qui nos vel semel deceperunt.

Sed forte, quamvis interdum sensus circa minuta quaedam et remotiora nos fallant, pleraque tamen alia sunt de quibus dubitari plane non potest, quamvis ab iisdem hauriantur: ut jam me hic esse, foco assidere, hyemali toga esse indutum, chartam istam manibus contrectare, et similia. Manus vero has ipsas, totumque hoc corpus meum esse, qua ratione posset negari? nisi me forte comparem nescio quibus insanis, quorum cerebella tam contumax vapor ex atra bile labefactat, ut constanter asseverent vel se esse reges, cum sunt pauperrimi, vel purpura indutos, cum sunt nudi, vel caput habere fictile, vel se totos esse cucurbitas, vel ex vitro conflatos; sed amentes sunt isti, nec minus ipse demens viderer, si quod ab iis exemplum ad me transferrem.

Praeclare sane, tanquam non sim homo qui soleam noctu dormire, et eadem omnia in somnis pati, vel etiam interdum minus verisimilia, quam quae isti vigilantes. Quam frequenter vero usitata ista, me hic esse, toga vestiri, foco assidere, quies nocturna persuadet, cum tamen positis vestibus jaceo inter strata! Atqui nunc certe vigilantibus oculis intueor hanc chartam, non sopitum est hoc caput quod commoveo, manum istam prudens et sciens extendo et sentio; non tam distincta contingerent dormienti. Quasi scilicet non recorder a similibus etiam cogitationibus me alias in somnis fuisse delusum; quae dum cogito attentius, tam plane video nunquam certis indiciis vigiliam a somno posse distingui, ut obstupescam, et fere hic ipse stupor mihi opinionem somni confirmet.

Age ergo somniemus, nec particularia ista vera sint, nos oculos aperire, caput movere, manus extendere, nec forte etiam nos habere tales manus, nec tale totum corpus; tamen profecto fatendum est visa per quietem esse veluti quasdam pictas imagines, quae non nisi ad similitudinem rerum verarum fingi potuerunt; ideoque saltem generalia haec, oculos, caput, manus, totumque corpus, res quasdam non imaginarias, sed veras existere. Nam sane pictores ipsi, ne tum quidem, cum Sirenas

Whatever I have up till now accepted as most true I have acquired either from the senses or through the senses. But from time to time I have found that the senses deceive, and it is prudent never to trust completely those who have deceived us even once.

Yet perhaps, although the senses occasionally deceive us with respect to objects which are very small or in the distance, there are many other beliefs about which doubt is quite impossible, even though they are derived from the senses – for example, that I am here, sitting by the fire, wearing a winter dressing-gown, holding this piece of paper in my hands, and so on. Again, how could it be denied that these hands or this whole body are mine? Unless perhaps I were to liken myself to madmen, whose brains are so damaged by the persistent vapours of melancholia that they firmly maintain they are kings when they are paupers, or say they are dressed in purple when they are naked, or that their heads are made of earthenware, or that they are pumpkins, or made of glass. But such people are insane, and I would be thought equally mad if I took anything from them as a model for myself.

A brilliant piece of reasoning! As if I were not a man who sleeps at night, and regularly experiences the same things while asleep[1] as madmen do when awake – indeed sometimes even more improbable ones. How often, asleep at night, am I convinced of just such familiar events – that I am here in my dressing-gown, sitting by the fire – when in fact I am lying undressed in bed! Yet at the moment my eyes are certainly wide awake when I look at this piece of paper; I shake my head and it is not asleep; as I stretch out and feel my hand I do so deliberately, and I know what I am doing. All this would not happen with such distinctness to someone asleep. Indeed! As if I did not remember other occasions when I have been tricked by exactly similar thoughts while asleep! As I think about this more carefully, I see plainly that there are never any sure signs by means of which being awake can be distinguished from being asleep. The result is that I begin to feel dazed, and this very feeling only reinforces the notion that I may be asleep.

Suppose then that I am dreaming, and that these particulars – that my eyes are open, that I am moving my head and stretching out my hands – are not true. Perhaps, indeed, I do not even have such hands or such a body at all. Nonetheless, it must surely be admitted that the visions which come in sleep are like paintings, which must have been fashioned in the likeness of things that are real, and hence that at least these general kinds of things – eyes, head, hands and the body as a whole – are things which are not imaginary but are real and exist. For even when painters try to create sirens 20

---

[1] '. . . and I regularly in my dreams represent to myself the same things' (French version).

et Satyriscos maxime inusitatis formis fingere student, naturas omni ex parte novas iis possunt assignare, sed tantummodo diversorum animalium membra permiscent; vel si forte aliquid excogitent adeo novum, ut nihil omnino ei simile fuerit visum, atque ita plane fictitium sit et falsum, certe tamen ad minimum veri colores esse debent, ex quibus illud componant. Nec dispari ratione, quamvis etiam generalia haec, oculi, caput, manus, et similia, imaginaria esse possent, necessario tamen saltem alia quaedam adhuc magis simplicia et universalia vera esse fatendum est, ex quibus tanquam coloribus veris omnes istae, seu verae, seu falsae, quae in cogitatione nostra sunt, rerum imagines effinguntur.

Cujus generis esse videntur natura corporea in communi, ejusque extensio; item figura rerum extensarum; item quantitas, sive earumdem magnitudo et numerus; item locus in quo existant, tempusque per quod durent, et similia.

Quapropter ex his forsan non male concludemus Physicam, Astronomiam, Medicinam, disciplinasque alias omnes, quae a rerum compositarum consideratione dependent, dubias quidem esse; atqui Arithmeticam, Geometriam, aliasque ejusmodi, quae nonnisi de simplicissimis et maxime generalibus rebus tractant, atque utrum eae sint in rerum natura necne, parum curant, aliquid certi atque indubitati continere. Nam sive vigilem, sive dormiam, duo et tria simul juncta sunt quinque, quadratumque non plura habet latera quam quatuor; nec fieri posse videtur ut tam perspicuae veritates in suspicionem falsitatis incurrant.

21   Verumtamen infixa quaedam est meae menti vetus opinio, Deum esse qui potest omnia, et a quo talis, qualis existo, sum creatus. Unde autem scio illum non fecisse ut nulla plane sit terra, nullum coelum, nulla res extensa, nulla figura, nulla magnitudo, nullus locus, et tamen haec omnia non aliter quam nunc mihi videantur existere? Imo etiam, quemadmodum judico interdum alios errare circa ea quae se perfectissime scire arbitrantur, ita ego ut fallar quoties duo et tria simul addo, vel numero quadrati latera, vel si quid aliud facilius fingi potest? At forte noluit Deus ita me decipi, dicitur enim summe bonus; sed si hoc ejus bonitati repugnaret, talem me creasse ut semper fallar, ab eadem etiam videretur esse alienum permittere ut interdum fallar; quod ultimum tamen non potest dici.

and satyrs with the most extraordinary bodies, they cannot give them natures which are new in all respects; they simply jumble up the limbs of different animals. Or if perhaps they manage to think up something so new that nothing remotely similar has ever been seen before – something which is therefore completely fictitious and unreal – at least the colours used in the composition must be real. By similar reasoning, although these general kinds of things – eyes, head, hands and so on – could be imaginary, it must at least be admitted that certain other even simpler and more universal things are real. These are as it were the real colours from which we form all the images of things, whether true or false, that occur in our thought.

This class appears to include corporeal nature in general, and its extension; the shape of extended things; the quantity, or size and number, of these things; the place in which they may exist, the time through which they may endure,[1] and so on.

So a reasonable conclusion from this might be that physics, astronomy, medicine, and all other disciplines which depend on the study of composite things, are doubtful; while arithmetic, geometry and other subjects of this kind, which deal only with the simplest and most general things, regardless of whether they really exist in nature or not, contain something certain and indubitable. For whether I am awake or asleep, two and three added together are five, and a square has no more than four sides. It seems impossible that such transparent truths should incur any suspicion of being false.

And yet firmly rooted in my mind is the long-standing opinion that 21 there is an omnipotent God who made me the kind of creature that I am. How do I know that he has not brought it about that there is no earth, no sky, no extended thing, no shape, no size, no place, while at the same time ensuring that all these things appear to me to exist just as they do now? What is more, just as I consider that others sometimes go astray in cases where they think they have the most perfect knowledge, how do I know that God has not brought it about that I too go wrong every time I add two and three or count the sides of a square, or in some even simpler matter, if that is imaginable? But perhaps God would not have allowed me to be deceived in this way, since he is said to be supremely good. But if it were inconsistent with his goodness to have created me such that I am deceived all the time, it would seem equally foreign to his goodness to allow me to be deceived even occasionally; yet this last assertion cannot be made.[2]

---

[1] '. . . the place where they are, the time which measures their duration' (French version).
[2] '. . . yet I cannot doubt that he does allow this' (French version).

Essent vero fortasse nonnulli qui tam potentem aliquem Deum mallent negare, quam res alias omnes credere esse incertas. Sed iis non repugnemus, totumque hoc de Deo demus esse fictitium; at seu fato, seu casu, seu continuata rerum serie, seu quovis alio modo me ad id quod sum pervenisse supponant; quoniam falli et errare imperfectio quaedam esse videtur, quo minus potentem originis meae authorem assignabunt, eo probabilius erit me tam imperfectum esse ut semper fallar. Quibus sane argumentis non habeo quod respondeam, sed tandem cogor fateri nihil esse ex iis quae olim vera putabam, de quo non liceat dubitare, idque non per inconsiderantiam vel levitatem, sed propter validas et meditatas rationes; ideoque etiam ab iisdem, 22 non minus quam ab aperte falsis, accurate deinceps assensionem esse cohibendam, si quid certi velim invenire.

Sed nondum sufficit haec advertisse, curandum est ut recorder; assidue enim recurrunt consuetae opiniones, occupantque credulitatem meam tanquam longo usu et familiaritatis jure sibi devinctam, fere etiam me invito; nec unquam iis assentiri et confidere desuescam, quamdiu tales esse supponam quales sunt revera, nempe aliquo quidem modo dubias, ut jam jam ostensum est, sed nihilominus valde probabiles, et quas multo magis rationi consentaneum sit credere quam negare. Quapropter, ut opinor, non male agam, si, voluntate plane in contrarium versa, me ipsum fallam, illasque aliquandiu omnino falsas imaginariasque esse fingam, donec tandem, velut aequatis utrimque praejudiciorum ponderibus, nulla amplius prava consuetudo judicium meum a recta rerum perceptione detorqueat. Etenim scio nihil inde periculi vel erroris interim sequuturum, et me plus aequo diffidentiae indulgere non posse, quandoquidem nunc non rebus agendis, sed cognoscendis tantum incumbo.

Supponam igitur non optimum Deum, fontem veritatis, sed genium aliquem malignum, eundemque summe potentem et callidum, omnem suam industriam in eo posuisse, ut me falleret: putabo coelum, aërem, terram, colores, figuras, sonos, cunctaque externa nihil aliud esse quam ludificationes somniorum, quibus 23 insidias credulitati meae tetendit: considerabo meipsum tanquam manus non habentem, non oculos, non carnem, non sanguinem, non aliquem sensum, sed haec omnia me habere falso opinantem:

Perhaps there may be some who would prefer to deny the existence of so powerful a God rather than believe that everything else is uncertain. Let us not argue with them, but grant them that everything said about God is a fiction. According to their supposition, then, I have arrived at my present state by fate or chance or a continuous chain of events, or by some other means; yet since deception and error seem to be imperfections, the less powerful they make my original cause, the more likely it is that I am so imperfect as to be deceived all the time. I have no answer to these arguments, but am finally compelled to admit that there is not one of my former beliefs about which a doubt may not properly be raised; and this is not a flippant or ill-considered conclusion, but is based on powerful and well thought-out reasons. So in future I must withhold my assent from 22 these former beliefs just as carefully as I would from obvious falsehoods, if I want to discover any certainty.[1]

But it is not enough merely to have noticed this; I must make an effort to remember it. My habitual opinions keep coming back, and, despite my wishes, they capture my belief, which is as it were bound over to them as a result of long occupation and the law of custom. I shall never get out of the habit of confidently assenting to these opinions, so long as I suppose them to be what in fact they are, namely highly probable opinions – opinions which, despite the fact that they are in a sense doubtful, as has just been shown, it is still much more reasonable to believe than to deny. In view of this, I think it will be a good plan to turn my will in completely the opposite direction and deceive myself, by pretending for a time that these former opinions are utterly false and imaginary. I shall do this until the weight of preconceived opinion is counter-balanced and the distorting influence of habit no longer prevents my judgement from perceiving things correctly. In the meantime, I know that no danger or error will result from my plan, and that I cannot possibly go too far in my distrustful attitude. This is because the task now in hand does not involve action but merely the acquisition of knowledge.

I will suppose therefore that not God, who is supremely good and the source of truth, but rather some malicious demon of the utmost power and cunning has employed all his energies in order to deceive me. I shall think that the sky, the air, the earth, colours, shapes, sounds and all external things are merely the delusions of dreams which he has devised to ensnare my judgement. I shall consider myself as not having hands or eyes, or 23 flesh, or blood or senses, but as falsely believing that I have all these things.

---

[1] '. . . in the sciences' (added in French version).

manebo obstinate in hac meditatione defixus, atque ita, siquidem non in potestate mea sit aliquid veri cognoscere, at certe hoc quod in me est, ne falsis assentiar, nec mihi quidquam iste deceptor, quantumvis potens, quantumvis callidus, possit imponere, obfirmata mente cavebo. Sed laboriosum est hoc institutum, et desidia quaedam ad consuetudinem vitae me reducit. Nec aliter quam captivus, qui forte imaginaria libertate fruebatur in somnis, cum postea suspicari incipit se dormire, timet excitari, blandisque illusionibus lente connivet: sic sponte relabor in veteres opiniones, vereorque expergisci, ne placidae quieti laboriosa vigilia succedens, non in aliqua luce, sed inter inextricabiles jam motarum difficultatum tenebras, in posterum sit degenda.

I shall stubbornly and firmly persist in this meditation; and, even if it is not in my power to know any truth, I shall at least do what is in my power,[1] that is, resolutely guard against assenting to any falsehoods, so that the deceiver, however powerful and cunning he may be, will be unable to impose on me in the slightest degree. But this is an arduous undertaking, and a kind of laziness brings me back to normal life. I am like a prisoner who is enjoying an imaginary freedom while asleep; as he begins to suspect that he is asleep, he dreads being woken up, and goes along with the pleasant illusion as long as he can. In the same way, I happily slide back into my old opinions and dread being shaken out of them, for fear that my peaceful sleep may be followed by hard labour when I wake, and that I shall have to toil not in the light, but amid the inextricable darkness of the problems I have now raised.

---

[1] '... nevertheless it is in my power to suspend my judgement' (French version).

De natura mentis humanae: quod ipsa sit notior quam corpus

In tantas dubitationes hesterna meditatione conjectus sum, ut nequeam amplius earum oblivisci, nec videam tamen qua ratione solvendae sint; sed, tanquam in profundum gurgitem ex improviso delapsus, ita turbatus sum, ut nec possim in imo pedem figere, nec enatare ad summum. Enitar tamen et tentabo rursus eandem viam quam heri fueram ingressus, removendo scilicet illud omne quod vel minimum dubitationis admittit, nihilo secius quam si omnino falsum esse comperissem; pergamque porro donec aliquid certi, vel, si nihil aliud, saltem hoc ipsum pro certo, nihil esse certi, cognoscam. Nihil nisi punctum petebat Archimedes, quod esset firmum et immobile, ut integram terram loco dimoveret; magna quoque speranda sunt, si vel minimum quid invenero quod certum sit et inconcussum.

Suppono igitur omnia quae video falsa esse; credo nihil unquam extitisse eorum quae mendax memoria repraesentat; nullos plane habeo sensus; corpus, figura, extensio, motus, locusque sunt chimerae. Quid igitur erit verum? Fortassis hoc unum, nihil esse certi.

Sed unde scio nihil esse diversum ab iis omnibus quae jam jam recensui, de quo ne minima quidem occasio sit dubitandi? Nunquid est aliquis Deus, vel quocunque nomine illum vocem, qui mihi has ipsas cogitationes immittit? Quare vero hoc putem, cum forsan ipsemet illarum author esse possim? Nunquid ergo saltem ego aliquid sum? Sed jam negavi me habere ullos sensus, et ullum corpus. Haereo tamen; nam quid inde? Sumne ita corpori sensibusque alligatus, ut sine illis esse non possim? Sed mihi persuasi nihil plane esse in mundo, nullum coelum, nullam terram, nullas mentes, nulla corpora; nonne igitur etiam me non esse? Imo

24

25

32

SECOND MEDITATION

The nature of the human mind, and how it is better known than the body

So serious are the doubts into which I have been thrown as a result of yesterday's meditation that I can neither put them out of my mind nor see any way of resolving them. It feels as if I have fallen unexpectedly into a deep whirlpool which tumbles me around so that I can neither stand on the bottom nor swim up to the top. Nevertheless I will make an effort and once more attempt the same path which I started on yesterday. Anything which admits of the slightest doubt I will set aside just as if I had found it to be wholly false; and I will proceed in this way until I recognize something certain, or, if nothing else, until I at least recognize for certain that there is no certainty. Archimedes used to demand just one firm and immovable point in order to shift the entire earth; so I too can hope for great things if I manage to find just one thing, however slight, that is certain and unshakeable. 24

I will suppose, then, that everything I see is spurious. I will believe that my memory tells me lies, and that none of the things that it reports ever happened. I have no senses. Body, shape, extension, movement and place are chimeras. So what remains true? Perhaps just the one fact that nothing is certain.

Yet apart from everything I have just listed, how do I know that there is not something else which does not allow even the slightest occasion for doubt? Is there not a God, or whatever I may call him, who puts into me[1] the thoughts I am now having? But why do I think this, since I myself may perhaps be the author of these thoughts? In that case am not I, at least, something? But I have just said that I have no senses and no body. This is the sticking point: what follows from this? Am I not so bound up 25 with a body and with senses that I cannot exist without them? But I have convinced myself that there is absolutely nothing in the world, no sky, no earth, no minds, no bodies. Does it now follow that I too do not exist? No:

---

[1] '. . . puts into my mind' (French version).

33

certe ego eram, si quid mihi persuasi. Sed est deceptor nescio quis, summe potens, summe callidus, qui de industria me semper fallit. Haud dubie igitur ego etiam sum, si me fallit; et fallat quantum potest, nunquam tamen efficiet, ut nihil sim quamdiu me aliquid esse cogitabo. Adeo ut, omnibus satis superque pensitatis, denique statuendum sit hoc pronuntiatum, *Ego sum, ego existo*, quoties a me profertur, vel mente concipitur, necessario esse verum.

Nondum vero satis intelligo, quisnam sim ego ille, qui jam necessario sum; deincepsque cavendum est ne forte quid aliud imprudenter assumam in locum mei, sicque aberrem etiam in ea cognitione, quam omnium certissimam evidentissimamque esse contendo. Quare jam denuo meditabor quidnam me olim esse crediderim, priusquam in has cogitationes incidissem; ex quo deinde subducam quidquid allatis rationibus vel minimum potuit infirmari, ut ita tandem praecise remaneat illud tantum quod certum est et inconcussum.

Quidnam igitur antehac me esse putavi? Hominem scilicet. Sed quid est homo? Dicamne animal rationale? Non, quia postea quaerendum foret quidnam animal sit, et quid rationale, atque ita ex una quaestione in plures difficilioresque delaberer; nec jam mihi tantum otii est, ut illo velim inter istiusmodi subtilitates abuti. Sed hic potius attendam, quid sponte et natura duce cogitationi meae antehac occurrebat, quoties quid essem considerabam. Nempe occurrebat primo, me habere vultum, manus, brachia, totamque hanc membrorum machinam, qualis etiam in cadavere cernitur, et quam corporis nomine designabam. Occurrebat praeterea me nutriri, incedere, sentire, et cogitare: quas quidem actiones ad animam referebam. Sed quid esset haec anima, vel non advertebam, vel exiguum nescio quid imaginabar, instar venti, vel ignis, vel aetheris, quod crassioribus mei partibus esset infusum. De corpore vero ne dubitabam quidem, sed distincte me nosse arbitrabar ejus naturam, quam si forte, qualem mente concipiebam, describere tentassem, sic explicuissem: per corpus intelligo illud omne quod aptum est figura aliqua terminari, loco circumscribi, spatium sic replere, ut ex eo aliud omne corpus excludat; tactu, visu, auditu, gustu, vel odoratu percipi, necnon moveri pluribus modis, non quidem a seipso, sed ab alio

if I convinced myself of something[1] then I certainly existed. But there is a deceiver of supreme power and cunning who is deliberately and constantly deceiving me. In that case I too undoubtedly exist, if he is deceiving me; and let him deceive me as much as he can, he will never bring it about that I am nothing so long as I think that I am something. So after considering everything very thoroughly, I must finally conclude that this proposition, *I am, I exist,* is necessarily true whenever it is put forward by me or conceived in my mind.

But I do not yet have a sufficient understanding of what this 'I' is, that now necessarily exists. So I must be on my guard against carelessly taking something else to be this 'I', and so making a mistake in the very item of knowledge that I maintain is the most certain and evident of all. I will therefore go back and meditate on what I originally believed myself to be, before I embarked on this present train of thought. I will then subtract anything capable of being weakened, even minimally, by the arguments now introduced, so that what is left at the end may be exactly and only what is certain and unshakeable.

What then did I formerly think I was? A man. But what is a man? Shall I say 'a rational animal'? No; for then I should have to inquire what an animal is, what rationality is, and in this way one question would lead me down the slope to other harder ones, and I do not now have the time to waste on subtleties of this kind. Instead I propose to concentrate on what came into my thoughts spontaneously and quite naturally whenever I used 26 to consider what I was. Well, the first thought to come to mind was that I had a face, hands, arms and the whole mechanical structure of limbs which can be seen in a corpse, and which I called the body. The next thought was that I was nourished, that I moved about, and that I engaged in sense-perception and thinking; and these actions I attributed to the soul. But as to the nature of this soul, either I did not think about this or else I imagined it to be something tenuous, like a wind or fire or ether, which permeated my more solid parts. As to the body, however, I had no doubts about it, but thought I knew its nature distinctly. If I had tried to describe the mental conception I had of it, I would have expressed it as follows: by a body I understand whatever has a determinable shape and a definable location and can occupy a space in such a way as to exclude any other body; it can be perceived by touch, sight, hearing, taste or smell, and can be moved in various ways, not by itself but by whatever else comes into contact with it. For, according to my judgement, the power of self-movement, like the

---

[1] '. . . or thought anything at all' (French version).

quopiam a quo tangatur: namque habere vim seipsum movendi,
item sentiendi, vel cogitandi, nullo pacto ad naturam corporis
pertinere judicabam; quinimo mirabar potius tales facultates in
quibusdam corporibus reperiri.

    Quid autem nunc, ubi suppono deceptorem aliquem potentissi-
mum, et, si fas est dicere, malignum, data opera in omnibus, quantum
potuit, me delusisse? Possumne affirmare me habere vel minimum quid
27 ex iis omnibus, quae jam dixi ad naturam corporis pertinere? Attendo,
cogito, revolvo, nihil occurrit; fatigor eadem frustra repetere. Quid
vero ex iis quae animae tribuebam? Nutriri vel incedere? Quandoquidem jam corpus non habeo, haec quoque nihil sunt nisi figmenta.
Sentire? Nempe etiam hoc non fit sine corpore, et permulta sentire
visus sum in somnis quae deinde animadverti me non sensisse. Cogitare? Hic invenio: cogitatio est; haec sola a me divelli nequit. Ego
sum, ego existo; certum est. Quandiu autem? Nempe quandiu cogito; nam forte etiam fieri posset, si cessarem ab omni cogitatione,
ut illico totus esse desinerem. Nihil nunc admitto nisi quod necessario sit verum; sum igitur praecise tantum res cogitans, id est, mens,
sive animus, sive intellectus, sive ratio, voces mihi prius significationis
ignotae. Sum autem res vera, et vere existens; sed qualis res? Dixi,
cogitans.

    Quid praeterea? Imaginabor: non sum compages illa membro-
rum, quae corpus humanum appellatur; non sum etiam tenuis
aliquis aër istis membris infusus, non ventus, non ignis, non
vapor, non halitus, non quidquid mihi fingo: supposui enim
ista nihil esse. Maneat positio: nihilominus tamen ego aliquid sum. Fortassis vero contingit, ut haec ipsa, quae suppono nihil esse, quia mihi sunt ignota, tamen in rei veritate non differant ab eo me quem novi? Nescio, de hac
re jam non disputo; de iis tantum quae mihi nota sunt,

power of sensation or of thought, was quite foreign to the nature of a body; indeed, it was a source of wonder to me that certain bodies were found to contain faculties of this kind.

But what shall I now say that I am, when I am supposing that there is some supremely powerful and, if it is permissible to say so, malicious deceiver, who is deliberately trying to trick me in every way he can? Can I now assert that I possess even the most insignificant of all the attributes which I have just said belong to the nature of a body? I scrutinize them, 27 think about them, go over them again, but nothing suggests itself; it is tiresome and pointless to go through the list once more. But what about the attributes I assigned to the soul? Nutrition or movement? Since now I do not have a body, these are mere fabrications. Sense-perception? This surely does not occur without a body, and besides, when asleep I have appeared to perceive through the senses many things which I afterwards realized I did not perceive through the senses at all. Thinking? At last I have discovered it – thought; this alone is inseparable from me. I am, I exist – that is certain. But for how long? For as long as I am thinking. For it could be that were I totally to cease from thinking, I should totally cease to exist. At present I am not admitting anything except what is necessarily true. I am, then, in the strict sense only a thing that thinks;[1] that is, I am a mind, or intelligence, or intellect, or reason – words whose meaning I have been ignorant of until now. But for all that I am a thing which is real and which truly exists. But what kind of a thing? As I have just said – a thinking thing.

What else am I? I will use my imagination.[2] I am not that structure of limbs which is called a human body. I am not even some thin vapour which permeates the limbs – a wind, fire, air, breath, or whatever I depict in my imagination; for these are things which I have supposed to be nothing. Let this supposition stand;[3] for all that I am still something. And yet may it not perhaps be the case that these very things which I am supposing to be nothing, because they are unknown to me, are in reality identical with the 'I' of which I am aware? I do not know, and for the moment I shall not argue the point, since I can make judgements only about things which

---

[1] The word 'only' is most naturally taken as going with 'a thing that thinks', and this interpretation is followed in the French version. When discussing this passage with Gassendi, however, Descartes suggests that he meant the 'only' to govern 'in the strict sense'; cf. AT IXA 215: CSM II 276.

[2] '. . . to see if I am not something more' (added in French version).

[3] Lat. *maneat* ('let it stand'), first edition. The second edition has the indicative *manet*: 'The proposition still stands, viz. that I am nonetheless something.' The French version reads: 'without changing this supposition, I find that I am still certain that I am something'.

judicium ferre possum. Novi me existere; quaero quis sim ego ille quem
novi. Certissimum est hujus sic praecise sumpti notitiam non pendere
28 ab iis quae existere nondum novi; non igitur ab iis ullis, quae imaginatione effingo. Atque hoc verbum, *effingo*, admonet me erroris mei:
nam fingerem revera, si quid me esse imaginarer, quia nihil aliud est
imaginari quam rei corporeae figuram, seu imaginem, contemplari.
Jam autem certo scio me esse, simulque fieri posse ut omnes istae
imagines, et generaliter quaecunque ad corporis naturam referuntur,
nihil sint praeter insomnia. Quibus animadversis, non minus ineptire
videor, dicendo: imaginabor, ut distinctius agnoscam quisnam sim,
quam si dicerem: jam quidem sum experrectus, videoque nonnihil
veri, sed quia nondum video satis evidenter, data opera obdormiam,
ut hoc ipsum mihi somnia verius evidentiusque repraesentent. Itaque
cognosco nihil eorum quae possum imaginationis ope comprehendere, ad hanc quam de me habeo notitiam pertinere, mentemque
ab illis diligentissime esse avocandam, ut suam ipsa naturam quam
distinctissime percipiat.

Sed quid igitur sum? Res cogitans. Quid est hoc? Nempe dubitans,
intelligens, affirmans, negans, volens, nolens, imaginans quoque, et
sentiens.

Non pauca sane haec sunt, si cuncta ad me pertineant. Sed
quidni pertinerent? Nonne ego ipse sum qui jam dubito fere
de omnibus, qui nonnihil tamen intelligo, qui hoc unum verum
esse affirmo, nego caetera, cupio plura nosse, nolo decipi, multa
vel invitus imaginor, multa etiam tanquam a sensibus venien-
29 tia animadverto? Quid est horum, quamvis semper dormiam,
quamvis etiam is qui me creavit, quantum in se est, me delu-
dat, quod non aeque verum sit ac me esse? Quid est quod a
mea cogitatione distinguatur? Quid est quod a me ipso sepa-
ratum dici possit? Nam quod ego sim qui dubitem, qui intelligam, qui velim, tam manifestum est, ut nihil occurrat per quod
evidentius explicetur. Sed vero etiam ego idem sum qui imaginor; nam quamvis forte, ut supposui, nulla prorsus res imagi-
nata vera sit, vis tamen ipsa imaginandi revera existit, et cogitationis meae partem facit. Idem denique ego sum qui sentio,
sive qui res corporeas tanquam per sensus animadverto: videlicet

are known to me. I know that I exist; the question is, what is this 'I' that I know? If the 'I' is understood strictly as we have been taking it, then it is quite certain that knowledge of it does not depend on things of whose existence I am as yet unaware; so it cannot depend on any of the things 28 which I invent in my imagination. And this very word 'invent' shows me my mistake. It would indeed be a case of fictitious invention if I used my imagination to establish that I was something or other; for imagining is simply contemplating the shape or image of a corporeal thing. Yet now I know for certain both that I exist and at the same time that all such images, and, in general, everything relating to the nature of body, could be mere dreams <and chimeras>. Once this point has been grasped, to say 'I will use my imagination to get to know more distinctly what I am' would seem to be as silly as saying 'I am now awake, and see some truth; but since my vision is not yet clear enough, I will deliberately fall asleep so that my dreams may provide a truer and clearer representation.' I thus realize that none of the things that the imagination enables me to grasp is at all relevant to this knowledge of myself which I possess, and that the mind must therefore be most carefully diverted from such things[1] if it is to perceive its own nature as distinctly as possible.

But what then am I? A thing that thinks. What is that? A thing that doubts, understands, affirms, denies, is willing, is unwilling, and also imagines and has sensory perceptions.

This is a considerable list, if everything on it belongs to me. But does it? Is it not one and the same 'I' who is now doubting almost everything, who nonetheless understands some things, who affirms that this one thing is true, denies everything else, desires to know more, is unwilling to be deceived, imagines many things even involuntarily, and is aware of many things which apparently come from the senses? Are not all these things just as true as the fact that I exist, even if I am asleep all the time, and 29 even if he who created me is doing all he can to deceive me? Which of all these activities is distinct from my thinking? Which of them can be said to be separate from myself? The fact that it is I who am doubting and understanding and willing is so evident that I see no way of making it any clearer. But it is also the case that the 'I' who imagines is the same 'I'. For even if, as I have supposed, none of the objects of imagination are real, the power of imagination is something which really exists and is part of my thinking. Lastly, it is also the same 'I' who has sensory perceptions, or is aware of bodily things as it were through the senses. For example, I am

---

[1] '... from this manner of conceiving things' (French version).

jam lucem video, strepitum audio, calorem sentio. Falsa haec sunt,
dormio enim. At certe videre videor, audire, calescere. Hoc falsum
esse non potest; hoc est proprie quod in me sentire appellatur;
atque hoc praecise sic sumptum nihil aliud est quam cogitare.

Ex quibus equidem aliquanto melius incipio nosse quisnam sim;
sed adhuc tamen videtur, nec possum abstinere quin putem, res corporeas, quarum imagines cogitatione formantur, et quas ipsi sensus explorant, multo distinctius agnosci quam istud nescio quid
mei, quod sub imaginationem non venit: quanquam profecto sit
mirum, res quas animadverto esse dubias, ignotas, a me alienas,
distinctius quam quod verum est, quod cognitum, quam denique
me ipsum, a me comprehendi. Sed video quid sit: gaudet aberrare mens mea, necdum se patitur intra veritatis limites cohiberi.
30 Esto igitur, et adhuc semel laxissimas habenas ei permittamus,
ut, illis paulo post opportune reductis, facilius se regi patiatur.

Consideremus res illas quae vulgo putantur omnium distinctissime comprehendi: corpora scilicet, quae tangimus, quae videmus;
non quidem corpora in communi, generales enim istae perceptiones aliquanto magis confusae esse solent, sed unum in particulari. Sumamus, exempli causa, hanc ceram: nuperrime ex favis fuit
educta; nondum amisit omnem saporem sui mellis; nonnihil retinet
odoris florum ex quibus collecta est; ejus color, figura, magnitudo,
manifesta sunt; dura est, frigida est, facile tangitur, ac, si artic-
ulo ferias, emittet sonum; omnia denique illi adsunt quae requiri
videntur, ut corpus aliquod possit quam distinctissime cognosci.
Sed ecce, dum loquor, igni admovetur: saporis reliquiae purgan-
tur, odor expirat, color mutatur, figura tollitur, crescit magnitudo,
fit liquida, fit calida, vix tangi potest, nec jam, si pulses, emittet
sonum. Remanetne adhuc eadem cera? Remanere fatendum est; nemo
negat, nemo aliter putat. Quid erat igitur in ea quod tam distincte
comprehendebatur? Certe nihil eorum quae sensibus attingebam;
nam quaecunque sub gustum, vel odoratum, vel visum, vel tactum,
vel auditum veniebant, mutata jam sunt: remanet cera.

Fortassis illud erat quod nunc cogito: nempe ceram ipsam
non quidem fuisse istam dulcedinem mellis, nec florum fra-
grantiam, nec istam albedinem, nec figuram, nec sonum, sed corpus quod mihi apparebat paulo ante modis istis conspicuum,
nunc diversis. Quid est autem hoc praecise quod sic imaginor?

now seeing light, hearing a noise, feeling heat. But I am asleep, so all this is false. Yet I certainly *seem* to see, to hear, and to be warmed. This cannot be false; what is called 'having a sensory perception' is strictly just this, and in this restricted sense of the term it is simply thinking.

From all this I am beginning to have a rather better understanding of what I am. But it still appears – and I cannot stop thinking this – that the corporeal things of which images are formed in my thought, and which the senses investigate, are known with much more distinctness than this puzzling 'I' which cannot be pictured in the imagination. And yet it is surely surprising that I should have a more distinct grasp of things which I realize are doubtful, unknown and foreign to me, than I have of that which is true and known – my own self. But I see what it is: my mind enjoys wandering off and will not yet submit to being restrained within the bounds of truth. Very well then; just this once let us give it a completely free rein, so that after a while, when it is time to tighten the reins, it may more readily submit to being curbed. 30

Let us consider the things which people commonly think they under-stand most distinctly of all; that is, the bodies which we touch and see. I do not mean bodies in general – for general perceptions are apt to be somewhat more confused – but one particular body. Let us take, for exam-ple, this piece of wax. It has just been taken from the honeycomb; it has not yet quite lost the taste of the honey; it retains some of the scent of the flowers from which it was gathered; its colour, shape and size are plain to see; it is hard, cold and can be handled without difficulty; if you rap it with your knuckle it makes a sound. In short, it has everything which appears necessary to enable a body to be known as distinctly as possible. But even as I speak, I put the wax by the fire, and look: the residual taste is eliminated, the smell goes away, the colour changes, the shape is lost, the size increases; it becomes liquid and hot; you can hardly touch it, and if you strike it, it no longer makes a sound. But does the same wax remain? It must be admitted that it does; no one denies it, no one thinks otherwise. So what was it in the wax that I understood with such distinctness? Evidently none of the features which I arrived at by means of the senses; for whatever came under taste, smell, sight, touch or hearing has now altered – yet the wax remains.

Perhaps the answer lies in the thought which now comes to my mind; namely, the wax was not after all the sweetness of the honey, or the fragrance of the flowers, or the whiteness, or the shape, or the sound, but was rather a body which presented itself to me in these various forms a little while ago, but which now exhibits different ones. But what exactly is it that I am now

31 Attendamus, et, remotis iis quae ad ceram non pertinent, videamus quid supersit: nempe nihil aliud quam extensum quid, flexibile, mutabile. Quid vero est hoc flexibile, mutabile? An quod imaginor, hanc ceram ex figura rotunda in quadratam, vel ex hac in triangularem verti posse? Nullo modo; nam innumerabilium ejusmodi mutationum capacem eam esse comprehendo, nec possum tamen innumerabiles imaginando percurrere; nec igitur comprehensio haec ab imaginandi facultate perficitur. Quid extensum? Nunquid etiam ipsa ejus extensio est ignota? Nam in cera liquescente fit major, major in ferventi, majorque rursus, si calor augeatur; nec recte judicarem quid sit cera, nisi putarem hanc etiam plures secundum extensionem varietates admittere, quam fuerim unquam imaginando complexus. Superest igitur ut concedam, me nequidem imaginari quid sit haec cera, sed sola mente percipere; dico hanc in particulari, de cera enim in communi clarius est. Quaenam vero est haec cera, quae non nisi mente percipitur? Nempe eadem quam video, quam tango, quam imaginor, eadem denique quam ab initio esse arbitrabar. Atqui, quod notandum est, ejus perceptio non visio, non tactio, non imaginatio est, nec unquam fuit, quamvis prius ita videretur, sed solius mentis inspectio, quae vel imperfecta esse potest et confusa, ut prius erat, vel clara et distincta, ut nunc est, prout minus vel magis ad illa ex quibus constat attendo.

Miror vero interim quam prona sit mea mens in errores;
32 nam quamvis haec apud me tacitus et sine voce considerem, haereo tamen in verbis ipsis, et fere decipior ab ipso usu loquendi. Dicimus enim nos videre ceram ipsammet, si adsit, non ex colore vel figura eam adesse judicare. Unde concluderem statim: ceram ergo visione oculi, non solius mentis inspectione, cognosci; nisi jam forte respexissem ex fenestra homines in platea transeuntes, quos etiam ipsos non minus usitate quam ceram dico me videre. Quid autem video praeter pileos et vestes, sub quibus latere possent automata? Sed judico homines esse.

imagining? Let us concentrate, take away everything which does not belong 31
to the wax, and see what is left: merely something extended, flexible and
changeable. But what is meant here by 'flexible' and 'changeable'? Is it what
I picture in my imagination: that this piece of wax is capable of changing
from a round shape to a square shape, or from a square shape to a triangular
shape? Not at all; for I can grasp that the wax is capable of countless changes
of this kind, yet I am unable to run through this immeasurable number
of changes in my imagination, from which it follows that it is not the
faculty of imagination that gives me my grasp of the wax as flexible and
changeable. And what is meant by 'extended'? Is the extension of the wax
also unknown? For it increases if the wax melts, increases again if it boils,
and is greater still if the heat is increased. I would not be making a correct
judgement about the nature of wax unless I believed it capable of being
extended in many more different ways than I will ever encompass in my
imagination. I must therefore admit that the nature of this piece of wax is
in no way revealed by my imagination, but is perceived by the mind alone.
(I am speaking of this particular piece of wax; the point is even clearer
with regard to wax in general.) But what is this wax which is perceived by
the mind alone?[1] It is of course the same wax which I see, which I touch,
which I picture in my imagination, in short the same wax which I thought
it to be from the start. And yet, and here is the point, the perception I have
of it[2] is a case not of vision or touch or imagination – nor has it ever been,
despite previous appearances – but of purely mental scrutiny; and this can
be imperfect and confused, as it was before, or clear and distinct as it is
now, depending on how carefully I concentrate on what the wax consists
in.

But as I reach this conclusion I am amazed at how <weak and> prone
to error my mind is. For although I am thinking about these matters within
myself, silently and without speaking, nonetheless the actual words bring 32
me up short, and I am almost tricked by ordinary ways of talking. We say
that we see the wax itself, if it is there before us, not that we judge it to be
there from its colour or shape; and this might lead me to conclude without
more ado that knowledge of the wax comes from what the eye sees, and not
from the scrutiny of the mind alone. But then if I look out of the window
and see men crossing the square, as I just happen to have done, I normally
say that I see the men themselves, just as I say that I see the wax. Yet do I
see any more than hats and coats which could conceal automatons? I *judge*

---

[1] '. . . which can be conceived only by the understanding or the mind' (French version).
[2] '. . . or rather the act whereby it is perceived' (added in French version).

Atque ita id quod putabam me videre oculis, sola judicandi facultate, quae in mente mea est, comprehendo.

Sed pudeat supra vulgus sapere cupientem, ex formis loquendi quas vulgus invenit dubitationem quaesivisse; pergamusque deinceps, attendendo utrum ego perfectius evidentiusque percipiebam quid esset cera, cum primum aspexi, credidique me illam ipso sensu externo, vel saltem sensu communi, ut vocant, id est potentia imaginatrice, cognoscere? an vero potius nunc, postquam diligentius investigavi tum quid ea sit, tum quomodo cognoscatur? Certe hac de re dubitare esset ineptum; nam quid fuit in prima perceptione distinctum? Quid quod non a quovis animali haberi posse videretur? At vero cum ceram ab externis formis distinguo, et tanquam vestibus detractis nudam considero, sic illam revera, quamvis adhuc error in judicio meo esse possit, non possum tamen sine humana mente percipere.

33   Quid autem dicam de hac ipsa mente, sive de me ipso? Nihildum enim aliud admitto in me esse praeter mentem. Quid, inquam, ego qui hanc ceram videor tam distincte percipere? Nunquid me ipsum non tantum multo verius, multo certius, sed etiam multo distinctius evidentiusque, cognosco? Nam, si judico ceram existere, ex eo quod hanc videam, certe multo evidentius efficitur me ipsum etiam existere, ex eo ipso quod hanc videam. Fieri enim potest ut hoc quod video non vere sit cera; fieri potest ut ne quidem oculos habeam, quibus quidquam videatur; sed fieri plane non potest, cum videam, sive (quod jam non distinguo) cum cogitem me videre, ut ego ipse cogitans non aliquid sim. Simili ratione, si judico ceram esse, ex eo quod hanc tangam, idem rursus efficietur, videlicet me esse. Si ex eo quod imaginer, vel quavis alia ex causa, idem plane. Sed et hoc ipsum quod de cera animadverto, ad reliqua omnia, quae sunt extra me posita, licet applicare. Porro autem, si magis distincta visa sit cerae perceptio, postquam mihi, non ex solo visu vel tactu, sed pluribus ex causis innotuit, quanto distinctius me ipsum a me nunc cognosci fatendum est, quandoquidem nullae rationes vel ad

that they are men. And so something which I thought I was seeing with my eyes is in fact grasped solely by the faculty of judgement which is in my mind.

However, one who wants to achieve knowledge above the ordinary level should feel ashamed at having taken ordinary ways of talking as a basis for doubt. So let us proceed, and consider on which occasion my perception of the nature of the wax was more perfect and evident. Was it when I first looked at it, and believed I knew it by my external senses, or at least by what they call the 'common' sense[1] – that is, the power of imagination? Or is my knowledge more perfect now, after a more careful investigation of the nature of the wax and of the means by which it is known? Any doubt on this issue would clearly be foolish; for what distinctness was there in my earlier perception? Was there anything in it which an animal could not possess? But when I distinguish the wax from its outward forms – take the clothes off, as it were, and consider it naked – then although my judgement may still contain errors, at least my perception now requires a human mind.

But what am I to say about this mind, or about myself? (So far, remember,   33 I am not admitting that there is anything else in me except a mind.) What, I ask, is this 'I' which seems to perceive the wax so distinctly? Surely my awareness of my own self is not merely much truer and more certain than my awareness of the wax, but also much more distinct and evident. For if I judge that the wax exists from the fact that I see it, clearly this same fact entails much more evidently that I myself also exist. It is possible that what I see is not really the wax; it is possible that I do not even have eyes with which to see anything. But when I see, or think I see (I am not here distinguishing the two), it is simply not possible that I who am now thinking am not something. By the same token, if I judge that the wax exists from the fact that I touch it, the same result follows, namely that I exist. If I judge that it exists from the fact that I imagine it, or for any other reason, exactly the same thing follows. And the result that I have grasped in the case of the wax may be applied to everything else located outside me. Moreover, if my perception of the wax seemed more distinct[2] after it was established not just by sight or touch but by many other considerations, it must be admitted that I now know myself even more distinctly. This is because every consideration whatsoever which contributes to my perception of the

---

[1] See note p. 121 below.
[2] The French version has 'more clear and distinct' and, at the end of this sentence, 'more evidently, distinctly and clearly'.

cerae, vel ad cujuspiam alterius corporis perceptionem possint juvare, quin eaedem omnes mentis meae naturam melius probent! Sed et alia insuper tam multa sunt in ipsa mente, ex quibus ejus notitia distinctior reddi potest, ut ea, quae ex corpore ad illam emanant, vix numeranda videantur.

34   Atque ecce tandem sponte sum reversus eo quo volebam; nam cum mihi nunc notum sit ipsamet corpora, non proprie a sensibus, vel ab imaginandi facultate, sed a solo intellectu percipi, nec ex eo percipi quod tangantur aut videantur, sed tantum ex eo quod intelligantur aperte cognosco nihil facilius aut evidentius mea mente posse a me percipi. Sed quia tam cito deponi veteris opinionis consuetudo non potest, placet hic consistere, ut altius haec nova cognitio memoriae meae diuturnitate meditationis infigatur.

wax, or of any other body, cannot but establish even more effectively the nature of my own mind. But besides this, there is so much else in the mind itself which can serve to make my knowledge of it more distinct, that it scarcely seems worth going through the contributions made by considering bodily things.

I see that without any effort I have now finally got back to where I wanted. I now know that even bodies are not strictly perceived by the 34 senses or the faculty of imagination but by the intellect alone, and that this perception derives not from their being touched or seen but from their being understood; and in view of this I know plainly that I can achieve an easier and more evident perception of my own mind than of anything else. But since the habit of holding on to old opinions cannot be set aside so quickly, I should like to stop here and meditate for some time on this new knowledge I have gained, so as to fix it more deeply in my memory.

De Deo, quod existat

Claudam nunc oculos, aures obturabo, avocabo omnes sensus, imagines etiam rerum corporalium omnes vel ex cogitatione mea delebo, vel certe, quia hoc fieri vix potest, illas ut inanes et falsas nihili pendam, meque solum alloquendo et penitius inspiciendo, meipsum paulatim mihi magis notum et familiarem reddere conabor. Ego sum res cogitans, id est dubitans, affirmans, negans, pauca intelligens, multa ignorans, volens, nolens, imaginans etiam et sentiens; ut enim ante animadverti, quamvis illa quae sentio vel imaginor extra me fortasse nihil sint, illos tamen cogitandi 35 modos, quos sensus et imaginationes appello, quatenus cogitandi quidam modi tantum sunt, in me esse sum certus.

Atque his paucis omnia recensui quae vere scio, vel saltem quae me scire hactenus animadverti. Nunc circumspiciam diligentius an forte adhuc apud me alia sint ad quae nondum respexi. Sum certus me esse rem cogitantem. Nunquid ergo etiam scio quid requiratur ut de aliqua re sim certus? Nempe in hac prima cognitione nihil aliud est, quam clara quaedam et distincta perceptio ejus quod affirmo; quae sane non sufficeret ad me certum de rei veritate reddendum, si posset unquam contingere, ut aliquid, quod ita clare et distincte perciperem, falsum esset; ac proinde jam videor pro regula generali posse statuere, illud omne esse verum, quod valde clare et distincte percipio.

Verumtamen multa prius ut omnino certa et manifesta admisi, quae tamen postea dubia esse deprehendi. Qualia ergo ista fuere? Nempe terra, coelum, sydera et caetera

The existence of God

I will now shut my eyes, stop my ears, and withdraw all my senses. I will eliminate from my thoughts all images of bodily things, or rather, since this is hardly possible, I will regard all such images as vacuous, false and worthless. I will converse with myself and scrutinize myself more deeply; and in this way I will attempt to achieve, little by little, a more intimate knowledge of myself. I am a thing that thinks: that is, a thing that doubts, affirms, denies, understands a few things, is ignorant of many things,[1] is willing, is unwilling, and also which imagines and has sensory perceptions; for as I have noted before, even though the objects of my sensory experience and imagination may have no existence outside me, nonetheless the modes of thinking which I refer to as cases of sensory perception and imagination, 35 in so far as they are simply modes of thinking, do exist within me – of that I am certain.

In this brief list I have gone through everything I truly know, or at least everything I have so far discovered that I know. Now I will cast around more carefully to see whether there may be other things within me which I have not yet noticed. I am certain that I am a thinking thing. Do I not therefore also know what is required for my being certain about anything? In this first item of knowledge there is simply a clear and distinct perception of what I am asserting; this would not be enough to make me certain of the truth of the matter if it could ever turn out that something which I perceived with such clarity and distinctness was false. So I now seem to be able to lay it down as a general rule that whatever I perceive very clearly and distinctly is true.[2]

Yet I previously accepted as wholly certain and evident many things which I afterwards realized were doubtful. What were these? The earth,

---

[1] The French version here inserts 'loves, hates'.
[2] '... all the things which we conceive very clearly and very distinctly are true' (French version).

omnia quae sensibus usurpabam. Quid autem de illis clare percipiebam? Nempe ipsas talium rerum ideas, sive cogitationes, menti meae
obversari. Sed ne nunc quidem illas ideas in me esse inficior. Aliud
autem quiddam erat quod affirmabam, quodque etiam ob consuetudinem credendi clare me percipere arbitrabar, quod tamen revera
non percipiebam: nempe res quasdam extra me esse, a quibus ideae
istae procedebant, et quibus omnino similes erant. Atque hoc erat,
in quo vel fallebar, vel certe, si verum judicabam, id non ex vi meae
perceptionis contingebat.

36   Quid vero? Cum circa res Arithmeticas vel Geometricas aliquid
valde simplex et facile considerabam, ut quod duo et tria simul juncta
sint quinque, vel similia, nunquid saltem illa satis perspicue intuebar,
ut vera esse affirmarem? Equidem non aliam ob causam de iis dubitandum esse postea judicavi, quam quia veniebat in mentem forte
aliquem Deum talem mihi naturam indere potuisse, ut etiam circa illa
deciperer, quae manifestissima viderentur. Sed quoties haec praecon-
cepta de summa Dei potentia opinio mihi occurrit, non possum non
fateri, siquidem velit, facile illi esse efficere ut errem, etiam in iis quae
me puto mentis oculis quam evidentissime intueri. Quoties vero ad
ipsas res, quas valde clare percipere arbitror, me converto, tam plane
ab illis persuadeor, ut sponte erumpam in has voces: fallat me quisquis
potest, nunquam tamen efficiet ut nihil sim, quandiu me aliquid esse
cogitabo; vel ut aliquando verum sit me nunquam fuisse, cum jam
verum sit me esse; vel forte etiam ut duo et tria simul juncta plura vel
pauciora sint quam quinque, vel similia, in quibus scilicet repugnan-
tiam agnosco manifestam. Et certe cum nullam occasionem habeam
existimandi aliquem Deum esse deceptorem, nec quidem adhuc satis
sciam utrum sit aliquis Deus, valde tenuis et, ut ita loquar, Metaphysica
dubitandi ratio est, quae tantum ex ea opinione dependet. Ut autem
etiam illa tollatur, quamprimum occurret occasio, examinare debeo
an sit Deus, et, si sit, an possit esse deceptor; hac enim re ignorata,
non videor de ulla alia plane certus esse unquam posse.

37   Nunc autem ordo videtur exigere, ut prius omnes meas cogitationes in certa genera distribuam, et in quibusnam ex illis veritas

sky, stars, and everything else that I apprehended with the senses. But what was it about them that I perceived clearly? Just that the ideas, or thoughts, of such things appeared before my mind. Yet even now I am not denying that these ideas occur within me. But there was something else which I used to assert, and which through habitual belief I thought I perceived clearly, although I did not in fact do so. This was that there were things outside me which were the sources of my ideas and which resembled them in all respects. Here was my mistake; or at any rate, if my judgement was true, it was not thanks to the strength of my perception.[1]

But what about when I was considering something very simple and straightforward in arithmetic or geometry, for example that two and three added together make five, and so on? Did I not see at least these things clearly enough to affirm their truth? Indeed, the only reason for my later judgement that they were open to doubt was that it occurred to me that perhaps some God could have given me a nature such that I was deceived even in matters which seemed most evident. But whenever my preconceived belief in the supreme power of God comes to mind, I cannot but admit that it would be easy for him, if he so desired, to bring it about that I go wrong even in those matters which I think I see utterly clearly with my mind's eye. Yet whenever I turn to the things themselves which I think I perceive very clearly, I am so convinced by them that I spontaneously declare: let whoever can do so deceive me, he will never bring it about that I am nothing, so long as I continue to think I am something; or make it true at some future time that I have never existed, since it is now true that I exist; or bring it about that two and three added together are more or less than five, or anything of this kind in which I see a manifest contradiction. And since I have no cause to think that there is a deceiving God, and I do not yet even know for sure whether there is a God at all, any reason for doubt which depends simply on this supposition is a very slight and, so to speak, metaphysical one. But in order to remove even this slight reason for doubt, as soon as the opportunity arises I must examine whether there is a God, and, if there is, whether he can be a deceiver. For if I do not know this, it seems that I can never be quite certain about anything else.

First, however, considerations of order appear to dictate that I now classify all my thoughts into definite kinds,[2] and ask which of them

36

37

---

[1] '...it was not because of any knowledge I possessed' (French version).

[2] The opening of this sentence is greatly expanded in the French version: 'In order that I may have the opportunity of examining this without interrupting the order of meditating which I have decided upon, which is to start only from those notions which I find first of all in my mind and pass gradually to those which I may find later on, I must here divide my thoughts...'

aut falsitas proprie consistat, inquiram. Quaedam ex his tanquam rerum imagines sunt, quibus solis proprie convenit ideae nomen: ut cum hominem, vel Chimaeram, vel Coelum, vel Angelum, vel Deum cogito. Aliae vero alias quasdam praeterea formas habent: ut, cum volo, cum timeo, cum affirmo, cum nego, semper quidem aliquam rem ut subjectum meae cogitationis apprehendo, sed aliquid etiam amplius quam istius rei similitudinem cogitatione complector; et ex his aliae voluntates, sive affectus, aliae autem judicia appellantur.

Jam quod ad ideas attinet, si solae in se spectentur, nec ad aliud quid illas referam, falsae proprie esse non possunt; nam sive capram, sive chimaeram imaginer, non minus verum est me unam imaginari quam alteram. Nulla etiam in ipsa voluntate, vel affectibus, falsitas est timenda; nam, quamvis prava, quamvis etiam ea quae nusquam sunt, possim optare, non tamen ideo non verum est illa me optare. Ac proinde sola supersunt judicia, in quibus mihi cavendum est ne fallar. Praecipuus autem error et frequentissimus qui possit in illis reperiri, consistit in eo quod ideas, quae in me sunt, judicem rebus quibusdam extra me positis similes esse sive conformes; nam profecto, si tantum ideas ipsas ut cogitationis meae quosdam modos considerarem, nec ad quidquam aliud referrem, vix mihi ullam errandi materiam dare possent.

38   Ex his autem ideis aliae innatae, aliae adventitiae, aliae a me ipso factae mihi videntur: nam quod intelligam quid sit res, quid sit veritas, quid sit cogitatio, haec non aliunde habere videor quam ab ipsamet mea natura; quod autem nunc strepitum audiam, solem videam, ignem sentiam, a rebus quibusdam extra me positis procedere hactenus judicavi; ac denique Syrenes, Hippogryphes, et similia, a me ipso finguntur. Vel forte etiam omnes esse adventitias possum putare, vel omnes innatas, vel omnes factas: nondum enim veram illarum originem clare perspexi.

Sed hic praecipue de iis est quaerendum, quas tanquam a rebus extra me existentibus desumptas considero, quaenam me moveat ratio ut illas istis rebus similes esse existimem. Nempe ita videor doctus a natura. Et praeterea experior illas non a mea voluntate nec proinde a me ipso pendere; saepe enim vel invito obversantur: ut jam, sive velim, sive nolim, sentio calorem, et ideo puto sensum illum, sive ideam

can properly be said to be the bearers of truth and falsity. Some of my thoughts are as it were the images of things, and it is only in these cases that the term 'idea' is strictly appropriate – for example, when I think of a man, or a chimera, or the sky, or an angel, or God. Other thoughts have various additional forms: thus when I will, or am afraid, or affirm, or deny, there is always a particular thing which I take as the object of my thought, but my thought includes something more than the likeness of that thing. Some thoughts in this category are called volitions or emotions, while others are called judgements.

Now as far as ideas are concerned, provided they are considered solely in themselves and I do not refer them to anything else, they cannot strictly speaking be false; for whether it is a goat or a chimera that I am imagining, it is just as true that I imagine the former as the latter. As for the will and the emotions, here too one need not worry about falsity; for even if the things which I may desire are wicked or even non-existent, that does not make it any less true that I desire them. Thus the only remaining thoughts where I must be on my guard against making a mistake are judgements. And the chief and most common mistake which is to be found here consists in my judging that the ideas which are in me resemble, or conform to, things located outside me. Of course, if I considered just the ideas themselves simply as modes of my thought, without referring them to anything else, they could scarcely give me any material for error.

Among my ideas, some appear to be innate, some to be adventitious,[1] and others to have been invented by me. My understanding of what a 38 thing is, what truth is, and what thought is, seems to derive simply from my own nature. But my hearing a noise, as I do now, or seeing the sun, or feeling the fire, comes from things which are located outside me, or so I have hitherto judged. Lastly, sirens, hippogriffs and the like are my own invention. But perhaps all my ideas may be thought of as adventitious, or they may all be innate, or all made up; for as yet I have not clearly perceived their true origin.

But the chief question at this point concerns the ideas which I take to be derived from things existing outside me: what is my reason for thinking that they resemble these things? Nature has apparently taught me to think this. But in addition I know by experience that these ideas do not depend on my will, and hence that they do not depend simply on me. Frequently I notice them even when I do not want to: now, for example, I feel the heat whether I want to or not, and this is why I think that this sensation or idea

---

[1] '. . . foreign to me and coming from outside' (French version).

caloris, a re a me diversa, nempe ab ignis cui assideo calore, mihi advenire. Nihilque magis obvium est, quam ut judicem istam rem suam similitudinem potius quam aliud quid in me immittere.

Quae rationes, an satis firmae sint, jam videbo. Cum hic dico me ita doctum esse a natura, intelligo tantum spontaneo quodam impetu me ferri ad hoc credendum, non lumine aliquo naturali mihi ostendi esse verum. Quae duo multum discrepant; nam quaecumque lumine naturali mihi ostenduntur, ut quod ex eo quod dubitem sequatur me esse, et similia, nullo modo dubia esse possunt, quia nulla alia facultas esse potest, cui aeque 39 fidam ac lumini isti, quaeque illa non vera esse possit docere; sed quantum ad impetus naturales, jam saepe olim judicavi me ab illis in deteriorem partem fuisse impulsum, cum de bono eligendo ageretur, nec video cur iisdem in ulla alia re magis fidam.

Deinde, quamvis ideae illae a voluntate mea non pendeant, non ideo constat ipsas a rebus extra me positis necessario procedere. Ut enim impetus illi, de quibus mox loquebar, quamvis in me sint, a voluntate tamen mea diversi esse videntur, ita forte etiam aliqua alia est in me facultas, nondum mihi satis cognita, istarum idearum effectrix, ut hactenus semper visum est illas, dum somnio, absque ulla rerum externarum ope, in me formari.

Ac denique, quamvis a rebus a me diversis procederent, non inde sequitur illas rebus istis similes esse debere. Quinimo in multis saepe magnum discrimen videor deprehendisse: ut, exempli causa, duas diversas solis ideas apud me invenio, unam tanquam a sensibus haustam, et quae maxime inter illas quas adventitias existimo est recensenda, per quam mihi valde parvus apparet, aliam vero ex rationibus Astronomiae desumptam, hoc est ex notionibus quibusdam mihi innatis elicitam, vel quocumque alio modo a me factam, per quam aliquoties major quam terra exhibetur; utraque profecto similis eidem soli extra me existenti esse non potest, et ratio persuadet illam ei maxime esse dissimilem, quae quam proxime ab ipso videtur emanasse.

of heat comes to me from something other than myself, namely the heat of the fire by which I am sitting. And the most obvious judgement for me to make is that the thing in question transmits to me its own likeness rather than something else.

I will now see if these arguments are strong enough. When I say 'Nature taught me to think this', all I mean is that a spontaneous impulse leads me to believe it, not that its truth has been revealed to me by some natural light. There is a big difference here. Whatever is revealed to me by the natural light – for example that from the fact that I am doubting it follows that I exist, and so on – cannot in any way be open to doubt. This is because there cannot be another faculty[1] both as trustworthy as the natural light and also capable of showing me that such things are not true. But as for my natural impulses, I have often judged in the past that they were pushing me in the wrong direction when it was a question of choosing the good, and I do not see why I should place any greater confidence in them in other matters.[2]

Then again, although these ideas do not depend on my will, it does not follow that they must come from things located outside me. Just as the impulses which I was speaking of a moment ago seem opposed to my will even though they are within me, so there may be some other faculty not yet fully known to me, which produces these ideas without any assistance from external things; this is, after all, just how I have always thought ideas are produced in me when I am dreaming.

And finally, even if these ideas did come from things other than myself, it would not follow that they must resemble those things. Indeed, I think I have often discovered a great disparity <between an object and its idea> in many cases. For example, there are two different ideas of the sun which I find within me. One of them, which is acquired as it were from the senses and which is a prime example of an idea which I reckon to come from an external source, makes the sun appear very small. The other idea is based on astronomical reasoning, that is, it is derived from certain notions which are innate in me (or else it is constructed by me in some other way), and this idea shows the sun to be several times larger than the earth. Obviously both these ideas cannot resemble the sun which exists outside me; and reason persuades me that the idea which seems to have emanated most directly from the sun itself has in fact no resemblance to it at all.

---

[1] '. . . or power for distinguishing truth from falsehood' (French version).
[2] '. . . concerning truth and falsehood' (French version).

40 Quae omnia satis demonstrant me non hactenus ex certo judicio, sed tantum ex caeco aliquo impulsu, credidisse res quasdam a me diversas existere, quae ideas sive imagines suas per organa sensuum, vel quolibet alio pacto, mihi immittant.

Sed alia quaedam adhuc via mihi occurrit ad inquirendum an res aliquae, ex iis quarum ideae in me sunt, extra me existant. Nempe, quatenus ideae istae cogitandi quidam modi tantum sunt, non agnosco ullam inter ipsas inaequalitatem, et omnes a me eodem modo procedere videntur; sed, quatenus una unam rem, alia aliam repraesentat, patet easdem esse ab invicem valde diversas. Nam proculdubio illae quae substantias mihi exhibent, majus aliquid sunt, atque, ut ita loquar, plus realitatis objectivae in se continent, quam illae quae tantum modos, sive accidentia, repraesentant; et rursus illa per quam summum aliquem Deum, aeternum, infinitum, omniscium, omnipotentem, rerumque omnium, quae praeter ipsum sunt, creatorem intelligo, plus profecto realitatis objectivae in se habet, quam illae per quas finitae substantiae exhibentur.

Jam vero lumine naturali manifestum est tantumdem ad minimum esse debere in causa efficiente et totali, quantum in ejusdem causae effectu. Nam, quaeso, undenam posset assumere realitatem suam effectus, nisi a causa? Et quomodo illam ei causa dare posset, nisi etiam haberet? Hinc autem sequitur, nec posse aliquid a nihilo fieri, nec etiam id quod magis perfectum est, hoc est quod plus real-

41 itatis in se continet, ab eo quod minus. Atque hoc non modo perspicue verum est de iis effectibus, quorum realitas est actualis sive formalis, sed etiam de ideis, in quibus consideratur tantum realitas objectiva. Hoc est, non modo non potest, exempli causa, aliquis lapis, qui prius non fuit, nunc incipere esse, nisi producatur ab aliqua re in qua totum illud sit vel formaliter vel eminenter, quod ponitur in lapide; nec potest calor in subjectum quod prius non

All these considerations are enough to establish that it is not reliable 40 judgement but merely some blind impulse that has made me believe up till now that there exist things distinct from myself which transmit to me ideas or images of themselves through the sense organs or in some other way.

But it now occurs to me that there is another way of investigating whether some of the things of which I possess ideas exist outside me. In so far as the ideas are <considered> simply <as> modes of thought, there is no recognizable inequality among them: they all appear to come from within me in the same fashion. But in so far as different ideas <are considered as images which> represent different things, it is clear that they differ widely. Undoubtedly, the ideas which represent substances to me amount to something more and, so to speak, contain within themselves more objective[1] reality than the ideas which merely represent modes or accidents. Again, the idea that gives me my understanding of a supreme God, eternal, infinite, <immutable,> omniscient, omnipotent and the creator of all things that exist apart from him, certainly has in it more objective reality than the ideas that represent finite substances.

Now it is manifest by the natural light that there must be at least as much <reality> in the efficient and total cause as in the effect of that cause. For where, I ask, could the effect get its reality from, if not from the cause? And how could the cause give it to the effect unless it possessed it? It follows from this both that something cannot arise from nothing, and also that what is more perfect – that is, contains in itself more reality – cannot arise from what is less perfect. And this is transparently true not only in 41 the case of effects which possess <what the philosophers call> actual or formal reality, but also in the case of ideas, where one is considering only <what they call> objective reality. A stone, for example, which previously did not exist, cannot begin to exist unless it is produced by something which contains, either formally or eminently, everything to be found in the stone;[2] similarly, heat cannot be produced in an object which was not

---

[1] '. . . i.e. participate by representation in a higher degree of being or perfection' (added in French version). According to the scholastic distinction invoked in the paragraphs that follow, the 'formal' reality of anything is its own intrinsic reality, while the 'objective' reality of an idea is a function of its representational content. Thus if an idea *A* represents some object *X* which is *F*, then *F*-ness will be contained 'formally' in *X* but 'objectively' in *A*. See below, pp. 165–7.

[2] '. . . i.e. it will contain in itself the same things as are in the stone or other more excellent things' (added in French version). In scholastic terminology, to possess a property 'formally' is to possess it literally, in accordance with its definition; to possess it 'eminently' is to possess it in some higher form.

calebat induci, nisi a re quae sit ordinis saltem aeque perfecti atque
est calor, et sic de caeteris; sed praeterea etiam non potest in me
esse idea caloris, vel lapidis, nisi in me posita sit ab aliqua causa, in
qua tantumdem ad minimum sit realitatis quantum esse in calore
vel lapide concipio. Nam quamvis ista causa nihil de sua realitate
actuali sive formali in meam ideam transfundat, non ideo putandum
est illam minus realem esse debere, sed talem esse naturam ipsius
ideae, ut nullam aliam ex se realitatem formalem exigat, praeter illam
quam mutuatur a cogitatione mea, cujus est modus. Quod autem
haec idea realitatem objectivam hanc vel illam contineat potius quam
aliam, hoc profecto habere debet ab aliqua causa in qua tantumdem
sit ad minimum realitatis formalis quantum ipsa continet objectivae.
Si enim ponamus aliquid in idea reperiri, quod non fuerit in ejus
causa, hoc igitur habet a nihilo; atqui quantumvis imperfectus sit
iste essendi modus, quo res est objective in intellectu per ideam, non
tamen profecto plane nihil est, nec proinde a nihilo esse potest.

    Nec etiam debeo suspicari, cum realitas quam considero in meis
42 ideis sit tantum objectiva, non opus esse ut eadem realitas sit formaliter
in causis istarum idearum, sed sufficere, si sit in iis etiam objective.
Nam quemadmodum iste modus essendi objectivus competit ideis ex
ipsarum natura, ita modus essendi formalis competit idearum causis,
saltem primis et praecipuis, ex earum natura. Et quamvis forte una
idea ex alia nasci possit, non tamen hic datur progressus in infinitum,
sed tandem ad aliquam primam debet deveniri, cujus causa sit instar
archetypi, in quo omnis realitas formaliter contineatur, quae est in
idea tantum objective. Adeo ut lumine naturali mihi sit perspicuum
ideas in me esse veluti quasdam imagines, quae possunt quidem facile
deficere a perfectione rerum a quibus sunt desumptae, non autem
quicquam majus aut perfectius continere.

    Atque haec omnia, quo diutius et curiosius examino, tanto clarius
et distinctius vera esse cognosco. Sed quid tandem ex his concludam?
Nempe si realitas objectiva alicujus ex meis ideis sit tanta ut certus
sim eandem nec formaliter nec eminenter in me esse, nec proinde
me ipsum ejus ideae causam esse posse, hinc necessario sequi, non
me solum esse in mundo, sed aliquam aliam rem, quae istius ideae
est causa, etiam existere. Si vero nulla talis in me idea reperiatur,

previously hot, except by something of at least the same order <degree or kind> of perfection as heat, and so on. But it is also true that the *idea* of heat, or of a stone, cannot exist in me unless it is put there by some cause which contains at least as much reality as I conceive to be in the heat or in the stone. For although this cause does not transfer any of its actual or formal reality to my idea, it should not on that account be supposed that it must be less real.[1] The nature of an idea is such that of itself it requires no formal reality except what it derives from my thought, of which it is a mode.[2] But in order for a given idea to contain such and such objective reality, it must surely derive it from some cause which contains at least as much formal reality as there is objective reality in the idea. For if we suppose that an idea contains something which was not in its cause, it must have got this from nothing; yet the mode of being by which a thing exists objectively <or representatively> in the intellect by way of an idea, imperfect though it may be, is certainly not nothing, and so it cannot come from nothing.

And although the reality which I am considering in my ideas is merely objective reality, I must not on that account suppose that the same reality 42 need not exist formally in the causes of my ideas, but that it is enough for it to be present in them objectively. For just as the objective mode of being belongs to ideas by their very nature, so the formal mode of being belongs to the causes of ideas – or at least the first and most important ones – by *their* very nature. And although one idea may perhaps originate from another, there cannot be an infinite regress here; eventually one must reach a primary idea, the cause of which will be like an archetype which contains formally <and in fact> all the reality <or perfection> which is present only objectively <or representatively> in the idea. So it is clear to me, by the natural light, that the ideas in me are like <pictures, or> images which can easily fall short of the perfection of the things from which they are taken, but which cannot contain anything greater or more perfect.

The longer and more carefully I examine all these points, the more clearly and distinctly I recognize their truth. But what is my conclusion to be? If the objective reality of any of my ideas turns out to be so great that I am sure the same reality does not reside in me, either formally or eminently, and hence that I myself cannot be its cause, it will necessarily follow that I am not alone in the world, but that some other thing which is the cause of this idea also exists. But if no such idea is to be found in me,

---

[1] '... that this cause must be less real' (French version).
[2] '... i.e. a manner or way of thinking' (added in French version).

nullum plane habebo argumentum quod me de alicujus rei a me diversae existentia certum reddat; omnia enim diligentissime circumspexi,
et nullum aliud potui hactenus reperire.

Ex his autem meis ideis, praeter illam quae me ipsum mihi exhibet,
43 de qua hic nulla difficultas esse potest, alia est quae Deum, aliae quae
res corporeas et inanimes, aliae quae Angelos, aliae quae animalia, ac
denique aliae quae alios homines mei similes repraesentant.

Et quantum ad ideas quae alios homines, vel animalia, vel Angelos
exhibent, facile intelligo illas ex iis quas habeo mei ipsius et rerum
corporalium et Dei posse componi, quamvis nulli praeter me homines,
nec animalia, nec Angeli, in mundo essent.

Quantum autem ad ideas rerum corporalium, nihil in illis occurrit, quod sit tantum ut non videatur a me ipso potuisse proficisci;
nam si penitius inspiciam, et singulas examinem eo modo quo heri
examinavi ideam cerae, animadverto perpauca tantum esse quae in illis
clare et distincte percipio: nempe magnitudinem, sive extensionem in
longum, latum, et profundum; figuram, quae ex terminatione istius
extensionis exsurgit; situm, quem diversa figurata inter se obtinent;
et motum, sive mutationem istius situs; quibus addi possunt substantia, duratio, et numerus: caetera autem, ut lumen et colores, soni,
odores, sapores, calor et frigus, aliaeque tactiles qualitates, nonnisi
valde confuse et obscure a me cogitantur, adeo ut etiam ignorem an
sint verae, vel falsae, hoc est, an ideae, quas de illis habeo, sint rerum
quarundam ideae, an non rerum. Quamvis enim falsitatem proprie
dictam, sive formalem, nonnisi in judiciis posse reperiri paulo ante
notaverim, est tamen profecto quaedam alia falsitas materialis in ideis,
cum non rem tanquam rem repraesentant: ita, exempli causa, ideae
44 quas habeo caloris et frigoris, tam parum clarae et distinctae sunt, ut
ab iis discere non possim, an frigus sit tantum privatio caloris, vel
calor privatio frigoris, vel utrumque sit realis qualitas, vel neutrum. Et
quia nullae ideae nisi tanquam rerum esse possunt, siquidem verum
sit frigus nihil aliud esse quam privationem caloris, idea quae mihi
illud tanquam reale quid et positivum repraesentat, non immerito
falsa dicetur, et sic de caeteris.

Quibus profecto non est necesse ut aliquem authorem a me
diversum assignem; nam, si quidem sint falsae, hoc est nullas res

I shall have no argument to convince me of the existence of anything apart from myself. For despite a most careful and comprehensive survey, this is the only argument I have so far been able to find.

Among my ideas, apart from the idea which gives me a representation of myself, which cannot present any difficulty in this context, there are ideas 43 which variously represent God, corporeal and inanimate things, angels, animals and finally other men like myself.

As far as concerns the ideas which represent other men, or animals, or angels, I have no difficulty in understanding that they could be put together from the ideas I have of myself, of corporeal things and of God, even if the world contained no men besides me, no animals and no angels.

As to my ideas of corporeal things, I can see nothing in them which is so great <or excellent> as to make it seem impossible that it originated in myself. For if I scrutinize them thoroughly and examine them one by one, in the way in which I examined the idea of the wax yesterday, I notice that the things which I perceive clearly and distinctly in them are very few in number. The list comprises size, or extension in length, breadth and depth; shape, which is a function of the boundaries of this extension; position, which is a relation between various items possessing shape; and motion, or change in position; to these may be added substance, duration and number. But as for all the rest, including light and colours, sounds, smells, tastes, heat and cold and the other tactile qualities, I think of these only in a very confused and obscure way, to the extent that I do not even know whether they are true or false, that is, whether the ideas I have of them are ideas of real things or of non-things.[1] For although, as I have noted before, falsity in the strict sense, or formal falsity, can occur only in judgements, there is another kind of falsity, material falsity, which occurs in ideas, when they represent non-things as things. For example, the ideas which I have of heat and cold contain so little clarity and distinctness that 44 they do not enable me to tell whether cold is merely the absence of heat or vice versa, or whether both of them are real qualities, or neither is. And since there can be no ideas which are not as it were of things,[2] if it is true that cold is nothing but the absence of heat, the idea which represents it to me as something real and positive deserves to be called false; and the same goes for other ideas of this kind.

Such ideas obviously do not require me to posit a source distinct from myself. For on the one hand, if they are false, that is, represent non-things,

---

[1] '...chimerical things which cannot exist' (French version).
[2] 'And since ideas, being like images, must in each case appear to us to represent something' (French version).

repraesentent, lumine naturali notum mihi est illas a nihilo procedere, hoc est, non aliam ob causam in me esse quam quia deest aliquid naturae meae, nec est plane perfecta; si autem sint verae, quia tamen tam parum realitatis mihi exhibent, ut ne quidem illud a non re possim distinguere, non video cur a me ipso esse non possint.

Ex iis vero quae in ideis rerum corporalium clara et distincta sunt, quaedam ab idea mei ipsius videor mutuari potuisse, nempe substantiam, durationem, numerum, et si quae alia sint ejusmodi; nam cum cogito lapidem esse substantiam, sive esse rem quae per se apta est existere, itemque me esse substantiam, quamvis concipiam me esse rem cogitantem et non extensam, lapidem vero esse rem extensam et non cogitantem, ac proinde maxima inter utrumque conceptum sit diversitas, in ratione tamen substantiae videntur convenire; itemque, cum percipio me nunc esse, et prius etiam aliquamdiu fuisse recordor, cumque varias habeo cogitationes quarum numerum intelligo, 45 acquiro ideas durationis et numeri, quas deinde ad quascunque alias res possum transferre. Caetera autem omnia ex quibus rerum corporearum ideae conflantur, nempe extensio, figura, situs, et motus, in me quidem, cum nihil aliud sim quam res cogitans, formaliter non continentur; sed quia sunt tantum modi quidam substantiae, ego autem substantia, videntur in me contineri posse eminenter.

Itaque sola restat idea Dei, in qua considerandum est an aliquid sit quod a me ipso non potuerit proficisci. Dei nomine intelligo substantiam quandam infinitam, independentem, summe intelligentem, summe potentem, et a qua tum ego ipse, tum aliud omne, si quid aliud extat, quodcumque extat, est creatum. Quae sane omnia talia sunt ut, quo diligentius attendo, tanto minus a me solo profecta esse posse videantur. Ideoque ex antedictis, Deum necessario existere, est concludendum.

Nam quamvis substantiae quidem idea in me sit ex hoc ipso quod sim substantia, non tamen idcirco esset idea substantiae infinitae, cum sim finitus, nisi ab aliqua substantia, quae revera esset infinita, procederet.

I know by the natural light that they arise from nothing – that is, they are in me only because of a deficiency and lack of perfection in my nature. If on the other hand they are true, then since the reality which they represent is so extremely slight that I cannot even distinguish it from a non-thing, I do not see why they cannot originate from myself.

With regard to the clear and distinct elements in my ideas of corporeal things, it appears that I could have borrowed some of these from my idea of myself, namely substance, duration, number and anything else of this kind. For example, I think that a stone is a substance, or is a thing capable of existing independently, and I also think that I am a substance. Admittedly I conceive of myself as a thing that thinks and is not extended, whereas I conceive of the stone as a thing that is extended and does not think, so that the two conceptions differ enormously; but they seem to agree with respect to the classification 'substance'.[1] Again, I perceive that I now exist, and remember that I have existed for some time; moreover, I have various thoughts which I can count; it is in these ways that I acquire the ideas of 45 duration and number which I can then transfer to other things. As for all the other elements which make up the ideas of corporeal things, namely extension, shape, position and movement, these are not formally contained in me, since I am nothing but a thinking thing; but since they are merely modes of a substance,[2] and I am a substance, it seems possible that they are contained in me eminently.

So there remains only the idea of God; and I must consider whether there is anything in the idea which could not have originated in myself. By the word 'God' I understand a substance that is infinite, <eternal, immutable,> independent, supremely intelligent, supremely powerful, and which created both myself and everything else (if anything else there be) that exists. All these attributes are such that, the more carefully I concentrate on them, the less possible it seems that they[3] could have originated from me alone. So from what has been said it must be concluded that God necessarily exists.

It is true that I have the idea of substance in me in virtue of the fact that I am a substance; but this would not account for my having the idea of an infinite substance, when I am finite, unless this idea proceeded from some substance which really was infinite.

---

[1] ' . . . in so far as they represent substances' (French version).
[2] ' . . . and as it were the garments under which corporeal substance appears to us' (French version).
[3] ' . . . that the idea I have of them' (French version).

Nec putare debeo me non percipere infinitum per veram ideam, sed tantum per negationem finiti, ut percipio quietem et tenebras per negationem motus et lucis; nam contra manifeste intelligo plus realitatis esse in substantia infinita quam in finita, ac proinde priorem quodammodo in me esse perceptionem infiniti quam finiti, hoc est Dei quam mei ipsius. Qua enim ratione intel-
46 ligerem me dubitare, me cupere, hoc est, aliquid mihi deesse, et me non esse omnino perfectum, si nulla idea entis perfectioris in me esset, ex cujus comparatione defectus meos agnoscerem?

Nec dici potest hanc forte ideam Dei materialiter falsam esse, ideoque a nihilo esse posse, ut paulo ante de ideis caloris et frigoris, et similium, animadverti; nam contra, cum maxime clara et distincta sit, et plus realitatis objectivae quam ulla alia contineat, nulla est per se magis vera, nec in qua minor falsitatis suspicio reperiatur. Est, inquam, haec idea entis summe perfecti et infiniti maxime vera; nam quamvis forte fingi possit tale ens non existere, non tamen fingi potest ejus ideam nihil reale mihi exhibere, ut de idea frigoris ante dixi. Est etiam maxime clara et distincta; nam quidquid clare et distincte percipio, quod est reale et verum, et quod perfectionem aliquam importat, totum in ea continetur. Nec obstat quod non comprehendam infinitum, vel quod alia innumera in Deo sint, quae nec comprehendere, nec forte etiam attingere cogitatione, ullo modo possum; est enim de ratione infiniti, ut a me, qui sum finitus, non comprehendatur; et sufficit me hoc ipsum intelligere, ac judicare, illa omnia quae clare percipio, et perfectionem aliquam importare scio, atque etiam forte alia innumera quae ignoro, vel formaliter vel eminenter in Deo esse, ut idea quam de illo habeo sit omnium quae in me sunt maxime vera, et maxime clara et distincta.

Sed forte majus aliquid sum quam ipse intelligam, omnesque illae perfectiones quas Deo tribuo, potentia quodammodo in
47 me sunt, etiamsi nondum sese exerant, neque ad actum reducantur. Experior enim jam cognitionem meam paulatim augeri; nec video quid obstet quominus ita magis et magis

And I must not think that, just as my conceptions of rest and darkness are arrived at by negating movement and light, so my perception of the infinite is arrived at not by means of a true idea but merely by negating the finite. On the contrary, I clearly understand that there is more reality in an infinite substance than in a finite one, and hence that my perception of the infinite, that is God, is in some way prior to my perception of the finite, that is myself. For how could I understand that I doubted or desired – that is, lacked something – and that I was not wholly perfect, unless there were in me some idea of a more perfect being which enabled me to recognize my own defects by comparison?

Nor can it be said that this idea of God is perhaps materially false and so could have come from nothing,[1] which is what I observed just a moment ago in the case of the ideas of heat and cold, and so on. On the contrary, it is utterly clear and distinct, and contains in itself more objective reality than any other idea; hence there is no idea which is in itself truer or less liable to be suspected of falsehood. This idea of a supremely perfect and infinite being is, I say, true in the highest degree; for although perhaps one may imagine that such a being does not exist, it cannot be supposed that the idea of such a being represents something unreal, as I said with regard to the idea of cold. The idea is, moreover, utterly clear and distinct; for whatever I clearly and distinctly perceive as being real and true, and implying any perfection, is wholly contained in it. It does not matter that I do not grasp the infinite, or that there are countless additional attributes of God which I cannot in any way grasp, and perhaps cannot even reach in my thought; for it is in the nature of the infinite not to be grasped by a finite being like myself. It is enough that I understand[2] the infinite, and that I judge that all the attributes which I clearly perceive and know to imply some perfection – and perhaps countless others of which I am ignorant – are present in God either formally or eminently. This is enough to make the idea that I have of God the truest and most clear and distinct of all my ideas.

But perhaps I am something greater than I myself understand, and all the perfections which I attribute to God are somehow in me potentially, though not yet emerging or actualized. For I am now experiencing a gradual increase in my knowledge, and I see nothing to prevent its increasing more

---

[1] '... i.e. could be in me in virtue of my imperfection' (added in French version).
[2] According to Descartes one can know or understand something without fully grasping it: 'In the same way we can touch a mountain with our hands but we cannot put our arms around it ... To grasp something is to embrace it in one's thought; to know something, it is sufficient to touch it with one's thought' (letter to Mersenne, 27 May 1630, AT I 152: CSMK 25).

augeatur in infinitum, nec etiam cur, cognitione sic aucta, non possim
ejus ope reliquas omnes Dei perfectiones adipisci; nec denique cur
potentia ad istas perfectiones, si jam in me est, non sufficiat ad illarum
ideam producendam.

Imo nihil horum esse potest. Nam primo, ut verum sit cognitionem
meam gradatim augeri, et multa in me esse potentia quae actu nondum sunt, nihil tamen horum ad ideam Dei pertinet, in qua nempe
nihil omnino est potentiale; namque hoc ipsum, gradatim augeri, certissimum est imperfectionis argumentum. Praeterea, etiamsi cognitio
mea semper magis et magis augeatur, nihilominus intelligo nunquam
illam idcirco fore actu infinitam, quia nunquam eo devenietur, ut
majoris adhuc incrementi non sit capax; Deum autem ita judico esse
actu infinitum, ut nihil ejus perfectioni addi possit. Ac denique percipio esse objectivum ideae non a solo esse potentiali, quod proprie
loquendo nihil est, sed tantummodo ab actuali sive formali posse
produci.

Neque profecto quicquam est in his omnibus, quod diligenter
attendenti non sit lumine naturali manifestum; sed quia, cum minus
attendo, et rerum sensibilium imagines mentis aciem excaecant, non
ita facile recordor cur idea entis me perfectioris necessario ab ente
48   aliquo procedat quod sit revera perfectius, ulterius quaerere libet
an ego ipse habens illam ideam esse possem, si tale ens nullum
existeret.

Nempe a quo essem? A me scilicet, vel a parentibus, vel ab aliis
quibuslibet Deo minus perfectis; nihil enim ipso perfectius, nec etiam
aeque perfectum, cogitari aut fingi potest.

Atqui, si a me essem, nec dubitarem, nec optarem, nec omnino
quicquam mihi deesset; omnes enim perfectiones quarum idea aliqua in me est, mihi dedissem, atque ita ipsemet Deus essem. Nec
putare debeo illa forsan quae mihi desunt difficilius acquiri posse,
quam illa quae jam in me sunt; nam contra, manifestum est longe
difficilius fuisse me, hoc est rem sive substantiam cogitantem, ex
nihilo emergere, quam multarum rerum quas ignoro cognitiones,
quae tantum istius substantiae accidentia sunt, acquirere. Ac certe,
si majus illud a me haberem, non mihi illa saltem, quae facilius

and more to infinity. Further, I see no reason why I should not be able to use this increased knowledge to acquire all the other perfections of God. And finally, if the potentiality for these perfections is already within me, why should not this be enough to generate the idea of such perfections?

But all this is impossible. First, though it is true that there is a gradual increase in my knowledge, and that I have many potentialities which are not yet actual, this is all quite irrelevant to the idea of God, which contains absolutely nothing that is potential;[1] indeed, this gradual increase in knowledge is itself the surest sign of imperfection. What is more, even if my knowledge always increases more and more, I recognize that it will never actually be infinite, since it will never reach the point where it is not capable of a further increase; God, on the other hand, I take to be actually infinite, so that nothing can be added to his perfection. And finally, I perceive that the objective being of an idea cannot be produced merely by potential being, which strictly speaking is nothing, but only by actual or formal being.

If one concentrates carefully, all this is quite evident by the natural light. But when I relax my concentration, and my mental vision is blinded by the images of things perceived by the senses, it is not so easy for me to remember why the idea of a being more perfect than myself must necessarily proceed from some being which is in reality more perfect. I should therefore like 48 to go further and inquire whether I myself, who have this idea, could exist if no such being existed.

From whom, in that case, would I derive my existence? From myself presumably, or from my parents, or from some other beings less perfect than God; for nothing more perfect than God, or even as perfect, can be thought of or imagined.

Yet if I derived my existence from myself,[2] then I should neither doubt nor want, nor lack anything at all; for I should have given myself all the perfections of which I have any idea, and thus I should myself be God. I must not suppose that the items I lack would be more difficult to acquire than those I now have. On the contrary, it is clear that, since I am a thinking thing or substance, it would have been far more difficult for me to emerge out of nothing than merely to acquire knowledge of the many things of which I am ignorant – such knowledge being merely an accident of that substance. And if I had derived my existence from myself, which is a greater achievement, I should certainly not have denied myself the knowledge in

---

[1] '. . . but only what is actual and real' (added in French version).
[2] '. . . and were independent of every other being' (added in French version).

haberi possunt, denegassem, sed neque etiam ulla alia ex iis, quae in idea Dei contineri percipio; quia nempe nulla difficiliora factu mihi videntur; si quae autem difficiliora factu essent, certe etiam mihi difficiliora viderentur, siquidem reliqua quae habeo, a me haberem, quoniam in illis potentiam meam terminari experirer.

Neque vim harum rationum effugio, si supponam me forte semper fuisse ut nunc sum, tanquam si inde sequeretur, nullum existentiae meae authorem esse quaerendum. Quoniam enim omne 49 tempus vitae in partes innumeras dividi potest, quarum singulae a reliquis nullo modo dependent, ex eo quod paulo ante fuerim, non sequitur me nunc debere esse, nisi aliqua causa me quasi rursus creet ad hoc momentum, hoc est me conservet. Perspicuum enim est attendenti ad temporis naturam, eadem plane vi et actione opus esse ad rem quamlibet singulis momentis quibus durat conservandam, qua opus esset ad eandem de novo creandam, si nondum existeret; adeo ut conservationem sola ratione a creatione differre, sit etiam unum ex iis quae lumine naturali manifesta sunt.

Itaque debeo nunc interrogare me ipsum, an habeam aliquam vim per quam possim efficere ut ego ille, qui jam sum, paulo post etiam sim futurus: nam, cum nihil aliud sim quam res cogitans, vel saltem cum de ea tantum mei parte praecise nunc agam quae est res cogitans, si quae talis vis in me esset, ejus proculdubio conscius essem. Sed et nullam esse experior, et ex hoc ipso evidentissime cognosco me ab aliquo ente a me diverso pendere.

Forte vero illud ens non est Deus, sumque vel a parentibus productus, vel a quibuslibet aliis causis Deo minus perfectis. Imo, ut jam ante dixi, perspicuum est tantumdem ad minimum esse debere in causa quantum est in effectu; et idcirco, cum sim res cogitans, ideamque quandam Dei in me habens, qualiscunque tandem mei causa assignetur, illam etiam esse rem cogitantem, et omnium perfectionum, quas Deo tribuo, ideam habere fatendum est. Potestque de illa rursus quaeri, an sit a se, vel ab alia. Nam si 50 a se, patet ex dictis illam ipsam Deum esse, quia nempe, cum vim habeat per se existendi, habet proculdubio etiam vim possidendi actu

question, which is something much easier to acquire, or indeed any of the attributes which I perceive to be contained in the idea of God; for none of them seem any harder to achieve. And if any of them were harder to achieve, they would certainly appear so to me, if I had indeed got all my other attributes from myself, since I should experience a limitation of my power in this respect.

I do not escape the force of these arguments by supposing that I have always existed as I do now, as if it followed from this that there was no need to look for any author of my existence. For a lifespan can be divided into countless parts, each completely independent of the others, so that it does not follow from the fact that I existed a little while ago that I must exist now, unless there is some cause which as it were creates me afresh at this moment – that is, which preserves me. For it is quite clear to anyone who attentively considers the nature of time that the same power and action are needed to preserve anything at each individual moment of its duration as would be required to create that thing anew if it were not yet in existence. Hence the distinction between preservation and creation is only a conceptual one,[1] and this is one of the things that are evident by the natural light.

I must therefore now ask myself whether I possess some power enabling me to bring it about that I who now exist will still exist a little while from now. For since I am nothing but a thinking thing – or at least since I am now concerned only and precisely with that part of me which is a thinking thing – if there were such a power in me, I should undoubtedly be aware of it. But I experience no such power, and this very fact makes me recognize most clearly that I depend on some being distinct from myself.

But perhaps this being is not God, and perhaps I was produced either by my parents or by other causes less perfect than God. No; for as I have said before, it is quite clear that there must be at least as much in the cause as in the effect.[2] And therefore whatever kind of cause is eventually proposed, since I am a thinking thing and have within me some idea of God, it must be admitted that what caused me is itself a thinking thing and possesses the idea of all the perfections which I attribute to God. In respect of this cause one may again inquire whether it derives its existence from itself or from another cause. If from itself, then it is clear from what has been said that it is itself God, since if it has the power of existing through its own might,[3] then undoubtedly it also has the power of actually possessing all

49

50

---

[1] Cf. *Principles*, Part 1, art. 62 (AT VIII 30: CSM I 214).
[2] '... at least as much reality in the cause as in its effect' (French version).
[3] Lat. *per se*; literally 'through itself'.

omnes perfectiones quarum ideam in se habet, hoc est omnes quas in Deo esse concipio. Si autem sit ab alia, rursus eodem modo de hac altera quaeretur, an sit a se, vel ab alia, donec tandem ad causam ultimam deveniatur, quae erit Deus.

Satis enim apertum est nullum hic dari posse progressum in infinitum, praesertim cum non tantum de causa, quae me olim produxit, hic agam, sed maxime etiam de illa quae me tempore praesenti conservat.

Nec fingi potest plures forte causas partiales ad me efficiendum concurrisse, et ab una ideam unius ex perfectionibus quas Deo tribuo, ab alia ideam alterius me accepisse, adeo ut omnes quidem illae perfectiones alicubi in universo reperiantur, sed non omnes simul junctae in uno aliquo, qui sit Deus. Nam contra, unitas, simplicitas, sive inseparabilitas eorum omnium quae in Deo sunt, una est ex praecipuis perfectionibus quas in eo esse intelligo. Nec certe istius omnium ejus perfectionum unitatis idea in me potuit poni ab ulla causa, a qua etiam aliarum perfectionum ideas non habuerim: neque enim efficere potuit ut illas simul junctas et inseparabiles intelligerem, nisi simul effecerit ut quaenam illae essent agnoscerem.

Quantum denique ad parentes attinet, ut omnia vera sint quae de illis unquam putavi, non tamen profecto illi me conservant, nec etiam ullo modo me, quatenus sum res cogitans, effecerunt; sed tantum dispositiones quasdam in ea materia posuerunt, cui me, hoc
51 est mentem, quam solam nunc pro me accipio, inesse judicavi. Ac proinde hic nulla de iis difficultas esse potest; sed omnino est concludendum, ex hoc solo quod existam, quaedamque idea entis perfectissimi, hoc est Dei, in me sit, evidentissime demonstrari Deum etiam existere.

Superest tantum ut examinem qua ratione ideam istam a Deo accepi; neque enim illam sensibus hausi, nec unquam non expectanti mihi advenit, ut solent rerum sensibilium ideae, cum istae res externis sensuum organis occurrunt, vel occurrere videntur; nec etiam a me efficta est, nam nihil ab illa detrahere, nihil illi superaddere plane possum; ac proinde superest ut mihi sit innata, quemadmodum etiam mihi est innata idea mei ipsius.

the perfections of which it has an idea – that is, all the perfections which I conceive to be in God. If, on the other hand, it derives its existence from another cause, then the same question may be repeated concerning this further cause, namely whether it derives its existence from itself or from another cause, until eventually the ultimate cause is reached, and this will be God.

It is clear enough that an infinite regress is impossible here, especially since I am dealing not just with the cause that produced me in the past, but also and most importantly with the cause that preserves me at the present moment.

Nor can it be supposed that several partial causes contributed to my creation, or that I received the idea of one of the perfections which I attribute to God from one cause and the idea of another from another – the supposition here being that all the perfections are to be found somewhere in the universe but not joined together in a single being, God. On the contrary, the unity, the simplicity, or the inseparability of all the attributes of God is one of the most important of the perfections which I understand him to have. And surely the idea of the unity of all his perfections could not have been placed in me by any cause which did not also provide me with the ideas of the other perfections; for no cause could have made me understand the interconnection and inseparability of the perfections without at the same time making me recognize what they were.

Lastly, as regards my parents, even if everything I have ever believed about them is true, it is certainly not they who preserve me; and in so far as I am a thinking thing, they did not even make me; they merely placed certain dispositions in the matter which I have always regarded as containing me, or rather my mind, for that is all I now take myself to be. So 51 there can be no difficulty regarding my parents in this context. Altogether then, it must be concluded that the mere fact that I exist and have within me an idea of a most perfect being, that is, God, provides a very clear proof that God does indeed exist.

It only remains for me to examine how I received this idea from God. For I did not acquire it from the senses; it has never come to me unexpectedly, as usually happens with the ideas of things that are perceivable by the senses, when these things present themselves to the external sense organs – or seem to do so. And it was not invented by me either; for I am plainly unable either to take away anything from it or to add anything to it. The only remaining alternative is that it is innate in me, just as the idea of myself is innate in me.

Et sane non mirum est Deum, me creando, ideam illam mihi indidisse, ut esset tanquam nota artificis operi suo impressa; nec etiam opus est ut nota illa sit aliqua res ab opere ipso diversa. Sed ex hoc uno quod Deus me creavit, valde credibile est me quodammodo ad imaginem et similitudinem ejus factum esse, illamque similitudinem, in qua Dei idea continetur, a me percipi per eandem facultatem, per quam ego ipse a me percipior: hoc est, dum in meipsum mentis aciem converto, non modo intelligo me esse rem incompletam et ab alio dependentem, remque ad majora et majora sive meliora indefinite aspirantem; sed simul etiam intelligo illum, a quo pendeo, majora ista omnia non indefinite et potentia tantum, sed reipsa infinite in se habere, atque ita Deum esse. Totaque vis argumenti in eo est,

52   quod agnoscam fieri non posse ut existam talis naturae qualis sum, nempe ideam Dei in me habens, nisi revera Deus etiam existeret, Deus, inquam, ille idem cujus idea in me est, hoc est, habens omnes illas perfectiones, quas ego non comprehendere, sed quocunque modo attingere cogitatione possum, et nullis plane defectibus obnoxius. Ex quibus satis patet illum fallacem esse non posse; omnem enim fraudem et deceptionem a defectu aliquo pendere, lumine naturali manifestum est.

Sed priusquam hoc diligentius examinem, simulque in alias veritates quae inde colligi possunt inquiram, placet hic aliquandiu in ipsius Dei contemplatione immorari, ejus attributa apud me expendere, et immensi hujus luminis pulchritudinem, quantum caligantis ingenii mei acies ferre poterit, intueri, admirari, adorare. Ut enim in hac sola divinae majestatis contemplatione summam alterius vitae foelicitatem consistere fide credimus, ita etiam jam ex eadem, licet multo minus perfecta, maximam, cujus in hac vita capaces simus, voluptatem percipi posse experimur.

And indeed it is no surprise that God, in creating me, should have placed this idea in me to be, as it were, the mark of the craftsman stamped on his work – not that the mark need be anything distinct from the work itself. But the mere fact that God created me is a very strong basis for believing that I am somehow made in his image and likeness, and that I perceive that likeness, which includes the idea of God, by the same faculty which enables me to perceive myself. That is, when I turn my mind's eye upon myself, I understand that I am a thing which is incomplete and dependent on another and which aspires without limit to ever greater and better things; but I also understand at the same time that he on whom I depend has within him all those greater things, not just indefinitely and potentially but actually and infinitely, and hence that he is God. The whole force of the argument lies in this: I recognize that it would be impossible for me to exist 52 with the kind of nature I have – that is, having within me the idea of God – were it not also the case that God really existed. By 'God' I mean the very being the idea of whom is within me, that is, the possessor of all the perfections which I cannot grasp, but can somehow reach in my thought, who is subject to no defects whatsoever.[1] It is clear enough from this that he cannot be a deceiver, since it is manifest by the natural light that all fraud and deception depend on some defect.

But before examining this point more carefully and investigating other truths which may be derived from it, I should like to pause here and spend some time in the contemplation of God; to reflect on his attributes, and to gaze at, wonder at and adore the beauty of this immense light, so far as the eye of my darkened intellect can bear it. For just as we believe through faith that the supreme happiness of the next life consists solely in the contemplation of the divine majesty, so experience tells us that this same contemplation, albeit much less perfect, enables us to know the greatest joy of which we are capable in this life.

---

[1] '. . . and has not one of the things which indicate some imperfection' (added in French version).

De vero et falso

Ita me his diebus assuefeci in mente a sensibus abducenda, tamque
53 accurate animadverti perpauca esse quae de rebus corporeis vere per-
cipiantur, multoque plura de mente humana, multo adhuc plura de
Deo cognosci, ut jam absque ulla difficultate cogitationem a rebus
imaginabilibus ad intelligibiles tantum, atque ab omni materia secre-
tas, convertam. Et sane multo magis distinctam habeo ideam mentis
humanae, quatenus est res cogitans, non extensa in longum, latum, et
profundum, nec aliud quid a corpore habens, quam ideam ullius rei
corporeae. Cumque attendo me dubitare, sive esse rem incompletam et
dependentem, adeo clara et distincta idea entis independentis et com-
pleti, hoc est Dei, mihi occurrit; et ex hoc uno quod talis idea in me sit,
sive quod ego ideam illam habens existam, adeo manifeste concludo
Deum etiam existere, atque ab illo singulis momentis totam existentiam meam dependere, ut nihil evidentius, nihil certius ab humano
ingenio cognosci posse confidam. Jamque videre videor aliquam viam
per quam ab ista contemplatione veri Dei, in quo nempe sunt omnes
thesauri scientiarum et sapientiae absconditi, ad caeterarum rerum
cognitionem deveniatur.

In primis enim agnosco fieri non posse ut ille me unquam fallat; in
omni enim fallacia vel deceptione aliquid imperfectionis reperitur; et
quamvis posse fallere, nonnullum esse videatur acuminis aut potentiae
argumentum, proculdubio velle fallere, vel malitiam vel imbecillitatem
testatur, nec proinde in Deum cadit.

Deinde experior quandam in me esse judicandi facultatem, quam
54 certe, ut et reliqua omnia quae in me sunt, a Deo accepi; cumque

Truth and falsity

During these past few days I have accustomed myself to leading my mind away from the senses; and I have taken careful note of the fact that there is very little about corporeal things that is truly perceived, whereas much 53 more is known about the human mind, and still more about God. The result is that I now have no difficulty in turning my mind away from imaginable things[1] and towards things which are objects of the intellect alone and are totally separate from matter. And indeed the idea I have of the human mind, in so far as it is a thinking thing, which is not extended in length, breadth or height and has no other bodily characteristics, is much more distinct than the idea of any corporeal thing. And when I consider the fact that I have doubts, or that I am a thing that is incomplete and dependent, then there arises in me a clear and distinct idea of a being who is independent and complete, that is, an idea of God. And from the mere fact that there is such an idea within me, or that I who possess this idea exist, I clearly infer that God also exists, and that every single moment of my entire existence depends on him. So clear is this conclusion that I am confident that the human intellect cannot know anything that is more evident or more certain. And now, from this contemplation of the true God, in whom all the treasures of wisdom and the sciences lie hidden, I think I can see a way forward to the knowledge of other things.[2]

To begin with, I recognize that it is impossible that God should ever deceive me. For in every case of trickery or deception some imperfection is to be found; and although the ability to deceive appears to be an indication of cleverness or power, the will to deceive is undoubtedly evidence of malice or weakness, and so cannot apply to God.

Next, I know by experience that there is in me a faculty of judgement which, like everything else which is in me, I certainly received from God. 54

---

[1] '. . . from things which can be perceived by the senses or imagined' (French version).
[2] '. . . of the other things in the universe' (French version).

ille nolit me fallere, talem profecto non dedit, ut, dum ea recte utor, possim unquam errare.

Nec ullum de hac re dubium superesset, nisi inde sequi videretur, me igitur errare nunquam posse; nam si quodcunque in me est, a Deo habeo, nec ullam ille mihi dederit errandi facultatem, non videor posse unquam errare. Atque ita prorsus, quamdiu de Deo tantum cogito, totusque in eum me converto, nullam erroris aut falsitatis causam deprehendo; sed, postmodum ad me reversus, experior me tamen innumeris erroribus esse obnoxium, quorum causam inquirens animadverto non tantum Dei, sive entis summe perfecti, realem et positivam, sed etiam, ut ita loquar, nihili, sive ejus quod ab omni perfectione summe abest, negativam quandam ideam mihi obversari, et me tanquam medium quid inter Deum et nihil, sive inter summum ens et non ens ita esse constitutum, ut, quatenus a summo ente sum creatus, nihil quidem in me sit, per quod fallar aut in errorem inducar, sed quatenus etiam quodammodo de nihilo, sive de non ente, participo, hoc est quatenus non sum ipse summum ens, desuntque mihi quam plurima, non adeo mirum esse quod fallar. Atque ita certe intelligo errorem, quatenus error est, non esse quid reale quod a Deo dependeat, sed tantummodo esse defectum; nec proinde ad errandum mihi opus esse aliqua facultate in hunc finem a Deo tributa, sed contingere ut errem, ex eo quod facultas verum judicandi, quam ab illo habeo, non sit in me infinita.

55 Verumtamen hoc nondum omnino satisfacit; non enim error est pura negatio, sed privatio, sive carentia cujusdam cognitionis, quae in me quodammodo esse deberet; atque attendenti ad Dei naturam non videtur fieri posse, ut ille aliquam in me posuerit facultatem, quae non sit in suo genere perfecta, sive quae aliqua sibi debita perfectione sit privata. Nam si, quo peritior est artifex, eo perfectiora opera ab illo proficiscantur, quid potest a summo illo rerum omnium conditore factum esse, quod non sit omnibus numeris absolutum? Nec dubium est quin potuerit Deus me talem creare, ut nunquam fallerer; nec etiam dubium est quin velit semper id quod est optimum: anne ergo melius est me falli quam non falli?

Dum haec perpendo attentius, occurrit primo non mihi esse mirandum, si quaedam a Deo fiant quorum rationes non

And since God does not wish to deceive me, he surely did not give me the kind of faculty which would ever enable me to go wrong while using it correctly.

There would be no further doubt on this issue were it not that what I have just said appears to imply that I am incapable of ever going wrong. For if everything that is in me comes from God, and he did not endow me with a faculty for making mistakes, it appears that I can never go wrong. And certainly, so long as I think only of God, and turn my whole attention to him, I can find no cause of error or falsity. But when I turn back to myself, I know by experience that I am prone to countless errors. On looking for the cause of these errors, I find that I possess not only a real and positive idea of God, or a being who is supremely perfect, but also what may be described as a negative idea of nothingness, or of that which is farthest removed from all perfection. I realize that I am, as it were, something intermediate between God and nothingness, or between supreme being and non-being: my nature is such that in so far as I was created by the supreme being, there is nothing in me to enable me to go wrong or lead me astray; but in so far as I participate in nothingness or non-being, that is, in so far as I am not myself the supreme being and am lacking in countless respects, it is no wonder that I make mistakes. I understand, then, that error as such is not something real which depends on God, but merely a defect. Hence my going wrong does not require me to have a faculty specially bestowed on me by God; it simply happens as a result of the fact that the faculty of true judgement which I have from God is in my case not infinite.

But this is still not entirely satisfactory. For error is not a pure negation,[1] 55 but rather a privation or lack of some knowledge which somehow should be in me. And when I concentrate on the nature of God, it seems impossible that he should have placed in me a faculty which is not perfect of its kind, or which lacks some perfection which it ought to have. The more skilled the craftsman the more perfect the work produced by him; if this is so, how can anything produced by the supreme creator of all things not be complete and perfect in all respects? There is, moreover, no doubt that God could have given me a nature such that I was never mistaken; again, there is no doubt that he always wills what is best. Is it then better that I should make mistakes than that I should not do so?

As I reflect on these matters more attentively, it occurs to me first of all that it is no cause for surprise if I do not understand the reasons for some

---

[1] '. . . i.e. not simply the defect or lack of some perfection to which I have no proper claim' (added in French version).

intelligam; nec de ejus existentia ideo esse dubitandum, quod forte quaedam alia esse experiar, quae quare vel quomodo ab illo facta sint non comprehendo. Cum enim jam sciam naturam meam esse valde infirmam et limitatam, Dei autem naturam esse immensam, incomprehensibilem, infinitam, ex hoc satis etiam scio innumerabilia illum posse quorum causas ignorem; atque ob hanc unicam rationem totum illud causarum genus, quod a fine peti solet, in rebus Physicis nullum usum habere existimo; non enim absque temeritate me puto posse investigare fines Dei.

56 Occurrit etiam non unam aliquam creaturam separatim, sed omnem rerum universitatem esse spectandam, quoties an opera Dei perfecta sint inquirimus; quod enim forte non immerito, si solum esset, valde imperfectum videretur, ut habens in mundo rationem partis est perfectissimum; et quamvis, ex quo de omnibus volui dubitare, nihil adhuc praeter me et Deum existere certo cognovi, non possum tamen, ex quo immensam Dei potentiam animadverti, negare quin multa alia ab illo facta sint, vel saltem fieri possint, adeo ut ego rationem partis in rerum universitate obtineam.

Deinde, ad me propius accedens, et qualesnam sint errores mei (qui soli imperfectionem aliquam in me arguunt) investigans, adverto illos a duabus causis simul concurrentibus dependere, nempe a facultate cognoscendi quae in me est, et a facultate eligendi, sive ab arbitrii libertate, hoc est ab intellectu et simul a voluntate. Nam per solum intellectum percipio tantum ideas de quibus judicium ferre possum, nec ullus error proprie dictus in eo praecise sic spectato reperitur; quamvis enim innumerae fortasse res existant, quarum ideae nullae in me sunt, non tamen proprie illis privatus, sed negative tantum destitutus, sum dicendus, quia nempe rationem nullam possum afferre, qua probem Deum mihi majorem quam dederit cognoscendi facultatem dare debuisse; atque quantumvis peritum artificem esse intelligam, non tamen ideo puto illum in singulis ex suis operibus omnes perfectiones ponere debuisse, quas in aliquibus ponere potest. Nec vero etiam queri possum, quod non satis amplam et perfectam voluntatem, sive arbitrii libertatem,

of God's actions; and there is no call to doubt his existence if I happen to find that there are other instances where I do not grasp why or how certain things were made by him. For since I now know that my own nature is very weak and limited, whereas the nature of God is immense, incomprehensible and infinite, I also know without more ado that he is capable of countless things whose causes are beyond my knowledge. And for this reason alone I consider the customary search for final causes to be totally useless in physics; there is considerable rashness in thinking myself capable of investigating the <impenetrable> purposes of God.

It also occurs to me that whenever we are inquiring whether the works of God are perfect, we ought to look at the whole universe, not just at one created thing on its own. For what would perhaps rightly appear very imperfect if it existed on its own is quite perfect when its function as a part 56 of the universe is considered. It is true that, since my decision to doubt everything, it is so far only myself and God whose existence I have been able to know with certainty; but after considering the immense power of God, I cannot deny that many other things have been made by him, or at least could have been made, and hence that I may have a place in the universal scheme of things.

Next, when I look more closely at myself and inquire into the nature of my errors (for these are the only evidence of some imperfection in me), I notice that they depend on two concurrent causes, namely on the faculty of knowledge which is in me, and on the faculty of choice or freedom of the will; that is, they depend on both the intellect and the will simultaneously. Now all that the intellect on its own does is to enable me to perceive[1] the ideas which are subjects for possible judgements; and when regarded strictly in this light, it turns out to contain no error in the proper sense of that term. For although countless things may exist without there being any corresponding ideas in me, it should not, strictly speaking, be said that I am deprived of these ideas,[2] but merely that I lack them, in a negative sense. This is because I cannot produce any reason to prove that God ought to have given me a greater faculty of knowledge than he did; and no matter how skilled I understand a craftsman to be, this does not make me think he ought to have put into every one of his works all the perfections which he is able to put into some of them. Besides, I cannot complain that the will or freedom of choice which I received from God is not sufficiently

---

[1] '... without affirming or denying anything' (added in French version).
[2] '... it cannot be said that my understanding is deprived of these ideas, as if they were something to which its nature entitles it' (French version).

a Deo acceperim; nam sane nullis illam limitibus circumscribi expe-
57 rior. Et quod valde notandum mihi videtur, nulla alia in me sunt tam
perfecta aut tanta, quin intelligam perfectiora sive majora adhuc esse
posse. Nam si, exempli causa, facultatem intelligendi considero, statim agnosco perexiguam illam et valde finitam in me esse, simulque
alterius cujusdam multo majoris, imo maximae atque infinitae, ideam
formo, illamque ex hoc ipso quod ejus ideam formare possim, ad Dei
naturam pertinere percipio. Eadem ratione, si facultatem recordandi
vel imaginandi, vel quaslibet alias examinem, nullam plane invenio,
quam non in me tenuem et circumscriptam, in Deo immensam,
esse intelligam. Sola est voluntas, sive arbitrii libertas, quam tantam in me experior, ut nullius majoris ideam apprehendam; adeo
ut illa praecipue sit, ratione cujus imaginem quandam et similitudinem Dei me referre intelligo. Nam quamvis major absque comparatione in Deo quam in me sit, tum ratione cognitionis et potentiae quae illi adjunctae sunt, redduntque ipsam magis firmam et
efficacem, tum ratione objecti, quoniam ad plura se extendit, non
tamen, in se formaliter et praecise spectata, major videtur; quia tantum in eo consistit, quod idem vel facere vel non facere (hoc est
affirmare vel negare, prosequi vel fugere) possimus, vel potius in
eo tantum, quod ad id quod nobis ab intellectu proponitur affirmandum vel negandum, sive prosequendum vel fugiendum, ita fera-
mur, ut a nulla vi externa nos ad id determinari sentiamus. Neque
enim opus est me in utramque partem ferri posse, ut sim liber,
58 sed contra, quo magis in unam propendeo, sive quia rationem veri
et boni in ea evidenter intelligo, sive quia Deus intima cogitationis meae ita disponit, tanto liberius illam eligo; nec sane divina
gratia, nec naturalis cognitio unquam imminuunt libertatem, sed
potius augent et corroborant. Indifferentia autem illa, quam experior, cum nulla me ratio in unam partem magis quam in alteram
impellit, est infimus gradus libertatis, et nullam in ea perfectionem,
sed tantummodo in cognitione defectum, sive negationem quandam,
testatur; nam si semper quid verum et bonum sit clare viderem, nunquam de eo quod esset judicandum vel eligendum deliberarem; atque
ita, quamvis plane liber, nunquam tamen indifferens esse possem.

Ex his autem percipio nec vim volendi, quam a Deo habeo,
per se spectatam, causam esse errorum meorum, est enim amplis-
sima, atque in suo genere perfecta; neque etiam vim intelligendi,

extensive or perfect, since I know by experience that it is not restricted in any way. Indeed, I think it is very noteworthy that there is nothing else 57 in me which is so perfect and so great that the possibility of a further increase in its perfection or greatness is beyond my understanding. If, for example, I consider the faculty of understanding, I immediately recognize that in my case it is extremely slight and very finite, and I at once form the idea of an understanding which is much greater – indeed supremely great and infinite; and from the very fact that I can form an idea of it, I perceive that it belongs to the nature of God. Similarly, if I examine the faculties of memory or imagination, or any others, I discover that in my case each one of these faculties is weak and limited, while in the case of God it is immeasurable. It is only the will, or freedom of choice, which I experience within me to be so great that the idea of any greater faculty is beyond my grasp; so much so that it is above all in virtue of the will that I understand myself to bear in some way the image and likeness of God. For although God's will is incomparably greater than mine, both in virtue of the knowledge and power that accompany it and make it more firm and efficacious, and also in virtue of its object, in that it ranges over a greater number of items, nevertheless it does not seem any greater than mine when considered as will in the essential and strict sense. This is because the will simply consists in our ability to do or not do something (that is, to affirm or deny, to pursue or avoid); or rather, it consists simply in the fact that when the intellect puts something forward, we are moved to affirm or deny or to pursue or avoid it in such a way that we do not feel ourselves to be determined by any external force. For in order to be free, there is no need for me to be capable of going in each of two directions; on the contrary, the more I incline in one direction – either because I clearly understand that reasons of truth and goodness point that way, or because of a divinely 58 produced disposition of my inmost thoughts – the freer is my choice. Neither divine grace nor natural knowledge ever diminishes freedom; on the contrary, they increase and strengthen it. But the indifference I feel when there is no reason pushing me in one direction rather than another is the lowest grade of freedom; it is evidence not of any perfection of freedom, but rather of a defect in knowledge or a kind of negation. For if I always saw clearly what was true and good, I should never have to deliberate about the right judgement or choice; in that case, although I should be wholly free, it would be impossible for me ever to be in a state of indifference.

From these considerations I perceive that the power of willing which I received from God is not, when considered in itself, the cause of my mistakes; for it is both extremely ample and also perfect of its kind. Nor is

nam quidquid intelligo, cum a Deo habeam ut intelligam, proculdubio recte intelligo, nec in eo fieri potest ut fallar. Unde ergo nascuntur mei errores? Nempe ex hoc uno quod, cum latius pateat voluntas quam intellectus, illam non intra eosdem limites contineo, sed etiam ad illa quae non intelligo extendo; ad quae cum sit indifferens, facile a vero et bono deflectit, atque ita et fallor et pecco.

Exempli causa, cum examinarem hisce diebus an aliquid in mundo existeret, atque adverterem, ex hoc ipso quod illud examinarem, evidenter sequi me existere, non potui quidem non judicare illud quod tam clare intelligebam verum esse; non quod ab aliqua vi externa fuerim ad id coactus, sed quia ex magna luce in intellectu magna consequuta est propensio in voluntate, atque ita tanto magis sponte et libere illud credidi, quanto minus fui ad istud ipsum indifferens. Nunc autem, non tantum scio me, quatenus sum res quaedam cogitans, existere, sed praeterea etiam idea quaedam naturae corporeae mihi obversatur, contingitque ut dubitem an natura cogitans quae in me est, vel potius quae ego ipse sum, alia sit ab ista natura corporea, vel an ambae idem sint; et suppono nullam adhuc intellectui meo rationem occurrere, quae mihi unum magis quam aliud persuadeat. Certe ex hoc ipso sum indifferens ad utrumlibet affirmandum vel negandum, vel etiam ad nihil de ea re judicandum.

Quinimo etiam haec indifferentia non ad ea tantum se extendit de quibus intellectus nihil plane cognoscit, sed generaliter ad omnia quae ab illo non satis perspicue cognoscuntur eo ipso tempore, quo de iis a voluntate deliberatur: quantumvis enim probabiles conjecturae me trahant in unam partem, sola cognitio quod sint tantum conjecturae, non autem certae atque indubitabiles rationes, sufficit ad assensionem meam in contrarium impellendam. Quod satis his diebus sum expertus, cum illa omnia quae prius ut vera quammaxime credideram, propter hoc unum quod de iis aliquo modo posse dubitari deprehendissem, plane falsa esse supposui.

Cum autem quid verum sit non satis clare et distincte percipio, si quidem a judicio ferendo abstineam, clarum est me recte agere, et non falli. Sed si vel affirmem vel negem, tunc libertate arbitrii non recte utor; atque si in eam partem quae falsa est me convertam, plane fallar; si vero alteram amplectar, casu quidem incidam in veritatem, sed

my power of understanding to blame; for since my understanding comes from God, everything that I understand I undoubtedly understand correctly, and any error here is impossible. So what then is the source of my mistakes? It must be simply this: the scope of the will is wider than that of the intellect; but instead of restricting it within the same limits, I extend its use to matters which I do not understand. Since the will is indifferent in such cases, it easily turns aside from what is true and good, and this is the source of my error and sin.

For example, during these past few days I have been asking whether anything in the world exists, and I have realized that from the very fact of my raising this question it follows quite evidently that I exist. I could not but judge that something which I understood so clearly was true; but this was not because I was compelled so to judge by any external force, 59 but because a great light in the intellect was followed by a great inclination in the will, and thus the spontaneity and freedom of my belief was all the greater in proportion to my lack of indifference. But now, besides the knowledge that I exist, in so far as I am a thinking thing, an idea of corporeal nature comes into my mind; and I happen to be in doubt as to whether the thinking nature which is in me, or rather which I am, is distinct from this corporeal nature or identical with it. I am making the further supposition that my intellect has not yet come upon any persuasive reason in favour of one alternative rather than the other. This obviously implies that I am indifferent as to whether I should assert or deny either alternative, or indeed refrain from making any judgement on the matter.

What is more, this indifference does not merely apply to cases where the intellect is wholly ignorant, but extends in general to every case where the intellect does not have sufficiently clear knowledge at the time when the will deliberates. For although probable conjectures may pull me in one direction, the mere knowledge that they are simply conjectures, and not certain and indubitable reasons, is itself quite enough to push my assent the other way. My experience in the last few days confirms this: the mere fact that I found that all my previous beliefs were in some sense open to doubt was enough to turn my absolutely confident belief in their truth into the supposition that they were wholly false.

If, however, I simply refrain from making a judgement in cases where I do not perceive the truth with sufficient clarity and distinctness, then it is clear that I am behaving correctly and avoiding error. But if in such cases I either affirm or deny, then I am not using my free will correctly. If I go for 60 the alternative which is false, then obviously I shall be in error; if I take the other side, then it is by pure chance that I arrive at the truth, and I shall

non ideo culpa carebo, quia lumine naturali manifestum est perceptionem intellectus praecedere semper debere voluntatis determina-
tionem. Atque in hoc liberi arbitrii non recto usu privatio illa inest
quae formam erroris constituit: privatio, inquam, inest in ipsa operatione, quatenus a me procedit, sed non in facultate quam a Deo
accepi, nec etiam in operatione quatenus ab illo dependet.

Neque enim habeo causam ullam conquerendi, quod Deus mihi
non majorem vim intelligendi, sive non majus lumen naturale
dederit quam dedit, quia est de ratione intellectus finiti ut multa
non intelligat, et de ratione intellectus creati ut sit finitus; estque
quod agam gratias illi, qui mihi nunquam quicquam debuit, pro
eo quod largitus est, non autem quod putem me ab illo iis esse
privatum, sive illum mihi ea abstulisse, quae non dedit.

Non habeo etiam causam conquerendi, quod voluntatem dederit
latius patentem quam intellectum; cum enim voluntas in una
tantum re, et tanquam in indivisibili consistat, non videtur
ferre ejus natura ut quicquam ab illa demi possit; et sane quo
amplior est, tanto majores debeo gratias ejus datori.

Nec denique etiam queri debeo, quod Deus mecum concurrat
ad eliciendos illos actus voluntatis, sive illa judicia, in quibus fallor: illi enim actus sunt omnino veri et boni, quatenus a Deo
dependent, et major in me quodammodo perfectio est, quod
illos possim elicere, quam si non possem. Privatio autem, in
61 qua sola ratio formalis falsitatis et culpae consistit, nullo Dei
concursu indiget, quia non est res, neque ad illum relata ut
causam privatio, sed tantummodo negatio dici debet. Nam sane
nulla imperfectio in Deo est, quod mihi libertatem dederit assentiendi vel non assentiendi quibusdam, quorum claram et distinctam perceptionem in intellectu meo non posuit; sed proculdubio in me imperfectio est, quod ista libertate non bene
utar, et de iis, quae non recte intelligo, judicium feram. Video
tamen fieri a Deo facile potuisse, ut, etiamsi manerem liber,
et cognitionis finitae, nunquam tamen errarem: nempe si vel
intellectui meo claram et distinctam perceptionem omnium de

still be at fault since it is clear by the natural light that the perception of the intellect should always precede the determination of the will. In this incorrect use of free will may be found the privation which constitutes the essence of error. The privation, I say, lies in the operation of the will in so far as it proceeds from me, but not in the faculty of will which I received from God, nor even in its operation, in so far as it depends on him.

And I have no cause for complaint on the grounds that the power of understanding or the natural light which God gave me is no greater than it is; for it is in the nature of a finite intellect to lack understanding of many things, and it is in the nature of a created intellect to be finite. Indeed, I have reason to give thanks to him who has never owed me anything for the great bounty that he has shown me, rather than thinking myself deprived or robbed of any gifts he did not bestow.[1]

Nor do I have any cause for complaint on the grounds that God gave me a will which extends more widely than my intellect. For since the will consists simply of one thing which is, as it were, indivisible, it seems that its nature rules out the possibility of anything being taken away from it. And surely, the more widely my will extends, then the greater thanks I owe to him who gave it to me.

Finally, I must not complain that the forming of those acts of will or judgements in which I go wrong happens with God's concurrence. For in so far as these acts depend on God, they are wholly true and good; and my ability to perform them means that there is in a sense more perfection in me than would be the case if I lacked this ability. As for the privation involved – which is all that the essential definition of falsity and wrong 61 consists in – this does not in any way require the concurrence of God, since it is not a thing; indeed, when it is referred to God as its cause, it should be called not a privation but simply a negation.[2] For it is surely no imperfection in God that he has given me the freedom to assent or not to assent in those cases where he did not endow my intellect with a clear and distinct perception; but it is undoubtedly an imperfection in me to misuse that freedom and make judgements about matters which I do not fully understand. I can see, however, that God could easily have brought it about that without losing my freedom, and despite the limitations in my knowledge, I should nonetheless never make a mistake. He could, for example, have endowed my intellect with a clear and distinct perception

---

[1] '... rather than entertaining so unjust a thought as to imagine that he deprived me of, or unjustly withheld, the other perfections which he did not give me' (French version).
[2] '... understanding these terms in accordance with scholastic usage' (added in French version).

quibus unquam essem deliberaturus indidisset; vel tantum si adeo
firmiter memoriae impressisset, de nulla unquam re esse judicandum
quam clare et distincte non intelligerem, ut nunquam ejus possem
oblivisci. Et facile intelligo me, quatenus rationem habeo totius cujusdam, perfectiorem futurum fuisse quam nunc sum, si talis a Deo
factus essem. Sed non ideo possum negare quin major quodammodo
perfectio sit in tota rerum universitate, quod quaedam ejus partes ab
erroribus immunes non sint, aliae vero sint, quam si omnes plane similes essent. Et nullum habeo jus conquerendi quod eam me Deus in
mundo personam sustinere voluerit, quae non est omnium praecipua
et maxime perfecta.

Ac praeterea, etiam ut non possim ab erroribus abstinere priori
illo modo qui pendet ab evidenti eorum omnium perceptione de
quibus est deliberandum, possum tamen illo altero qui pendet ab eo
62 tantum, quod recorder, quoties de rei veritate non liquet, a judicio
ferendo esse abstinendum; nam, quamvis eam in me infirmitatem
esse experiar, ut non possim semper uni et eidem cognitioni defixus
inhaerere, possum tamen attenta et saepius iterata meditatione efficere,
ut ejusdem, quoties usus exiget, recorder, atque ita habitum quemdam
non errandi acquiram.

Qua in re cum maxima et praecipua hominis perfectio consistat, non
parum me hodierna meditatione lucratum esse existimo, quod erroris
et falsitatis causam investigarim. Et sane nulla alia esse potest ab ea
quam explicui; nam quoties voluntatem in judiciis ferendis ita contineo, ut ad ea tantum se extendat quae illi clare et distincte ab intellectu
exhibentur, fieri plane non potest ut errem, quia omnis clara et distincta perceptio proculdubio est aliquid, ac proinde a nihilo esse non
potest, sed necessario Deum authorem habet, Deum, inquam, illum
summe perfectum, quem fallacem esse repugnat; ideoque proculdubio est vera. Nec hodie tantum didici quid mihi sit cavendum ut
nunquam fallar, sed simul etiam quid agendum ut assequar veritatem;
assequar enim illam profecto, si tantum ad omnia quae perfecte intelligo satis attendam, atque illa a reliquis, quae confusius et obscurius
apprehendo, secernam. Cui rei diligenter imposterum operam dabo.

of everything about which I was ever likely to deliberate; or he could simply have impressed it unforgettably on my memory that I should never make a judgement about anything which I did not clearly and distinctly understand. Had God made me this way, then I can easily understand that, considered as a totality,[1] I would have been more perfect than I am now. But I cannot therefore deny that there may in some way be more perfection in the universe as a whole because some of its parts are not immune from error, while others are immune, than there would be if all the parts were exactly alike. And I have no right to complain that the role God wished me to undertake in the world is not the principal one or the most perfect of all.

What is more, even if I have no power to avoid error in the first way just mentioned, which requires a clear perception of everything I have to deliberate on, I can avoid error in the second way, which depends merely on 62 my remembering to withhold judgement on any occasion when the truth of the matter is not clear. Admittedly, I am aware of a certain weakness in me, in that I am unable to keep my attention fixed on one and the same item of knowledge at all times; but by attentive and repeated meditation I am nevertheless able to make myself remember it as often as the need arises, and thus get into the habit of avoiding error.

It is here that man's greatest and most important perfection is to be found, and I therefore think that today's meditation, involving an investigation into the cause of error and falsity, has been very profitable. The cause of error must surely be the one I have explained; for if, whenever I have to make a judgement, I restrain my will so that it extends to what the intellect clearly and distinctly reveals, and no further, then it is quite impossible for me to go wrong. This is because every clear and distinct perception is undoubtedly something,[2] and hence cannot come from nothing, but must necessarily have God for its author. Its author, I say, is God, who is supremely perfect, and who cannot be a deceiver on pain of contradiction; hence the perception is undoubtedly true. So today I have learned not only what precautions to take to avoid ever going wrong, but also what to do to arrive at the truth. For I shall unquestionably reach the truth, if only I give sufficient attention to all the things which I perfectly understand, and separate these from all the other cases where my apprehension is more confused and obscure. And this is just what I shall take good care to do from now on.

[1] '...as if there were only myself in the world' (added in French version).
[2] '...something real and positive' (French version).

De essentia rerum materialium; et iterum de Deo, quod existat

Multa mihi supersunt de Dei attributis, multa de mei ipsius sive mentis meae natura investiganda; sed illa forte alias resumam, jamque nihil magis urgere videtur (postquam animadverti quid cavendum atque agendum sit ad assequendam veritatem), quam ut ex dubiis, in quae superioribus diebus incidi, coner emergere, videamque an aliquid certi de rebus materialibus haberi possit.

Et quidem, priusquam inquiram an aliquae tales res extra me existant, considerare debeo illarum ideas, quatenus sunt in mea cogitatione, et videre quaenam ex iis sint distinctae, quaenam confusae.

Nempe distincte imaginor quantitatem, quam vulgo Philosophi appellant continuam, sive ejus quantitatis aut potius rei quantae extensionem in longum, latum et profundum; numero in ea varias partes; quaslibet istis partibus magnitudines, figuras, situs, et motus locales, motibusque istis quaslibet durationes assigno.

Nec tantum illa, sic in genere spectata, mihi plane nota et perspecta sunt, sed praeterea etiam particularia innumera de figuris, de numero, de motu, et similibus, attendendo percipio, quorum veritas 64 adeo aperta est et naturae meae consentanea, ut, dum illa primum detego, non tam videar aliquid novi addiscere, quam eorum quae jam ante sciebam reminisci, sive ad ea primum advertere, quae dudum quidem in me erant, licet non prius in illa obtutum mentis convertissem.

Quodque hic maxime considerandum puto, invenio apud me innumeras ideas quarumdam rerum, quae, etiam si extra me fortasse nullibi existant, non tamen dici possunt nihil esse; et quamvis a me quodammodo ad arbitrium cogitentur, non tamen a me finguntur, sed suas habent veras et immutabiles naturas. Ut cum, exempli causa, triangulum imaginor, etsi fortasse talis figura nullibi gentium

The essence of material things, and the existence of God considered a second time

There are many matters which remain to be investigated concerning the attributes of God and the nature of myself, or my mind; and perhaps I shall take these up at another time. But now that I have seen what to do and what to avoid in order to reach the truth, the most pressing task seems to be to try to escape from the doubts into which I fell a few days ago, and see whether any certainty can be achieved regarding material objects.

But before I inquire whether any such things exist outside me, I must consider the ideas of these things, in so far as they exist in my thought, and see which of them are distinct, and which confused.

Quantity, for example, or 'continuous' quantity as the philosophers commonly call it, is something I distinctly imagine. That is, I distinctly imagine the extension of the quantity (or rather of the thing which is quantified) in length, breadth and depth. I also enumerate various parts of the thing, and to these parts I assign various sizes, shapes, positions and local motions; and to the motions I assign various durations.

Not only are all these things very well known and transparent to me when regarded in this general way, but in addition there are countless particular features regarding shapes, number, motion and so on, which I perceive when I give them my attention. And the truth of these matters is so open and so much in harmony with my nature, that on first discovering them 64 it seems that I am not so much learning something new as remembering what I knew before; or it seems like noticing for the first time things which were long present within me although I had never turned my mental gaze on them before.

But I think the most important consideration at this point is that I find within me countless ideas of things which even though they may not exist anywhere outside me still cannot be called nothing; for although in a sense they can be thought of at will, they are not my invention but have their own true and immutable natures. When, for example, I imagine a triangle, even if perhaps no such figure exists, or has ever existed, anywhere

extra cogitationem meam existat, nec unquam extiterit, est tamen
profecto determinata quaedam ejus natura, sive essentia, sive forma,
immutabilis et aeterna, quae a me non efficta est, nec a mente mea
dependet; ut patet ex eo quod demonstrari possint variae proprietates
de isto triangulo, nempe quod ejus tres anguli sint aequales duobus
rectis, quod maximo ejus angulo maximum latus subtendatur, et similes, quas velim nolim clare nunc agnosco, etiamsi de iis nullo modo
antea cogitaverim, cum triangulum imaginatus sum, nec proinde a me
fuerint effictae.

Neque ad rem attinet, si dicam mihi forte a rebus externis per
organa sensuum istam trianguli ideam advenisse, quia nempe corpora triangularem figuram habentia interdum vidi; possum enim alias
innumeras figuras excogitare, de quibus nulla suspicio esse potest quod
65 mihi unquam per sensus illapsae sint, et tamen varias de iis, non minus
quam de triangulo, proprietates demonstrare. Quae sane omnes sunt
verae, quandoquidem a me clare cognoscuntur, ideoque aliquid sunt,
non merum nihil: patet enim illud omne quod verum est esse aliquid;
et jam fuse demonstravi illa omnia quae clare cognosco esse vera. Atque
quamvis id non demonstrassem, ea certe est natura mentis meae ut
nihilominus non possem iis non assentiri, saltem quamdiu ea clare percipio; meminique me semper, etiam ante hoc tempus, cum sensuum
objectis quammaxime inhaererem, ejusmodi veritates, quae nempe de
figuris, aut numeris, aliisve ad Arithmeticam vel Geometriam vel in
genere ad puram atque abstractam Mathesim pertinentibus, evidenter
agnoscebam, pro omnium certissimis habuisse.

Jam vero si ex eo solo, quod alicujus rei ideam possim ex cogitatione mea depromere, sequitur ea omnia, quae ad illam rem pertinere
clare et distincte percipio, revera ad illam pertinere, nunquid inde
haberi etiam potest argumentum, quo Dei existentia probetur? Certe
ejus ideam, nempe entis summe perfecti, non minus apud me invenio, quam ideam cujusvis figurae aut numeri; nec minus clare et
distincte intelligo ad ejus naturam pertinere ut semper existat, quam
id quod de aliqua figura aut numero demonstro ad ejus figurae aut
numeri naturam etiam pertinere; ac proinde, quamvis non omnia,
quae superioribus hisce diebus meditatus sum, vera essent, in eodem
66 ad minimum certitudinis gradu esse deberet apud me Dei existentia,
in quo fuerunt hactenus Mathematicae veritates.

outside my thought, there is still a determinate nature, or essence, or form of the triangle which is immutable and eternal, and not invented by me or dependent on my mind. This is clear from the fact that various properties can be demonstrated of the triangle, for example that its three angles equal two right angles, that its greatest side subtends its greatest angle, and the like; and since these properties are ones which I now clearly recognize whether I want to or not, even if I never thought of them at all when I previously imagined the triangle, it follows that they cannot have been invented by me.

It would be beside the point for me to say that since I have from time to time seen bodies of triangular shape, the idea of the triangle may have come to me from external things by means of the sense organs. For I can think up countless other shapes which there can be no suspicion of my ever having encountered through the senses, and yet I can demonstrate various properties of these shapes, just as I can with the triangle. All these properties 65 are certainly true, since I am clearly aware of them, and therefore they are something, and not merely nothing; for it is obvious that whatever is true is something; and I have already amply demonstrated that everything of which I am clearly aware is true. And even if I had not demonstrated this, the nature of my mind is such that I cannot but assent to these things, at least so long as I clearly perceive them. I also remember that even before, when I was completely preoccupied with the objects of the senses, I always held that the most certain truths of all were the kind which I recognized clearly in connection with shapes, or numbers or other items relating to arithmetic or geometry, or in general to pure and abstract mathematics.

But if the mere fact that I can produce from my thought the idea of something entails that everything which I clearly and distinctly perceive to belong to that thing really does belong to it, is not this a possible basis for another argument to prove the existence of God? Certainly, the idea of God, or a supremely perfect being, is one which I find within me just as surely as the idea of any shape or number. And my understanding that it belongs to his nature that he always exists[1] is no less clear and distinct than is the case when I prove of any shape or number that some property belongs to its nature. Hence, even if it turned out that not everything on which I have meditated in these past days is true, I ought still to regard the existence of God as having at least the same level of certainty as I have hitherto attributed to the truths of mathematics.[2]   66

---

[1] '. . . that actual and eternal existence belongs to his nature' (French version).
[2] '. . . which concern only figures and numbers' (added in French version).

Quanquam sane hoc prima fronte non est omnino perspicuum, sed quandam sophismatis speciem refert. Cum enim assuetus sim in omnibus aliis rebus existentiam ab essentia distinguere, facile mihi persuadeo illam etiam ab essentia Dei sejungi posse, atque ita Deum ut non existentem cogitari. Sed tamen diligentius attendenti fit manifestum, non magis posse existentiam ab essentia Dei separari, quam ab essentia trianguli magnitudinem trium ejus angulorum aequalium duobus rectis, sive ab idea montis ideam vallis: adeo ut non magis repugnet cogitare Deum (hoc est ens summe perfectum) cui desit existentia (hoc est cui desit aliqua perfectio), quam cogitare montem cui desit vallis.

Verumtamen, ne possim quidem cogitare Deum nisi existentem, ut neque montem sine valle, at certe, ut neque ex eo quod cogitem montem cum valle, ideo sequitur aliquem montem in mundo esse, ita neque ex eo quod cogitem Deum ut existentem, ideo sequi videtur Deum existere: nullam enim necessitatem cogitatio mea rebus imponit; et quemadmodum imaginari licet equum alatum, etsi nullus equus habeat alas, ita forte Deo existentiam possum affingere, quamvis nullus Deus existat.

Imo sophisma hic latet; neque enim, ex eo quod non possim cogitare montem nisi cum valle, sequitur alicubi montem et vallem existere,
67 sed tantum montem et vallem, sive existant, sive non existant, a se mutuo sejungi non posse. Atqui ex eo quod non possim cogitare Deum nisi existentem, sequitur existentiam a Deo esse inseparabilem, ac proinde illum revera existere; non quod mea cogitatio hoc efficiat, sive aliquam necessitatem ulli rei imponat, sed contra quia ipsius rei, nempe existentiae Dei, necessitas me determinat ad hoc cogitandum: neque enim mihi liberum est Deum absque existentia (hoc est ens summe perfectum absque summa perfectione) cogitare, ut liberum est equum vel cum alis vel sine alis imaginari.

Neque etiam hic dici debet, necesse quidem esse ut ponam Deum existentem, postquam posui illum habere omnes perfectiones, quandoquidem existentia una est ex illis, sed priorem positionem necessariam non fuisse; ut neque necesse est me putare figuras omnes quadrilateras circulo inscribi, sed posito quod hoc putem, necesse erit me fateri rhombum circulo inscribi, quod aperte tamen est falsum. Nam, quamvis non necesse sit ut incidam unquam in ullam de Deo cogitationem, quoties tamen de ente primo et summo libet cogitare, atque

At first sight, however, this is not transparently clear, but has some appearance of being a sophism. Since I have been accustomed to distinguish between existence and essence in everything else, I find it easy to persuade myself that existence can also be separated from the essence of God, and hence that God can be thought of as not existing. But when I concentrate more carefully, it is quite evident that existence can no more be separated from the essence of God than the fact that its three angles equal two right angles can be separated from the essence of a triangle, or than the idea of a mountain can be separated from the idea of a valley. Hence it is just as much of a contradiction to think of God (that is, a supremely perfect being) lacking existence (that is, lacking a perfection), as it is to think of a mountain without a valley.

However, even granted that I cannot think of God except as existing, just as I cannot think of a mountain without a valley, it certainly does not follow from the fact that I think of a mountain with a valley that there is any mountain in the world; and similarly, it does not seem to follow from the fact that I think of God as existing that he does exist. For my thought does not impose any necessity on things; and just as I may imagine a winged horse even though no horse has wings, so I may be able to attach existence to God even though no God exists.

But there is a sophism concealed here. From the fact that I cannot think of a mountain without a valley, it does not follow that a mountain and valley exist anywhere, but simply that a mountain and a valley, whether 67 they exist or not, are mutually inseparable. But from the fact that I cannot think of God except as existing, it follows that existence is inseparable from God, and hence that he really exists. It is not that my thought makes it so, or imposes any necessity on any thing; on the contrary, it is the necessity of the thing itself, namely the existence of God, which determines my thinking in this respect. For I am not free to think of God without existence (that is, a supremely perfect being without a supreme perfection) as I am free to imagine a horse with or without wings.

And it must not be objected at this point that while it is indeed necessary for me to suppose God exists, once I have made the supposition that he has all perfections (since existence is one of the perfections), nevertheless the original supposition was not necessary. Similarly, the objection would run, it is not necessary for me to think that all quadrilaterals can be inscribed in a circle; but given this supposition, it will be necessary for me to admit that a rhombus can be inscribed in a circle – which is patently false. Now admittedly, it is not necessary that I ever light upon any thought of God; but whenever I do choose to think of the first and supreme being, and

ejus ideam tanquam ex mentis meae thesauro depromere, necesse est
ut illi omnes perfectiones attribuam, etsi nec omnes tunc enumerem,
nec ad singulas attendam: quae necessitas plane sufficit ut postea,
cum animadverto existentiam esse perfectionem, recte concludam ens
primum et summum existere: quemadmodum non est necesse me
ullum triangulum unquam imaginari, sed quoties volo figuram recti-
lineam tres tantum angulos habentem considerare, necesse est ut illi
68 ea tribuam, ex quibus recte infertur ejus tres angulos non majores
esse duobus rectis, etiamsi hoc ipsum tunc non advertam. Cum vero
examino quaenam figurae circulo inscribantur, nullo modo necesse est
ut putem omnes quadrilateras ex eo numero esse; imo etiam idipsum
nequidem fingere possum, quamdiu nihil volo admittere nisi quod
clare et distincte intelligo. Ac proinde magna differentia est inter ejusmodi falsas positiones, et ideas veras mihi ingenitas, quarum prima et
praecipua est idea Dei. Nam sane multis modis intelligo illam non esse
quid fictitium a cogitatione mea dependens, sed imaginem verae et
immutabilis naturae: ut, primo, quia nulla alia res potest a me excogitari, ad cujus essentiam existentia pertineat, praeter solum Deum;
deinde, quia non possum duos aut plures ejusmodi Deos intelligere,
et quia, posito quod jam unus existat, plane videam esse necessarium
ut et ante ab aeterno extiterit, et in aeternum sit mansurus; ac denique,
quod multa alia in Deo percipiam, quorum nihil a me detrahi potest
nec mutari.

Sed vero, quacumque tandem utar probandi ratione, semper eo
res redit, ut ea me sola plane persuadeant, quae clare et distincte percipio. Et quidem ex iis quae ita percipio, etsi nonnulla
unicuique obvia sint, alia vero nonnisi ab iis qui propius inspici-
unt et diligenter investigant deteguntur, postquam tamen detecta
sunt, haec non minus certa quam illa existimantur. Ut quamvis
69 non tam facile appareat in triangulo rectangulo quadratum basis
aequale esse quadratis laterum, quam istam basim maximo ejus
angulo subtendi, non tamen minus creditur, postquam semel est
perspectum. Quod autem ad Deum attinet, certe nisi praejudiciis
obruerer, et rerum sensibilium imagines cogitationem meam omni
ex parte obsiderent, nihil illo prius aut facilius agnoscerem; nam

bring forth the idea of God from the treasure house of my mind as it were, it is necessary that I attribute all perfections to him, even if I do not at that time enumerate them or attend to them individually. And this necessity plainly guarantees that, when I later realize that existence is a perfection, I am correct in inferring that the first and supreme being exists. In the same way, it is not necessary for me ever to imagine a triangle; but whenever I do wish to consider a rectilinear figure having just three angles, it is necessary that I attribute to it the properties which license the inference that its three 68 angles equal no more than two right angles, even if I do not notice this at the time. By contrast, when I examine what figures can be inscribed in a circle, it is in no way necessary for me to think that this class includes all quadrilaterals. Indeed, I cannot even imagine this, so long as I am willing to admit only what I clearly and distinctly understand. So there is a great difference between this kind of false supposition and the true ideas which are innate in me, of which the first and most important is the idea of God. There are many ways in which I understand that this idea is not something fictitious which is dependent on my thought, but is an image of a true and immutable nature. First of all, there is the fact that, apart from God, there is nothing else of which I am capable of thinking such that existence belongs[1] to its essence. Second, I cannot understand how there could be two or more Gods of this kind; and after supposing that one God exists, I plainly see that it is necessary that he has existed from eternity and will abide for eternity. And finally, I perceive many other attributes of God, none of which I can remove or alter.

But whatever method of proof I use, I am always brought back to the fact that it is only what I clearly and distinctly perceive that completely convinces me. Some of the things I clearly and distinctly perceive are obvious to everyone, while others are discovered only by those who look more closely and investigate more carefully; but once they have been discovered, the latter are judged to be just as certain as the former. In the case of a right-angled triangle, for example, the fact that the square on the hypotenuse 69 is equal to the square on the other two sides is not so readily apparent as the fact that the hypotenuse subtends the largest angle; but once one has seen it, one believes it just as strongly. But as regards God, if I were not overwhelmed by preconceived opinions, and if the images of things perceived by the senses did not besiege my thought on every side, I would certainly acknowledge him sooner and more easily than anything else. For

---

[1] '. . . necessarily belongs' (French version).

quid ex se est apertius, quam summum ens esse, sive Deum, ad cujus solius essentiam existentia pertinet, existere?

Atque, quamvis mihi attenta consideratione opus fuerit ad hoc ipsum percipiendum, nunc tamen non modo de eo aeque certus sum ac de omni alio quod certissimum videtur, sed praeterea etiam animadverto caeterarum rerum certitudinem ab hoc ipso ita pendere, ut absque eo nihil unquam perfecte sciri possit.

Etsi enim ejus sim naturae ut, quamdiu aliquid valde clare et distincte percipio, non possim non credere verum esse, quia tamen ejus etiam sum naturae ut non possim obtutum mentis in eandem rem semper defigere ad illam clare percipiendam, recurratque saepe memoria judicii ante facti, cum non amplius attendo ad rationes propter quas tale quid judicavi, rationes aliae afferri possunt quae me, si Deum ignorarem, facile ab opinione dejicerent, atque ita de nulla unquam re veram et certam scientiam, sed vagas tantum et mutabiles opiniones, haberem. Sic, exempli causa, cum naturam trianguli considero, evidentissime quidem mihi, utpote Geometriae principiis imbuto, apparet ejus tres angulos aequales esse duobus rectis, nec possum non credere 70   id verum esse, quamdiu ad ejus demonstrationem attendo; sed statim atque mentis aciem ab illa deflexi, quantumvis adhuc recorder me illam clarissime perspexisse, facile tamen potest accidere ut dubitem an sit vera, si quidem Deum ignorem. Possum enim mihi persuadere me talem a natura factum esse, ut interdum in iis fallar quae me puto quam evidentissime percipere, cum praesertim meminerim me saepe multa pro veris et certis habuisse, quae postmodum, aliis rationibus adductus, falsa esse judicavi.

Postquam vero percepi Deum esse, quia simul etiam intellexi caetera omnia ab eo pendere, illumque non esse fallacem; atque inde collegi illa omnia, quae clare et distincte percipio, necessario esse vera; etiamsi non attendam amplius ad rationes propter quas istud verum esse judicavi, modo tantum recorder me clare et distincte perspexisse, nulla ratio contraria afferri potest, quae me ad dubitandum impellat, sed veram et certam de hoc habeo scientiam. Neque de hoc tantum, sed et de reliquis omnibus quae memini me aliquando demonstrasse, ut de Geometricis et similibus. Quid enim nunc mihi opponctur? Mene talem factum esse ut saepe

what is more self-evident than the fact that the supreme being exists, or that God, to whose essence alone existence belongs,[1] exists?

Although it needed close attention for me to perceive this, I am now just as certain of it as I am of everything else which appears most certain. And what is more, I see that the certainty of all other things depends on this, so that without it nothing can ever be perfectly known.

Admittedly my nature is such that so long as[2] I perceive something very clearly and distinctly I cannot but believe it to be true. But my nature is also such that I cannot fix my mental vision continually on the same thing, so as to keep perceiving it clearly; and often the memory of a previously made judgement may come back, when I am no longer attending to the arguments which led me to make it. And so other arguments can now occur to me which might easily undermine my opinion, if I were unaware of God; and I should thus never have true and certain knowledge about anything, but only shifting and changeable opinions. For example, when I consider the nature of a triangle, it appears most evident to me, steeped as I am in the principles of geometry, that its three angles are equal to two right angles; and so long as I attend to the proof, I cannot but believe this to be true. But as soon as I turn my mind's eye away from the proof, then in spite of still remembering that I perceived it very clearly, I can easily fall into doubt about its truth, if I am unaware of God. For I can convince myself that I have a natural disposition to go wrong from time to time in matters which I think I perceive as evidently as can be. This will seem even more likely when I remember that there have been frequent cases where I have regarded things as true and certain, but have later been led by other arguments to judge them to be false. 70

Now, however, I have perceived that God exists, and at the same time I have understood that everything else depends on him, and that he is no deceiver; and I have drawn the conclusion that everything which I clearly and distinctly perceive is of necessity true. Accordingly, even if I am no longer attending to the arguments which led me to judge that this is true, as long as I remember that I clearly and distinctly perceived it, there are no counter-arguments which can be adduced to make me doubt it, but on the contrary I have true and certain knowledge of it. And I have knowledge not just of this matter, but of all matters which I remember ever having demonstrated, in geometry and so on. For what objections can now be raised?[3] That the way I am made makes me prone to frequent

---

[1] '. . . in the idea of whom alone necessary and eternal existence is comprised' (French version).
[2] '. . . as soon as' (French version).
[3] '. . . to oblige me to call these matters into doubt' (added in French version).

fallar? At jam scio me in iis, quae perspicue intelligo, falli non posse. Mene multa alias pro veris et certis habuisse, quae postea falsa esse deprehendi? Atqui nulla ex iis clare et distincte perceperam, sed hujus regulae veritatis ignarus ob alias causas forte credideram, quas postea minus firmas esse detexi. Quid ergo dicetur? Anne (ut nuper mihi objiciebam) me forte somniare, sive illa omnia, quae jam cogito, non magis vera esse quam ea quae dormienti occurrunt? Imo etiam hoc nihil mutat; nam certe, quamvis somniarem, si quid intellectui meo sit evidens, illud omnino est verum.

71

Atque ita plane video omnis scientiae certitudinem et veritatem ab una veri Dei cognitione pendere, adeo ut, priusquam illum nossem, nihil de ulla alia re perfecte scire potuerim. Jam vero innumera, tum de ipso Deo aliisque rebus intellectualibus, tum etiam de omni illa natura corporea, quae est purae Matheseos objectum, mihi plane nota et certa esse possunt.

error? But I now know that I am incapable of error in those cases where my understanding is transparently clear. Or can it be objected that I have in the past regarded as true and certain many things which I afterwards recognized to be false? But none of these were things which I clearly and distinctly perceived: I was ignorant of this rule for establishing the truth, and believed these things for other reasons which I later discovered to be less reliable. So what is left to say? Can one raise the objection I put to myself a while ago, that I may be dreaming, or that everything which I am now thinking has as little truth as what comes to the mind of one who is asleep? Yet even this does not change anything. For even though I might 71 be dreaming, if there is anything which is evident to my intellect, then it is wholly true.

Thus I see plainly that the certainty and truth of all knowledge depends uniquely on my awareness of the true God, to such an extent that I was incapable of perfect knowledge about anything else until I became aware of him. And now it is possible for me to achieve full and certain knowledge of countless matters, both concerning God himself and other things whose nature is intellectual, and also concerning the whole of that corporeal nature which is the subject matter of pure mathematics.[1]

---

[1] '...and also concerning things which belong to corporeal nature in so far as it can serve as the object of geometrical demonstrations which have no concern with whether that object exists' (French version).

De rerum materialium existentia, et reali mentis a corpore distinctione

Reliquum est ut examinem an res materiales existant. Et quidem jam ad minimum scio illas, quatenus sunt purae Matheseos objectum, posse existere, quandoquidem ipsas clare et distincte percipio. Non enim dubium est quin Deus sit capax ea omnia efficiendi quae ego sic percipiendi sum capax; nihilque unquam ab illo fieri non posse judicavi, nisi propter hoc quod illud a me distincte percipi repugnaret. Praeterea ex imaginandi facultate, qua me uti experior, dum circa res istas materiales versor, sequi videtur illas existere; nam attentius considerati quidnam sit imaginatio, nihil aliud esse apparet quam quaedam applicatio facultatis cognoscitivae ad corpus ipsi intime praesens, ac proinde existens.

Quod ut planum fiat, primo examino differentiam quae est inter imaginationem et puram intellectionem. Nempe, exempli causa, cum triangulum imaginor, non tantum intelligo illud esse figuram tribus lineis comprehensam, sed simul etiam istas tres lineas tanquam praesentes acie mentis intueor, atque hoc est quod imaginari appello. Si vero de chiliogono velim cogitare, equidem aeque bene intelligo illud esse figuram constantem mille lateribus, ac intelligo triangulum esse figuram constantem tribus; sed non eodem modo illa mille latera imaginor, sive tanquam praesentia intueor. Et quamvis tunc, propter consuetudinem aliquid semper imaginandi, quoties de re corporea cogito, figuram forte aliquam confuse mihi repraesentem, patet tamen illam non esse chiliogonum, quia nulla in re est diversa ab ea quam mihi etiam repraesentarem, si de myriogono aliave quavis figura plurimorum laterum cogitarem; nec quicquam juvat ad eas proprietates, quibus chiliogonum ab aliis polygonis differt, agnoscendas. Si vero de pentagono quaestio sit, possum quidem ejus figuram intelligere, sicut figuram chiliogoni, absque ope imaginationis; sed possum etiam eandem imaginari, applicando scilicet aciem

The existence of material things, and the real distinction between mind and body [1]

It remains for me to examine whether material things exist. And at least I now know they are capable of existing, in so far as they are the subject matter of pure mathematics, since I perceive them clearly and distinctly. For there is no doubt that God is capable of creating everything that I am capable of perceiving in this manner; and I have never judged that something could not be made by him except on the grounds that there would be a contradiction in my perceiving it distinctly. The conclusion that material things exist is also suggested by the faculty of imagination, which I am aware of using when I turn my mind to material things. For when I give more attentive consideration to what imagination is, it seems 72 to be nothing else but an application of the cognitive faculty to a body which is intimately present to it, and which therefore exists.

To make this clear, I will first examine the difference between imagination and pure understanding. When I imagine a triangle, for example, I do not merely understand that it is a figure bounded by three lines, but at the same time I also see the three lines with my mind's eye as if they were present before me; and this is what I call imagining. But if I want to think of a chiliagon, although I understand that it is a figure consisting of a thousand sides just as well as I understand the triangle to be a three-sided figure, I do not in the same way imagine the thousand sides or see them as if they were present before me. It is true that since I am in the habit of imagining something whenever I think of a corporeal thing, I may construct in my mind a confused representation of some figure; but it is clear that this is not a chiliagon. For it differs in no way from the representation I should form if I were thinking of a myriagon, or any figure with very many sides. Moreover, such a representation is useless for recognizing the properties which distinguish a chiliagon from other polygons. But suppose I am dealing with a pentagon: I can of course understand the figure of a pentagon, just as I can the figure of a chiliagon, without the help of the imagination; but I can also imagine a pentagon, by applying my mind's eye

---

[1] '. . . between the soul and body of a man' (French version).

101

mentis ad ejus quinque latera, simulque ad aream iis contentam; et
73 manifeste hic animadverto mihi peculiari quadam animi contentione
opus esse ad imaginandum, qua non utor ad intelligendum: quae nova
animi contentio differentiam inter imaginationem et intellectionem
puram clare ostendit.

Ad haec considero istam vim imaginandi quae in me est, prout differt a vi intelligendi, ad mei ipsius, hoc est ad mentis meae essentiam
non requiri; nam quamvis illa a me abesset, procul dubio manerem
nihilominus ille idem qui nunc sum; unde sequi videtur illam ab aliqua re a me diversa pendere. Atque facile intelligo, si corpus aliquod
existat cui mens sit ita conjuncta ut ad illud veluti inspiciendum pro
arbitrio se applicet, fieri posse ut per hoc ipsum res corporeas imaginer; adeo ut hic modus cogitandi in eo tantum a pura intellectione
differat, quod mens, dum intelligit, se ad seipsam quodammodo convertat, respiciatque aliquam ex ideis quae illi ipsi insunt; dum autem
imaginatur, se convertat ad corpus, et aliquid in eo ideae vel a se
intellectae vel sensu perceptae conforme intueatur. Facile, inquam,
intelligo imaginationem ita perfici posse, siquidem corpus existat; et
quia nullus alius modus aeque conveniens occurrit ad illam explicandam, probabiliter inde conjicio corpus existere; sed probabiliter
tantum, et quamvis accurate omnia investigem, nondum tamen video
ex ea naturae corporeae idea distincta, quam in imaginatione mea
invenio, ullum sumi posse argumentum, quod necessario concludat
aliquod corpus existere.

74 Soleo vero alia multa imaginari, praeter illam naturam corpoream,
quae est purae Matheseos objectum, ut colores, sonos, sapores,
dolorem, et similia, sed nulla tam distincte; et quia haec percipio
melius sensu, a quo videntur ope memoriae ad imaginationem pervenisse, ut commodius de ipsis agam, eadem opera etiam de sensu
est agendum, videndumque an ex iis quae isto cogitandi modo, quem
sensum appello, percipiuntur, certum aliquod argumentum pro rerum
corporearum existentia habere possim.

Et primo quidem apud me hic repetam quaenam illa sint quae
antehac, ut sensu percepta, vera esse putavi, et quas ob causas id
putavi; deinde etiam causas expendam propter quas eadem postea in
dubium revocavi; ac denique considerabo quid mihi nunc de iisdem
sit credendum.

Primo itaque sensi me habere caput, manus, pedes, et membra

to its five sides and the area contained within them. And in doing this
I notice quite clearly that imagination requires a peculiar effort of mind 73
which is not required for understanding; this additional effort of mind
clearly shows the difference between imagination and pure understanding.

Besides this, I consider that this power of imagining which is in me,
differing as it does from the power of understanding, is not a necessary
constituent of my own essence, that is, of the essence of my mind. For
if I lacked it, I should undoubtedly remain the same individual as I now
am; from which it seems to follow that it depends on something distinct
from myself. And I can easily understand that, if there does exist some
body to which the mind is so joined that it can apply itself to contemplate
it, as it were, whenever it pleases, then it may possibly be this very body
that enables me to imagine corporeal things. So the difference between this
mode of thinking and pure understanding may simply be this: when the
mind understands, it in some way turns towards itself and inspects one
of the ideas which are within it; but when it imagines, it turns towards
the body and looks at something in the body which conforms to an idea
understood by the mind or perceived by the senses. I can, as I say, easily
understand that this is how imagination comes about, if the body exists;
and since there is no other equally suitable way of explaining imagination
that comes to mind, I can make a probable conjecture that the body exists.
But this is only a probability; and despite a careful and comprehensive
investigation, I do not yet see how the distinct idea of corporeal nature
which I find in my imagination can provide any basis for a necessary
inference that some body exists.

But besides that corporeal nature which is the subject matter of pure 74
mathematics, there is much else that I habitually imagine, such as colours,
sounds, tastes, pain and so on – though not so distinctly. Now I perceive
these things much better by means of the senses, which is how, with the
assistance of memory, they appear to have reached the imagination. So
in order to deal with them more fully, I must pay equal attention to the
senses, and see whether the things which are perceived by means of that
mode of thinking which I call 'sensory perception' provide me with any
sure argument for the existence of corporeal things.

To begin with, I will go back over all the things which I previously took
to be perceived by the senses, and reckoned to be true; and I will go over my
reasons for thinking this. Next, I will set out my reasons for subsequently
calling these things into doubt. And finally I will consider what I should
now believe about them.

First of all then, I perceived by my senses that I had a head, hands,

caetera ex quibus constat illud corpus, quod tanquam mei partem, vel forte etiam tanquam me totum spectabam; sensique hoc corpus inter alia multa corpora versari, a quibus variis commodis vel incommodis affici potest, et commoda ista sensu quodam voluptatis, et incommoda sensu doloris metiebar. Atque, praeter dolorem et voluptatem, sentiebam etiam in me famem, sitim, aliosque ejusmodi appetitus; itemque corporeas quasdam propensiones ad hilaritatem, ad tristitiam, ad iram, similesque alios affectus; foris vero, praeter corporum extensionem, et figuras, et motus, sentiebam etiam in illis duritiem, et calorem, aliasque tactiles qualitates; ac praeterea lumen, et colores, et odores, et sapores, et sonos, ex quorum varietate caelum, terram, maria, et reliqua corpora ab invicem distinguebam. Nec sane absque ratione, ob ideas istarum omnium qualitatum quae cogitationi meae se offerebant, et quas solas proprie et immediate sentiebam, putabam me sentire res quasdam a mea cogitatione plane diversas, nempe corpora a quibus ideae istae procederent; experiebar enim illas absque ullo meo consensu mihi advenire, adeo ut neque possem objectum ullum sentire, quamvis vellem, nisi illud sensus organo esset praesens, nec possem non sentire cum erat praesens. Cumque ideae sensu perceptae essent multo magis vividae et expressae, et suo etiam modo magis distinctae, quam ullae ex iis quas ipse prudens et sciens meditando effingebam, vel memoriae meae impressas advertebam, fieri non posse videbatur ut a meipso procederent; ideoque supererat ut ab aliis quibusdam rebus advenirent. Quarum rerum cum nullam aliunde notitiam haberem quam ex istis ipsis ideis, non poterat aliud mihi venire in mentem quam illas iis similes esse. Atque etiam quia recordabar me prius usum fuisse sensibus quam ratione, videbamque ideas quas ipse effingebam non tam expressas esse, quam illae erant quas sensu percipiebam, et plerumque ex earum partibus componi, facile mihi persuadebam nullam plane me habere in intellectu, quam non prius habuissem in sensu. Non etiam sine ratione corpus illud, quod speciali quodam jure meum appellabam, magis ad me pertinere quam alia ulla arbitrabar: neque enim ab illo poteram unquam sejungi, ut a reliquis; omnes appetitus et affectus in illo et pro illo sentiebam; ac denique dolorem et titillationem voluptatis in ejus partibus, non autem in aliis extra illud positis, advertebam. Cur vero ex isto nescio quo doloris

feet and other limbs making up the body which I regarded as part of myself, or perhaps even as my whole self. I also perceived by my senses that this body was situated among many other bodies which could affect it in various favourable or unfavourable ways; and I gauged the favourable effects by a sensation of pleasure, and the unfavourable ones by a sensation of pain. In addition to pain and pleasure, I also had sensations within me of hunger, thirst and other such appetites, and also of physical propensities towards cheerfulness, sadness, anger and similar emotions. And outside me, besides the extension, shapes and movements of bodies, I also had 75 sensations of their hardness and heat, and of the other tactile qualities. In addition, I had sensations of light, colours, smells, tastes and sounds, the variety of which enabled me to distinguish the sky, the earth, the seas, and all other bodies, one from another. Considering the ideas of all these qualities which presented themselves to my thought, although the ideas were, strictly speaking, the only immediate objects of my sensory awareness, it was not unreasonable for me to think that the items which I was perceiving through the senses were things quite distinct from my thought, namely bodies which produced the ideas. For my experience was that these ideas came to me quite without my consent, so that I could not have sensory awareness of any object, even if I wanted to, unless it was present to my sense organs; and I could not avoid having sensory awareness of it when it was present. And since the ideas perceived by the senses were much more lively and vivid and even, in their own way, more distinct than any of those which I deliberately formed through meditating or which I found impressed on my memory, it seemed impossible that they should have come from within me; so the only alternative was that they came from other things. Since the sole source of my knowledge of these things was the ideas themselves, the supposition that the things resembled the ideas was bound to occur to me. In addition, I remembered that the use of my senses had come first, while the use of my reason came only later; and I saw that the ideas which I formed myself were less vivid than those which I perceived with the senses and were, for the most part, made up of elements of sensory ideas. In this way I easily convinced myself that I had nothing at all in the intellect which I had not previously had in sensation. As for the body which by some special right I called 'mine', 76 my belief that this body, more than any other, belonged to me had some justification. For I could never be separated from it, as I could from other bodies; and I felt all my appetites and emotions in, and on account of, this body; and finally, I was aware of pain and pleasurable ticklings in parts of this body, but not in other bodies external to it. But why should that

sensu quaedam animi tristitia, et ex sensu titillationis laetitia quaedam consequatur, curve illa nescio quae vellicatio ventriculi, quam famem voco, me de cibo sumendo admoneat, gutturis vero ariditas de potu, et ita de caeteris, non aliam sane habebam rationem, nisi quia ita doctus sum a natura; neque enim ulla plane est affinitas (saltem quam ego intelligam) inter istam vellicationem et cibi sumendi voluntatem, sive inter sensum rei dolorem inferentis, et cogitationem tristitiae ab isto sensu exortae. Sed et reliqua omnia, quae de sensuum objectis judicabam, videbar a natura didicisse: prius enim illa ita se habere mihi persuaseram, quam rationes ullas quibus hoc ipsum probaretur expendissem.

Postea vero multa paulatim experimenta fidem omnem quam sensibus habueram labefactarunt; nam et interdum turres, quae rotundae visae fuerant e longinquo, quadratae apparebant e propinquo, et statuae permagnae, in eorum fastigiis stantes, non magnae e terra spectanti videbantur; et talibus aliis innumeris in rebus sensuum externorum judicia falli deprehendebam. Nec externo-
77 rum duntaxat, sed etiam internorum; nam quid dolore intimius esse potest? Atqui audiveram aliquando ab iis, quibus crus aut brachium fuerat abscissum, se sibi videri adhuc interdum dolorem sentire in ea parte corporis qua carebant; ideoque etiam in me non plane certum esse videbatur membrum aliquod mihi dolere, quamvis sentirem in eo dolorem. Quibus etiam duas maxime generales dubitandi causas nuper adjeci: prima erat, quod nulla unquam, dum vigilo, me sentire crediderim, quae non etiam inter dormiendum possim aliquando putare me sentire; cumque illa, quae sentire mihi videor in somnis, non credam a rebus extra me positis mihi advenire, non advertebam quare id potius crederem de iis quae sentire mihi videor vigilando. Altera erat, quod cum authorem meae originis adhuc ignorarem, vel saltem ignorare me fingerem, nihil videbam obstare quominus essem natura ita constitutus ut fallerer, etiam in iis quae mihi verissima apparebant. Et quantum ad rationes quibus antea rerum sensibilium veritatem mihi persuaseram, non difficulter ad illas respondebam. Cum enim viderer ad multa impelli a natura, quae ratio dissuadebat, non multum fidendum esse putabam iis quae a natura docentur. Et quamvis sensuum perceptiones a voluntate mea non penderent, non ideo concludendum esse putabam illas a rebus a

curious sensation of pain give rise to a particular distress of mind; or why should a certain kind of delight follow on a tickling sensation? Again, why should that curious tugging in the stomach which I call hunger tell me that I should eat, or a dryness of the throat tell me to drink, and so on? I was not able to give any explanation of all this, except that nature taught me so. For there is absolutely no connection (at least that I can understand) between the tugging sensation and the decision to take food, or between the sensation of something causing pain and the mental apprehension of distress that arises from that sensation. These and other judgements that I made concerning sensory objects, I was apparently taught to make by nature; for I had already made up my mind that this was how things were, before working out any arguments to prove it.

Later on, however, I had many experiences which gradually undermined all the faith I had had in the senses. Sometimes towers which had looked round from a distance appeared square from close up; and enormous statues standing on their pediments did not seem large when observed from the ground. In these and countless other such cases, I found that the judgements of the external senses were mistaken. And this applied not just to the external senses but to the internal senses as well. For what can be more internal than pain? And yet I had heard that those who had had a leg or an arm amputated sometimes still seemed to feel pain intermittently in the missing part of the body. So even in my own case it was apparently not quite certain that a particular limb was hurting, even if I felt pain in it. To these reasons for doubting, I recently added two very general ones.[1] The first was that every sensory experience I have ever thought I was having while awake I can also think of myself as sometimes having while asleep; and since I do not believe that what I seem to perceive in sleep comes from things located outside me, I did not see why I should be any more inclined to believe this of what I think I perceive while awake. The second reason for doubt was that since I did not yet know the author of my being (or at least was pretending not to), I saw nothing to rule out the possibility that my natural constitution made me prone to error even in matters which seemed to me most true. As for the reasons for my previous confident belief in the truth of the things perceived by the senses, I had no trouble in refuting them. For since I apparently had natural impulses towards many things which reason told me to avoid, I reckoned that a great deal of confidence should not be placed in what I was taught by nature. And despite the fact that the perceptions of the senses were not dependent on my will, I did not think that I should on that account infer that they proceeded from things

77

[1] Cf. Med. I, pp. 25–7 above.

me diversis procedere, quia forte aliqua esse potest in meipso facultas, etsi mihi nondum cognita, illarum effectrix.

Nunc autem, postquam incipio meipsum meaeque authorem originis melius nosse, non quidem omnia, quae habere videor a 78 sensibus, puto esse temere admittenda; sed neque etiam omnia in dubium revocanda.

Et primo, quoniam scio omnia quae clare et distincte intelligo, talia a Deo fieri posse qualia illa intelligo, satis est quod possim unam rem absque altera clare et distincte intelligere, ut certus sim unam ab altera esse diversam, quia potest saltem a Deo seorsim poni; et non refert a qua potentia id fiat, ut diversa existimetur; ac proinde, ex hoc ipso quod sciam me existere, quodque interim nihil plane aliud ad naturam sive essentiam meam pertinere animadvertam, praeter hoc solum quod sim res cogitans, recte concludo meam essentiam in hoc uno consistere, quod sim res cogitans. Et quamvis fortasse (vel potius, ut postmodum dicam, pro certo) habeam corpus, quod mihi valde arcte conjunctum est, quia tamen ex una parte claram et distinctam habeo ideam mei ipsius, quatenus sum tantum res cogitans, non extensa, et ex alia parte distinctam ideam corporis, quatenus est tantum res extensa, non cogitans, certum est me a corpore meo revera esse distinctum, et absque illo posse existere.

Praeterea invenio in me facultates specialibus quibusdam modis cogitandi, puta facultates imaginandi et sentiendi, sine quibus totum me possum clare et distincte intelligere, sed non vice versa illas sine me, hoc est sine substantia intelligente cui insint: intellectionem enim nonnullam in suo formali conceptu includunt, unde percipio illas a me, ut modos a re, distingui. Agnosco etiam quasdam alias facultates, ut locum mutandi, varias figuras induendi, et similes, quae quidem non 79 magis quam praecedentes, absque aliqua substantia cui insint,

distinct from myself, since I might perhaps have a faculty not yet known to me which produced them.[1]

But now, when I am beginning to achieve a better knowledge of myself and the author of my being, although I do not think I should heedlessly accept everything I seem to have acquired from the senses, neither do I 78 think that everything should be called into doubt.

First, I know that everything which I clearly and distinctly understand is capable of being created by God so as to correspond exactly with my understanding of it. Hence the fact that I can clearly and distinctly understand one thing apart from another is enough to make me certain that the two things are distinct, since they are capable of being separated, at least by God. The question of what kind of power is required to bring about such a separation does not affect the judgement that the two things are distinct. Thus, simply by knowing that I exist and seeing at the same time that absolutely nothing else belongs to my nature or essence except that I am a thinking thing, I can infer correctly that my essence consists solely in the fact that I am a thinking thing. It is true that I may have (or, to anticipate, that I certainly have) a body that is very closely joined to me. But nevertheless, on the one hand I have a clear and distinct idea of myself, in so far as I am simply a thinking, non-extended thing; and on the other hand I have a distinct idea of body,[2] in so far as this is simply an extended, non-thinking thing. And accordingly, it is certain that I[3] am really distinct from my body, and can exist without it.

Besides this, I find in myself faculties for certain special modes of thinking,[4] namely imagination and sensory perception. Now I can clearly and distinctly understand myself as a whole without these faculties; but I cannot, conversely, understand these faculties without me, that is, without an intellectual substance to inhere in. This is because there is an intellectual act included in their essential definition; and hence I perceive that the distinction between them and myself corresponds to the distinction between the modes of a thing and the thing itself.[5] Of course I also recognize that there are other faculties (like those of changing position, of taking on various shapes, and so on) which, like sensory perception and imagination, cannot be understood apart from some substance for them to inhere in, 79

[1] Cf. Med. III, p. 53 above.
[2] The Latin term *corpus* as used here by Descartes is ambiguous as between 'body' (i.e. corporeal matter in general) and 'the body' (i.e. this particular body of mine). The French version preserves the ambiguity.
[3] '... that is, my soul, by which I am what I am' (added in French version).
[4] '... certain modes of thinking which are quite special and distinct from me' (French version).
[5] '... between the shapes, movements and other modes or accidents of a body and the body which supports them' (French version).

possunt intelligi, nec proinde etiam absque illa existere: sed manifestum est has, siquidem existant, inesse debere substantiae corporeae sive extensae, non autem intelligenti, quia nempe aliqua extensio, non autem ulla plane intellectio, in earum claro et distincto conceptu continetur. Jam vero est quidem in me passiva quaedam facultas sentiendi, sive ideas rerum sensibilium recipiendi et cognoscendi, sed ejus nullum usum habere possem, nisi quaedam activa etiam existeret, sive in me, sive in alio, facultas istas ideas producendi vel efficiendi. Atque haec sane in me ipso esse non potest, quia nullam plane intellectionem praesupponit, et me non cooperante, sed saepe etiam invito, ideae istae producuntur: ergo superest ut sit in aliqua substantia a me diversa, in qua quoniam omnis realitas vel formaliter vel eminenter inesse debet, quae est objective in ideis ab ista facultate productis (ut jam supra animadverti), vel haec substantia est corpus, sive natura corporea, in qua nempe omnia formaliter continentur quae in ideis objective; vel certe Deus est, vel aliqua creatura corpore nobilior, in qua continentur eminenter. Atqui, cum Deus non sit fallax, omnino manifestum est illum nec per se immediate istas ideas mihi immittere, nec etiam mediante aliqua creatura, in qua earum realitas objectiva, non formaliter, sed eminenter tantum contineatur. Cum enim nullam plane facultatem mihi dederit
80 ad hoc agnoscendum, sed contra magnam propensionem ad credendum illas a rebus corporeis emitti, non video qua ratione posset intelligi ipsum non esse fallacem, si aliunde quam a rebus corporeis emitterentur. Ac proinde res corporeae existunt. Non tamen forte omnes tales omnino existunt, quales illas sensu comprehendo, quoniam ista sensuum comprehensio in multis valde obscura est et confusa; sed saltem illa omnia in iis sunt, quae clare et distincte intelligo, id est omnia, generaliter spectata, quae in purae Matheseos objecto comprehenduntur.

Quantum autem attinet ad reliqua quae vel tantum particularia sunt, ut quod sol sit talis magnitudinis aut figurae etc., vel minus clare intellecta, ut lumen, sonus, dolor, et similia, quamvis valde dubia et incerta sint, hoc tamen ipsum, quod Deus non sit fallax, quodque idcirco fieri non possit ut ulla falsitas in meis opinionibus reperiatur,

and hence cannot exist without it. But it is clear that these other faculties, if they exist, must be in a corporeal or extended substance and not an intellectual one; for the clear and distinct conception of them includes extension, but does not include any intellectual act whatsoever. Now there is in me a passive faculty of sensory perception, that is, a faculty for receiving and recognizing the ideas of sensible objects; but I could not make use of it unless there was also an active faculty, either in me or in something else, which produced or brought about these ideas. But this faculty cannot be in me, since clearly it presupposes no intellectual act on my part,[1] and the ideas in question are produced without my cooperation and often even against my will. So the only alternative is that it is in another substance distinct from me – a substance which contains either formally or eminently all the reality which exists objectively[2] in the ideas produced by this faculty (as I have just noted). This substance is either a body, that is, a corporeal nature, in which case it will contain formally <and in fact> everything which is to be found objectively <or representatively> in the ideas; or else it is God, or some creature more noble than a body, in which case it will contain eminently whatever is to be found in the ideas. But since God is not a deceiver, it is quite clear that he does not transmit the ideas to me either directly from himself, or indirectly, via some creature which contains the objective reality of the ideas not formally but only eminently. For God has given me no faculty at all for recognizing any such source for these ideas; on the contrary, he has given me a great propensity to believe that 80 they are produced by corporeal things. So I do not see how God could be understood to be anything but a deceiver if the ideas were transmitted from a source other than corporeal things. It follows that corporeal things exist. They may not all exist in a way that exactly corresponds with my sensory grasp of them, for in many cases the grasp of the senses is very obscure and confused. But at least they possess all the properties which I clearly and distinctly understand, that is, all those which, viewed in general terms, are comprised within the subject matter of pure mathematics.

What of the other aspects of corporeal things which are either particular (for example that the sun is of such and such a size or shape etc.), or less clearly understood, such as light or sound or pain, and so on? Despite the high degree of doubt and uncertainty involved here, the very fact that God is not a deceiver, and the consequent impossibility of there being any falsity

---

[1] '... cannot be in me in so far as I am merely a thinking thing, since it does not presuppose any thought on my part' (French version).

[2] For the terms 'formally', 'eminently' and 'objectively', see notes on pp. 53 and 55 above.

nisi aliqua etiam sit in me facultas a Deo tributa ad illam emendandam, certam mihi spem ostendit veritatis etiam in iis assequendae. Et sane non dubium est quin ea omnia quae doceor a natura aliquid habeant veritatis: per naturam enim, generaliter spectatam, nihil nunc aliud quam vel Deum ipsum, vel rerum creatarum coordinationem a Deo institutam intelligo; nec aliud per naturam meam in particulari, quam complexionem eorum omnium quae mihi a Deo sunt tributa.

Nihil autem est quod me ista natura magis expresse doceat, quam quod habeam corpus, cui male est cum dolorem sentio, quod cibo vel potu indiget, cum famem aut sitim patior, et similia; nec proinde dubitare debeo, quin aliquid in eo sit veritatis.

81   Docet etiam natura, per istos sensus doloris, famis, sitis etc., me non tantum adesse meo corpori ut nauta adest navigio, sed illi arctissime esse conjunctum et quasi permixtum, adeo ut unum quid cum illo componam. Alioqui enim, cum corpus laeditur, ego, qui nihil aliud sum quam res cogitans, non sentirem idcirco dolorem, sed puro intellectu laesionem istam perciperem, ut nauta visu percipit si quid in nave frangatur; et cum corpus cibo vel potu indiget, hoc ipsum expresse intelligerem, non confusos famis et sitis sensus haberem. Nam certe isti sensus sitis, famis, doloris etc., nihil aliud sunt quam confusi quidam cogitandi modi ab unione et quasi permixtione mentis cum corpore exorti.

Praeterea etiam doceor a natura varia circa meum corpus alia corpora existere, ex quibus nonnulla mihi prosequenda sunt, alia fugienda. Et certe, ex eo quod valde diversos sentiam colores, sonos, odores, sapores, calorem, duritiem, et similia, recte concludo, aliquas esse in corporibus, a quibus variae istae sensuum perceptiones adveniunt, varietates iis respondentes, etiamsi forte iis non similes; atque ex eo quod quaedam ex illis perceptionibus mihi gratae sint, aliae ingratae, plane certum est meum corpus, sive potius me totum, quatenus ex corpore et mente sum compositus, variis commodis et incommodis a circumjacentibus corporibus affici posse.

82   Multa vero alia sunt quae, etsi videar a natura doctus esse, non tamen revera ab ipsa, sed a consuetudine quadam inconsiderate judicandi accepi, atque ideo falsa esse facile contingit: ut quod omne spatium,

in my opinions which cannot be corrected by some other faculty supplied by God, offers me a sure hope that I can attain the truth even in these matters. Indeed, there is no doubt that everything that I am taught by nature contains some truth. For if nature is considered in its general aspect, then I understand by the term nothing other than God himself, or the ordered system of created things established by God. And by my own nature in particular I understand nothing other than the totality of things bestowed on me by God.

There is nothing that my own nature teaches me more vividly than that I have a body, and that when I feel pain there is something wrong with the body, and that when I am hungry or thirsty the body needs food and drink, and so on. So I should not doubt that there is some truth in this.

Nature also teaches me, by these sensations of pain, hunger, thirst and 81 so on, that I am not merely present in my body as a sailor is present in a ship,[1] but that I am very closely joined and, as it were, intermingled with it, so that I and the body form a unit. If this were not so, I, who am nothing but a thinking thing, would not feel pain when the body was hurt, but would perceive the damage purely by the intellect, just as a sailor perceives by sight if anything in his ship is broken. Similarly, when the body needed food or drink, I should have an explicit understanding of the fact, instead of having confused sensations of hunger and thirst. For these sensations of hunger, thirst, pain and so on are nothing but confused modes of thinking which arise from the union and, as it were, intermingling of the mind with the body.

I am also taught by nature that various other bodies exist in the vicinity of my body, and that some of these are to be sought out and others avoided. And from the fact that I perceive by my senses a great variety of colours, sounds, smells and tastes, as well as differences in heat, hardness and the like, I am correct in inferring that the bodies which are the source of these various sensory perceptions possess differences corresponding to them, though perhaps not resembling them. Also, the fact that some of the perceptions are agreeable to me while others are disagreeable makes it quite certain that my body, or rather my whole self, in so far as I am a combination of body and mind, can be affected by the various beneficial or harmful bodies which surround it.

There are, however, many other things which I may appear to have 82 been taught by nature, but which in reality I acquired not from nature but from a habit of making ill-considered judgements; and it is therefore quite

---

[1] '...as a pilot in his ship' (French version).

in quo nihil plane occurrit quod meos sensus moveat, sit vacuum; quod in corpore, exempli gratia, calido aliquid sit plane simile ideae caloris quae in me est, in albo aut viridi sit eadem albedo aut viriditas quam sentio, in amaro aut dulci idem sapor, et sic de caeteris; quod et astra et turres, et quaevis alia remota corpora ejus sint tantum magnitudinis et figurae, quam sensibus meis exhibent, et alia ejusmodi. Sed ne quid in hac re non satis distincte percipiam, accuratius debeo definire quid proprie intelligam, cum dico me aliquid doceri a natura. Nempe hic naturam strictius sumo, quam pro complexione eorum omnium quae mihi a Deo tributa sunt; in hac enim complexione multa continentur quae ad mentem solam pertinent, ut quod percipiam id quod factum est infectum esse non posse, et reliqua omnia quae lumine naturali sunt nota, de quibus hic non est sermo; multa etiam quae ad solum corpus spectant, ut quod deorsum tendat, et similia, de quibus etiam non ago, sed de iis tantum quae mihi, ut composito ex mente et corpore, a Deo tributa sunt. Ideoque haec natura docet quidem ea refugere quae sensum doloris inferunt, et ea prosequi quae sensum voluptatis, et talia; sed non apparet illam praeterea nos docere ut quicquam ex istis sensuum perceptionibus sine praevio intellectus examine de rebus extra nos positis concludamus, quia de iis verum scire ad mentem solam, non autem ad compositum, videtur pertinere. Ita quamvis stella non magis oculum meum quam ignis exiguae facis afficiat, nulla tamen in eo realis sive positiva propensio est ad credendum illam non esse majorem, sed hoc sine ratione ab ineunte aetate judicavi; et quamvis ad ignem accedens sentio calorem, ut etiam ad eundem nimis prope accedens sentio dolorem, nulla profecto ratio est quae suadeat in igne aliquid esse simile isti calori, ut neque etiam isti dolori, sed tantummodo in eo aliquid esse, quodcunque demum sit, quod istos in nobis sensus caloris vel doloris efficiat; et quamvis etiam in aliquo spatio nihil sit quod moveat sensum, non ideo sequitur in eo nullum

83

possible that these are false. Cases in point are the belief that any space in which nothing is occurring to stimulate my senses must be empty; or that the heat in a body is something exactly resembling the idea of heat which is in me; or that when a body is white or green, the selfsame whiteness or greenness which I perceive through my senses is present in the body; or that in a body which is bitter or sweet there is the selfsame taste which I experience, and so on; or, finally, that stars and towers and other distant bodies have the same size and shape which they present to my senses, and other examples of this kind. But to make sure that my perceptions in this matter are sufficiently distinct, I must more accurately define exactly what I mean when I say that I am taught something by nature. In this context I am taking nature to be something more limited than the totality of things bestowed on me by God. For this includes many things that belong to the mind alone – for example my perception that what is done cannot be undone, and all other things that are known by the natural light;[1] but at this stage I am not speaking of these matters. It also includes much that relates to the body alone, like the tendency to move in a downward direction, and so on; but I am not speaking of these matters either. My sole concern here is with what God has bestowed on me as a combination of mind and body. My nature, then, in this limited sense, does indeed teach me to avoid what induces a feeling of pain and to seek out what induces feelings of pleasure, and so on. But it does not appear to teach us to draw any conclusions from these sensory perceptions about things located outside us without waiting until the intellect has examined[2] the matter. For knowledge of the truth about such things seems to belong to the mind alone, not to the combination of mind and body. Hence, 83 although a star has no greater effect on my eye than the flame of a small light, that does not mean that there is any real or positive inclination in me to believe that the star is no bigger than the light; I have simply made this judgement from childhood onwards without any rational basis. Similarly, although I feel heat when I go near a fire and feel pain when I go too near, there is no convincing argument for supposing that there is something in the fire which resembles the heat, any more than for supposing that there is something which resembles the pain. There is simply reason to suppose that there is something in the fire, whatever it may eventually turn out to be, which produces in us the feelings of heat or pain. And likewise, even though there is nothing in any given space that stimulates the senses, it does

[1] '. . . without any help from the body' (added in French version).
[2] '. . . carefully and maturely examined' (French version).

esse corpus: sed video me in his aliisque permultis ordinem naturae pervertere esse assuetum, quia nempe sensuum perceptionibus,
quae proprie tantum a natura datae sunt ad menti significandum
quaenam composito, cujus pars est, commoda sint vel incommoda,
et eatenus sunt satis clarae et distinctae, utor tanquam regulis certis
ad immediate dignoscendum quaenam sit corporum extra nos pos-
itorum essentia, de qua tamen nihil nisi valde obscure et confuse
significant.

Atqui jam ante satis perspexi qua ratione, non obstante Dei
bonitate, judicia mea falsa esse contingat. Sed nova hic occurrit
difficultas circa illa ipsa quae tanquam persequenda vel fugienda
mihi a natura exhibentur, atque etiam circa internos sensus in
quibus errores videor deprehendisse: ut cum quis, grato cibi alicu-
84 jus sapore delusus, venenum intus latens assumit. Sed nempe tunc
tantum a natura impellitur ad illud appetendum in quo gra-
tus sapor consistit, non autem ad venenum, quod plane ignorat; nihilque hinc aliud concludi potest, quam naturam istam
non esse omnisciam: quod non mirum, quia, cum homo sit
res limitata, non alia illi competit quam limitatae perfectionis.

At vero non raro etiam in iis erramus ad quae a natura impel-
limur: ut cum ii qui aegrotant, potum vel cibum appetunt sibi
paulo post nociturum. Dici forsan hic poterit, illos ob id errare,
quod natura eorum sit corrupta; sed hoc difficultatem non tollit, quia non minus vere homo aegrotus creatura Dei est quam
sanus; nec proinde minus videtur repugnare illum a Deo fallacem
naturam habere. Atque ut horologium ex rotis et ponderibus con-
fectum non minus accurate leges omnes naturae observat, cum
male fabricatum est et horas non recte indicat, quam cum omni
ex parte artificis voto satisfacit: ita, si considerem hominis corpus,
quatenus machinamentum quoddam est ex ossibus, nervis, mus-
culis, venis, sanguine et pellibus ita aptum et compositum, ut,
etiamsi nulla in eo mens existeret, eosdem tamen haberet omnes
motus qui nunc in eo non ab imperio voluntatis nec proinde a
mente procedunt, facile agnosco illi aeque naturale fore, si, exempli causa, hydrope laboret, eam faucium ariditatem pati, quae sitis
sensum menti inferre solet, atque etiam ab illa ejus nervos et

not follow that there is no body there. In these cases and many others I see that I have been in the habit of misusing the order of nature. For the proper purpose of the sensory perceptions given me by nature is simply to inform the mind of what is beneficial or harmful for the composite of which the mind is a part; and to this extent they are sufficiently clear and distinct. But I misuse them by treating them as reliable touchstones for immediate judgements about the essential nature of the bodies located outside us; yet this is an area where they provide only very obscure and confused information.

I have already looked in sufficient detail at how, notwithstanding the goodness of God, it may happen that my judgements are false. But a further problem now comes to mind regarding those very things which nature presents to me as objects which I should seek out or avoid, and also regarding the internal sensations, where I seem to have detected errors[1] – e.g. when someone is tricked by the pleasant taste of some food into eating the poison concealed inside it. Yet in this case, what the man's nature urges 84 him to go for is simply what is responsible for the pleasant taste, and not the poison, which his nature knows nothing about. The only inference that can be drawn from this is that his nature is not omniscient. And this is not surprising, since man is a limited thing, and so it is only fitting that his perfection should be limited.

And yet it is not unusual for us to go wrong even in cases where nature does urge us towards something. Those who are ill, for example, may desire food or drink that will shortly afterwards turn out to be bad for them. Perhaps it may be said that they go wrong because their nature is disordered, but this does not remove the difficulty. A sick man is no less one of God's creatures than a healthy one, and it seems no less a contradiction to suppose that he has received from God a nature which deceives him. Yet a clock constructed with wheels and weights observes all the laws of its nature just as closely when it is badly made and tells the wrong time as when it completely fulfils the wishes of the clockmaker. In the same way, I might consider the body of a man as a kind of machine equipped with and made up of bones, nerves, muscles, veins, blood and skin in such a way that, even if there were no mind in it, it would still perform all the same movements as it now does in those cases where movement is not under the control of the will or, consequently, of the mind.[2] I can easily see that if such a body suffers from dropsy, for example, and is affected by the dryness of the throat which normally produces in the mind the sensation

---

[1] '. . . and thus seem to have been directly deceived by my nature' (added in French version).
[2] '. . . but occurs merely as a result of the disposition of the organs' (French version).

reliquas partes ita disponi ut potum sumat ex quo morbus augea-
85 tur, quam, cum nullum tale in eo vitium est, a simili faucium
siccitate moveri ad potum sibi utile assumendum. Et quamvis,
respiciens ad praeconceptum horologii usum, dicere possim illud,
cum horas non recte indicat, a natura sua deflectere; atque
eodem modo, considerans machinamentum humani corporis tanquam comparatum ad motus qui in eo fieri solent, putem illud
etiam a natura sua aberrare, si ejus fauces sint aridae, cum
potus ad ipsius conservationem non prodest; satis tamen animadverto hanc ultimam naturae acceptionem ab altera multum differre: haec enim nihil aliud est quam denominatio a cogitatione
mea, hominem aegrotum et horologium male fabricatum cum
idea hominis sani et horologii recte facti comparante, dependens,
rebusque de quibus dicitur extrinseca; per illam vero aliquid intelligo quod revera in rebus reperitur, ac proinde nonnihil habet veritatis.

Ac certe, etiamsi respiciendo ad corpus hydrope laborans, sit tantum denominatio extrinseca, cum dicitur ejus natura esse corrupta,
ex eo quod aridas habeat fauces, nec tamen egeat potu; respiciendo
tamen ad compositum, sive ad mentem tali corpori unitam, non
est pura denominatio, sed verus error naturae, quod sitiat cum
potus est ipsi nociturus; ideoque hic remanet inquirendum, quo
pacto bonitas Dei non impediat quominus natura sic sumpta sit fallax.

Nempe imprimis hic adverto magnam esse differentiam inter
mentem et corpus, in eo quod corpus ex natura sua sit sem-
86 per divisibile, mens autem plane indivisibilis; nam sane cum hanc
considero, sive meipsum quatenus sum tantum res cogitans, nullas in me partes possum distinguere, sed rem plane unam et integram me esse intelligo; et quamvis toti corpori tota mens unita
esse videatur, abscisso tamen pede, vel brachio, vel quavis alia corporis parte, nihil ideo de mente subductum esse cognosco; neque
etiam facultates volendi, sentiendi, intelligendi etc. ejus partes
dici possunt, quia una et eadem mens est quae vult, quae sen-
tit, quae intelligit. Contra vero nulla res corporea sive extensa
potest a me cogitari, quam non facile in partes cogitatione divi-
dam, atque hoc ipso illam divisibilem esse intelligam: quod unum

of thirst, the resulting condition of the nerves and other parts will dispose the body to take a drink, with the result that the disease will be aggravated. Yet this is just as natural as the body's being stimulated by a similar dryness 85 of the throat to take a drink when there is no such illness and the drink is beneficial. Admittedly, when I consider the purpose of the clock, I may say that it is departing from its nature when it does not tell the right time; and similarly when I consider the mechanism of the human body, I may think that, in relation to the movements which normally occur in it, it too is deviating from its nature if the throat is dry at a time when drinking is not beneficial to its continued health. But I am well aware that 'nature' as I have just used it has a very different significance from 'nature' in the other sense. As I have just used it, 'nature' is simply a label which depends on my thought; it is quite extraneous to the things to which it is applied, and depends simply on my comparison between the idea of a sick man and a badly made clock, and the idea of a healthy man and a well-made clock. But by 'nature' in the other sense I understand something which is really to be found in the things themselves; in this sense, therefore, the term contains something of the truth.

When we say, then, with respect to the body suffering from dropsy, that it has a disordered nature because it has a dry throat and yet does not need drink, the term 'nature' is here used merely as an extraneous label. However, with respect to the composite, that is, the mind united with this body, what is involved is not a mere label, but a true error of nature, namely that it is thirsty at a time when drink is going to cause it harm. It thus remains to inquire how it is that the goodness of God does not prevent nature, in this sense, from deceiving us.

The first observation I make at this point is that there is a great difference between the mind and the body, inasmuch as the body is by its very nature always divisible, while the mind is utterly indivisible. For when I consider 86 the mind, or myself in so far as I am merely a thinking thing, I am unable to distinguish any parts within myself; I understand myself to be something quite single and complete. Although the whole mind seems to be united to the whole body, I recognize that if a foot or arm or any other part of the body is cut off, nothing has thereby been taken away from the mind. As for the faculties of willing, of sensory perception, of understanding and so on, these cannot be termed parts of the mind, since it is one and the same mind that wills, and has sensory perceptions and understands. By contrast, there is no corporeal or extended thing that I can think of which in my thought I cannot easily divide into parts; and this very fact makes me understand that it is divisible. This one argument would be enough to

sufficeret ad me docendum, mentem a corpore omnino esse diversam, si nondum illud aliunde satis scirem.

Deinde adverto mentem non ab omnibus corporis partibus immediate affici, sed tantummodo a cerebro, vel forte etiam ab una tantum exigua ejus parte, nempe ab ea in qua dicitur esse sensus communis; quae, quotiescunque eodem modo est disposita, menti idem exhibet, etiamsi reliquae corporis partes diversis interim modis possint se habere, ut probant innumera experimenta, quae hic recensere non est opus.

Adverto praeterea eam esse corporis naturam, ut nulla ejus pars possit ab alia parte aliquantum remota moveri, quin possit etiam moveri eodem modo a qualibet ex iis quae interjacent, quamvis illa remotior nihil agat. Ut, exempli causa, in 87 fune A, B, C, D, si trahatur ejus ultima pars D, non alio pacto movebitur prima A, quam moveri etiam posset, si traheretur una ex intermediis B vel C, et ultima D maneret immota. Nec dissimili ratione, cum sentio dolorem pedis, docuit me Physica sensum illum fieri ope nervorum per pedem sparsorum, qui, inde ad cerebrum usque funium instar extensi, dum trahuntur in pede, trahunt etiam intimas cerebri partes ad quas pertingunt, quemdamque motum in iis excitant, qui institutus est a natura ut mentem afficiat sensu doloris tanquam in pede existentis. Sed quia illi nervi per tibiam, crus, lumbos, dorsum, et collum transire debent, ut a pede ad cerebrum perveniant, potest contingere ut, etiamsi eorum pars, quae est in pede, non attingatur, sed aliqua tantum ex intermediis, idem plane ille motus fiat in cerebro qui fit pede male affecto, ex quo necesse erit ut mens sentiat eundem dolorem. Et idem de quolibet alio sensu est putandum.

Adverto denique, quandoquidem unusquisque ex motibus, qui fiunt in ea parte cerebri quae immediate mentem afficit, non nisi unum aliquem sensum illi infert, nihil hac in re melius posse excogitari, quam si eum inferat qui, ex omnibus quos inferre potest, ad hominis sani conservationem quammaxime et quam frequentissime conducit.

show me that the mind is completely different from the body, even if I did not already know as much from other considerations.

My next observation is that the mind is not immediately affected by all parts of the body, but only by the brain, or perhaps just by one small part of the brain, namely the part which is said to contain the 'common' sense.[1] Every time this part of the brain is in a given state, it presents the same signals to the mind, even though the other parts of the body may be in a different condition at the time. This is established by countless observations, which there is no need to review here.

I observe, in addition, that the nature of the body is such that whenever any part of it is moved by another part which is some distance away, it can always be moved in the same fashion by any of the parts which lie in between, even if the more distant part does nothing. For example, in a cord ABCD, if one end D is pulled so that the other end A moves, the exact same movement could have been brought about if one of the intermediate points B or C had been pulled, and D had not moved at all. In similar fashion, when I feel a pain in my foot, physiology tells me that this happens by means of nerves distributed throughout the foot, and that these nerves are like cords which go from the foot right up to the brain. When the nerves are pulled in the foot, they in turn pull on inner parts of the brain to which they are attached, and produce a certain motion in them; and nature has laid it down that this motion should produce in the mind a sensation of pain, as occurring in the foot. But since these nerves, in passing from the foot to the brain, must pass through the calf, the thigh, the lumbar region, the back and the neck, it can happen that, even if it is not the part in the foot but one of the intermediate parts which is being pulled, the same motion will occur in the brain as occurs when the foot is hurt, and so it will necessarily come about that the mind feels the same sensation of pain. And we must suppose the same thing happens with regard to any other sensation.

My final observation is that any given movement occurring in the part of the brain that immediately affects the mind produces just one corresponding sensation; and hence the best system that could be devised is that it should produce the one sensation which, of all possible sensations, is most especially and most frequently conducive to the preservation of the

87

---

[1] The supposed faculty which integrates the data from the five specialized senses (the notion goes back ultimately to Aristotle). 'The seat of the common sense must be very mobile, to receive all the impressions which come from the senses; but it must also be of such a kind as to be movable only by the spirits which transmit these impressions. Only the *conarion* [pineal gland] fits this description' (letter to Mersenne, 21 April 1641, AT III 362: CSMK 180).

Experientiam autem testari, tales esse omnes sensus nobis a natura inditos; ac proinde nihil plane in iis reperiri, quod non Dei

88 potentiam bonitatemque testetur. Ita, exempli causa, cum nervi qui sunt in pede vehementer et praeter consuetudinem moventur, ille eorum motus, per spinae dorsi medullam ad intima cerebri pertingens, ibi menti signum dat ad aliquid sentiendum, nempe dolorem tanquam in pede existentem, a quo illa excitatur ad ejus causam, ut pedi infestam, quantum in se est, amovendam. Potuisset vero natura hominis a Deo sic constitui, ut ille idem motus in cerebro quidvis aliud menti exhiberet: nempe vel seipsum, quatenus est in cerebro, vel quatenus est in pede, vel in aliquo ex locis intermediis, vel denique aliud quidlibet; sed nihil aliud ad corporis conservationem aeque conduxisset. Eodem modo, cum potu indigemus, quaedam inde oritur siccitas in gutture, nervos ejus movens et illorum ope cerebri interiora; hicque motus mentem afficit sensu sitis, quia nihil in toto hoc negotio nobis utilius est scire, quam quod potu ad conservationem valetudinis egeamus, et sic de caeteris.

Ex quibus omnino manifestum est, non obstante immensa Dei bonitate, naturam hominis ut ex mente et corpore compositi non posse non aliquando esse fallacem. Nam si quae causa, non in pede, sed in alia quavis ex partibus per quas nervi a pede ad cerebrum porriguntur, vel etiam in ipso cerebro, eundem plane motum excitet qui solet excitari pede male affecto, sentietur dolor tanquam in pede, sensusque naturaliter falletur, quia, cum ille idem motus in cerebro non possit nisi eundem semper sensum menti inferre, multoque frequentius oriri soleat a causa quae laedit pedem, quam ab

89 alia alibi existente, rationi consentaneum est ut pedis potius quam alterius partis dolorem menti semper exhibeat. Et si quando faucium ariditas, non ut solet ex eo quod ad corporis valetudinem potus conducat, sed ex contraria aliqua causa oriatur, ut in hydropico contingit, longe melius est illam tunc fallere, quam si contra semper falleret, cum corpus est bene constitutum; et sic de reliquis.

Atque haec consideratio plurimum juvat, non modo ut errores omnes quibus natura mea obnoxia est animadvertam, sed etiam ut illos aut emendare aut vitare facile possim. Nam sane, cum sciam

healthy man. And experience shows that the sensations which nature has given us are all of this kind; and so there is absolutely nothing to be found in them that does not bear witness to the power and goodness of God. For example, when the nerves in the foot are set in motion in a violent and unusual manner, this motion, by way of the spinal cord, reaches the inner parts of the brain, and there gives the mind its signal for having a certain sensation, namely the sensation of a pain as occurring in the foot. This stimulates the mind to do its best to get rid of the cause of the pain, which it takes to be harmful to the foot. It is true that God could have made the nature of man such that this particular motion in the brain indicated something else to the mind; it might, for example, have made the mind aware of the actual motion occurring in the brain, or in the foot, or in any of the intermediate regions; or it might have indicated something else entirely. But there is nothing else which would have been so conducive to the continued well-being of the body. In the same way, when we need drink, there arises a certain dryness in the throat; this sets in motion the nerves of the throat, which in turn move the inner parts of the brain. This motion produces in the mind a sensation of thirst, because the most useful thing for us to know about the whole business is that we need drink in order to stay healthy. And so it is in the other cases.

It is quite clear from all this that, notwithstanding the immense goodness of God, the nature of man as a combination of mind and body is such that it is bound to mislead him from time to time. For there may be some occurrence, not in the foot but in one of the other areas through which the nerves travel in their route from the foot to the brain, or even in the brain itself; and if this cause produces the same motion which is generally produced by injury to the foot, then pain will be felt as if it were in the foot. This deception of the senses is natural, because a given motion in the brain must always produce the same sensation in the mind; and the origin of the motion in question is much more often going to be something which is hurting the foot, rather than something existing elsewhere. So it is reasonable that this motion should always indicate to the mind a pain in the foot rather than in any other part of the body. Again, dryness of the throat may sometimes arise not, as it normally does, from the fact that a drink is necessary to the health of the body, but from some quite opposite cause, as happens in the case of the man with dropsy. Yet it is much better that it should mislead on this occasion than that it should always mislead when the body is in good health. And the same goes for the other cases.

This consideration is the greatest help to me, not only for noticing all the errors to which my nature is liable, but also for enabling me to correct

omnes sensus circa ea, quae ad corporis commodum spectant, multo frequentius verum indicare quam falsum, possimque uti fere semper pluribus ex iis ad eandem rem examinandam, et insuper memoria, quae praesentia cum praecedentibus connectit, et intellectu, qui jam omnes errandi causas perspexit; non amplius vereri debeo ne illa, quae mihi quotidie a sensibus exhibentur, sint falsa, sed hyperbolicae superiorum dierum dubitationes, ut risu dignae, sunt explodendae. Praesertim summa illa de somno, quem a vigilia non distinguebam; nunc enim adverto permagnum inter utrumque esse discrimen, in eo quod nunquam insomnia cum reliquis omnibus actionibus vitae a memoria conjungantur, ut ea quae vigilanti occurrunt; nam sane, si quis, dum vigilo, mihi derepente appareret, statimque postea dispareret, ut fit in somnis, ita scilicet ut nec unde venisset, nec quo abiret, 90 viderem, non immerito spectrum potius, aut phantasma in cerebro meo effictum, quam verum hominem esse judicarem. Cum vero eae res occurrunt, quas distincte, unde, ubi, et quando mihi adveniant, adverto, earumque perceptionem absque ulla interruptione cum tota reliqua vita connecto, plane certus sum, non in somnis, sed vigilanti occurrere. Nec de ipsarum veritate debeo vel minimum dubitare, si, postquam omnes sensus, memoriam et intellectum ad illas examinandas convocavi, nihil mihi, quod cum caeteris pugnet, ab ullo ex his nuntietur. Ex eo enim quod Deus non sit fallax, sequitur omnino in talibus me non falli. Sed quia rerum agendarum necessitas non semper tam accurati examinis moram concedit, fatendum est humanam vitam circa res particulares saepe erroribus esse obnoxiam, et naturae nostrae infirmitas est agnoscenda.

or avoid them without difficulty. For I know that in matters regarding the well-being of the body, all my senses report the truth much more frequently than not. Also, I can almost always make use of more than one sense to investigate the same thing; and in addition, I can use both my memory, which connects present experiences with preceding ones, and my intellect, which has by now examined all the causes of error. Accordingly, I should not have any further fears about the falsity of what my senses tell me every day; on the contrary, the exaggerated doubts of the last few days should be dismissed as laughable. This applies especially to the principal reason for doubt, namely my inability to distinguish between being asleep and being awake. For I now notice that there is a vast difference between the two, in that dreams are never linked by memory with all the other actions of life as waking experiences are. If, while I am awake, anyone were suddenly to appear to me and then disappear immediately, as happens in sleep, so that I could not see where he had come from or where he had gone to, it would not be unreasonable for me to judge that he was a ghost, or a vision created 90 in my brain,[1] rather than a real man. But when I distinctly see where things come from and where and when they come to me, and when I can connect my perceptions of them with the whole of the rest of my life without a break, then I am quite certain that when I encounter these things I am not asleep but awake. And I ought not to have even the slightest doubt of their reality if, after calling upon all the senses as well as my memory and my intellect in order to check them, I receive no conflicting reports from any of these sources. For from the fact that God is not a deceiver it follows that in cases like these I am completely free from error. But since the pressure of things to be done does not always allow us to stop and make such a meticulous check, it must be admitted that in this human life we are often liable to make mistakes about particular things, and we must acknowledge the weakness of our nature.

---

[1] '... like those that are formed in the brain when I sleep' (added in French version).

OBJECTIONES
DOCTORUM ALIQUOT VIRORUM IN PRAECENDENTES MEDITATIONES CUM RESPONSIONIBUS AUTHORIS

[CIRCA PRIMAM MEDITATIONEM]

(481) Utar hic exemplo valde familiari, ad facti mei rationem ipsi explicandam, ne deinceps illam non intelligat, aut se non intelligere ausit simulare. Si forte haberet corbem pomis plenam, et vereretur ne aliqua ex pomis istis essent putrida, velletque ipsa auferre, ne reliqua corrumperent, quo pacto id faceret? An non in primis omnia omnino ex corbe rejiceret? ac deinde singula ordine perlustrans, ea sola, quae agnosceret non esse corrupta, resumeret, atque in corbem reponeret, aliis relictis? Eadem ergo ratione, ii qui nunquam recte philosophati sunt, varias habent in mente sua opiniones, quas cum a pueritia coacervare coeperint, merito timent ne pleraeque ex iis non sint verae, ipsasque ab aliis separare conantur, ne ob earum misturam reddantur omnes incertae. Hocque nulla meliore via facere possunt, quam si omnes simul et semel, tanquam incertas falsasve, rejiciant; ac deinde singulas ordine perlustrantes, eas solas resumant, quas veras et indubitatas esse cognoscent. Atque ita non male initio omnia rejeci . . .

[Septimae Responsiones]

(332) Tametsi enim fallacia falsitasve sit, non in sensu, qui mere passive se habet, refertque solum ea quae apparent, quaeque talia ex suis causis apparere necessum est, sed in judicio, sive in mente, quae circumspecte satis non agit, neque advertit eas quae procul sunt, ex hisce aliisve causis

126

THE OBJECTIONS
OF VARIOUS LEARNED MEN
TO THE FOREGOING MEDITATIONS
WITH THE REPLIES OF THE AUTHOR
[SELECTIONS]

[ON THE FIRST MEDITATION]

[THE REJECTION OF PREVIOUS BELIEFS]

Here I shall employ an everyday example to explain to my critic the (481)
rationale for my procedure, so as to prevent him misunderstanding it, or
having the gall to pretend he does not understand it, in future. Suppose he
had a basket full of apples and, being worried that some of the apples were
rotten, wanted to take out the rotten ones to prevent the rot spreading.
How would he proceed? Would he not begin by tipping the whole lot out
of the basket? And would not the next step be to cast his eye over each
apple in turn, and pick up and put back in the basket only those he saw to
be sound, leaving the others? In just the same way, those who have never
philosophized correctly have various opinions in their minds which they
have begun to store up since childhood, and which they therefore have
reason to believe may in many cases be false. They then attempt to separate
the false beliefs from the others, so as to prevent their contaminating the
rest and making the whole lot uncertain. Now the best way they can
accomplish this is to reject all their beliefs together in one go, as if they
were all uncertain and false. They can then go over each belief in turn and
re-adopt only those which they recognize to be true and indubitable. Thus
I was right to begin by rejecting all my beliefs . . .

[*Seventh Replies*: CSM II 324]

[THE RELIABILITY OF THE SENSES]

Although there is deception or falsity, it is not to be found in the senses; (332)
for the senses are quite passive and report only appearances, which must
appear in the way they do owing to their causes. The error or falsity is
in the judgement or the mind, which is not circumspect enough and
does not notice that things at a distance will for one reason or another

127

apparere confusiora minoraque seipsis, dum prope sunt, et ita de caeteris: attamen, ubicumque fallacia sit, negandum non est quin aliqua sit. Solumque difficultas est, sicne semper sit, ut nunquam de rei cujuspiam sensibus perceptae veritate constare possit.

333   Sane vere nihil est necesse exempla obvia conquirere. Dico solum ad ea, quae profers sive potius objicis, constare omnino videri, cum turrim et prope spectamus et contingimus, certos nos esse quod sit quadrata, qui, remotiores, habueramus ansam judicandi rotundam, vel certe dubitandi, quadratane an rotunda an alterius figurae esset.

Sic sensus ille doloris, qui apparet adhuc esse in pede aut manu, postquam ea membra rescissa sunt, fallere aliquando potest, in iis scilicet quibus sunt rescissa, idque ob spiritus sensorios assuetos in ipsa deferre inque ipsis sensum exprimere; attamen qui integri sunt, tam certi sunt se in pede aut manu, quam compungi vident, dolorem sentire, ut dubitare non valeant.

Sic, cum vigilemus somniemusque per vices, donec vivimus, fallacia quidem per somnium est, quod ea videri coram appareant, quae coram non sunt; attamen nec semper somniamus, nec, dum revera vigilamus, dubitare possumus vigilemusne an somniemus potius.

[*Objectiones Quintae*]

Hic manifeste ostendis te praejudiciis tantum niti, nunquamque illa exuere, cum velis nos in iis, in quibus falsitatem nunquam deteximus, nullam falsitatem suspicari; atque ideo, *cum turrim et prope spectamus*
386 *et contingimus, certos nos esse quod sit quadrata*, si quadrata appareat; et cum revera vigilamus, *dubitare nos non posse vigilemusne an somniemus*, et talia. Nullam enim habes rationem existimandi omnia, in quibus error esse potest, jam olim a te fuisse animadversa; et facile probari posset, te in iis interdum falli quae certa esse sic admittis.

[*Quintae Responsiones*]

*   *   *

(418) Nonus denique scrupulus maxime nos urget, cum ais sensuum operationibus esse diffidendum, et intellectus certitudinem sensuum

appear smaller and more blurred than when they are nearby, and so on. Nevertheless, when deception occurs, we must not deny that it exists; the only difficulty is whether it occurs all the time, thus making it impossible for us ever to be sure of the truth of anything which we perceive by the senses.

It is quite unnecessary to look for obvious examples here. With regard 333 to the cases you mention, or rather put forward as presenting a problem, I will simply say that it seems to be quite uncontroversial that when we look at a tower from nearby, and touch it, we are sure that it is square, even though when we were further off we had occasion to judge it to be round, or at any rate to doubt whether it was square or round or some other shape.

Similarly the feeling of pain which still appears to occur in the foot or hand after these limbs have been amputated[1] may sometimes give rise to deception, because the spirits responsible for sensation have been accustomed to pass into the limbs and produce a sensation in them. But such deception occurs, of course, in people who have suffered amputation; those whose bodies are intact are so certain that they feel pain in the foot or hand when they see it is pricked, that they cannot be in doubt.

Again, since during our lives we are alternately awake or dreaming, a dream may give rise to deception because things may appear to be present when they are not in fact present. But we do not dream all the time, and for as long as we are really awake we cannot doubt whether we are awake or dreaming. [*Fifth Objections*: CSM II 230–1]

Here you show quite clearly that you are relying entirely on a preconceived opinion which you have never got rid of. You maintain that we never suspect any falsity in situations where we have never detected it, and hence that 'when we look at a tower from nearby and touch it we are sure that it is square', if it appears square. You also maintain that when we are really 386 awake, we 'cannot doubt whether we are awake or asleep', and so on. But you have no reason to think that you have previously noticed all the circumstances in which error can occur; moreover, it is easy to prove that you are from time to time mistaken in matters which you accept as certain. [*Fifth Replies*: CSM II 264]

* * *

Our *ninth* and most worrying difficulty is your assertion that we ought to (418) mistrust the operations of the senses and that the reliability of the intellect

---

[1] See Med. VI, p. 107 above.

certitudine longe majorem esse. Quid enim, si nulla possit intellectus certitudine gaudere, nisi prius eam a sensibus bene dispositis habeat? Siquidem non potest ille alicujus sensus errorem corrigere, nisi prius alter sensus praedictum emendet errorem. Apparet baculus fractus in aqua ob refractionem, qui tamen rectus sit: quis corriget illum errorem? An intellectus? Nusquam, sed tactus. Idemque de reliquis esto judicium. Itaque si sensus omnes rite dispositos adhibeas, qui semper idem renuntient, maximam omnium certitudinem, cujus homo sit naturaliter capax, assequeris; quae saepenumero te fugiet, si mentis operationi fidas, quae saepe aberrat in iis, de quibus nequidem dubitari posse credebat.

[*Objectiones Sextae*]

Cum itaque dicitur *baculum apparere fractum in aqua ob refractionem,* idem est ac si diceretur, eo illum modo nobis apparere, ex quo infans judicaret ipsum fractum esse, et ex quo etiam nos, secundum praejudi-
439 cia quibus ab ineunte aetate assuevimus, idem judicamus. Quod autem hic additur, nempe *illum errorem non intellectu, sed tactu corrigi,* non potest a me concedi: quia, etsi ex tactu baculum rectum esse judicamus, idque eo judicandi modo, cui ab infantia sumus assueti, quique idcirco *sensus* vocatur, non tamen hoc sufficit ad errorem visus emendandum, sed insuper operae est, ut aliquam rationem habeamus, quae nos doceat credendum esse hac de re judicio ex tactu, potius quam judicio ex viso, elicito: quae ratio, cum in nobis ab infantia non fuerit, non sensui, sed tantum intellectui, est tribuenda. Atque ideo in hoc ipso exemplo solus est intellectus, qui sensus errorem emendat; nec ullum unquam afferri potest, in quo error ex eo contingat, quod mentis operationi magis quam sensui fidamus.   [*Sextae Responsiones*]

171 Satis constat ex iis quae dicta sunt in hac Meditatione, nullum esse κριτήριον, quo somnia nostra a vigilia et sensione vera dignoscantur; et propterea phantasmata, quae vigilantes et sentientes habemus,

is much greater than that of the senses.[1] But how can the intellect enjoy any certainty unless it has previously derived it from the senses when they are working as they should? How can it correct a mistake made by one of the senses unless some other sense first corrects the mistake? Owing to refraction, a stick which is in fact straight appears bent in water. What corrects the error? The intellect? Not at all; it is the sense of touch. And the same sort of thing must be taken to occur in other cases. Hence if you have recourse to all your senses when they are in good working order, and they all give the same report, you will achieve the greatest certainty of which man is naturally capable. But you will often fail to achieve it if you trust the operations of the mind; for the mind often goes astray in just those areas where it had previously supposed doubt to be impossible.

[*Sixth Objections*: CSM II 281–2]

When people say that a stick in water 'appears bent because of refraction', this is the same as saying that it appears to us in a way which would lead a child to judge that it was bent – and which may even lead us to make the same judgement, following the preconceived opinions which we have become accustomed to accept from our earliest years. But I cannot grant 439 my critics' further comment that this error is corrected 'not by the intellect but by the sense of touch'. As a result of touching it, we may judge that the stick is straight, and the kind of judgement involved may be the kind we have been accustomed to make since childhood, and which is therefore referred to as the 'sense' of touch. But the sense alone does not suffice to correct the visual error: in addition we need to have some degree of reason which tells us that in this case we should believe the judgement based on touch rather than that elicited by vision. And since we did not have this power of reasoning in our infancy, it must be attributed not to the senses but to the intellect. Thus even in the very example my critics produce, it is the intellect alone which corrects the error of the senses; and it is not possible to produce any case in which error results from our trusting the operation of the mind more than the senses. [*Sixth Replies*: CSM II 296]

[THE DREAMING ARGUMENT]

From what is said in this Meditation it is clear enough that there is no 171 criterion enabling us to distinguish our dreams from the waking state and from veridical sensations. And hence the images we have when we are awake

---

[1] See above, Med. I, p. 25; Med. II, p. 43; Med. VI, p. 115.

non esse accidentia objectis externis inhaerentia, neque argumento esse talia objecta externa omnino existere. Ideoque si sensus nostros sine alia ratiocinatione sequamur, merito dubitabimus an aliquid existat, necne. Veritatem ergo hujus Meditationis agnoscimus. Sed quoniam de eadem incertitudine sensibilium disputavit Plato et alii antiquorum Philosophorum, et vulgo observatur difficultas dignoscendi vigiliam ab insomniis, nolim excellentissum authorem novarum speculationum illa vetera publicare.

[*Objectiones Tertiae*]

Dubitandi rationes, quae hic a Philosopho admittuntur ut verae, non a me nisi tanquam verisimiles fuere propositae; iisque usus sum, non ut pro novis venditarem, sed partim ut lectorum animos 172 praepararem ad res intellectuales considerandas, illasque a corporeis distinguendas, ad quod omnino necessariae mihi videntur; partim ut ad ipsas in sequentibus Meditationibus responderem; et partim etiam ut ostenderem quam firmae sint veritates quas postea pro-pono, quandoquidem ab istis Metaphysicis dubitationibus labefac-tari non possunt. Itaque nullam ex earum recensione laudem quae-sivi; sed non puto me magis ipsas omittere potuisse, quam medic-inae scriptor morbi descriptionem, cujus curandi methodum vult docere.

[*Tertiae Responsiones*]

An tibi nunquam contigit, quod bene multis, ut somnianti certa et clara ea viderentur, quae dubia postea, quae falsa compereris? Sane *pru-* 457 *dentiae est nunquam illis plane confidere, qui te vel semel decepere.* At, ais, alia summe certorum ratio est. Sunt ea istiusmodi, ut vel somniantibus aut deliris apparere non possint dubia. Serione loqueris, amabo te, qui illa summe certa sic confingas, ut ne somniantibus quidem aut deliris apparere possint dubia? Quae sunt illa porro? Ac si dormientibus, si male sanis, quae ridicula sunt, quae absurda, certa interdum videntur,

and having sensations are not accidents that inhere in external objects, and are no proof that any such external object exists at all. So if we follow our senses, without exercising our reason in any way, we shall be justified in doubting whether anything exists. I acknowledge the correctness of this Meditation. But since Plato and other ancient philosophers discussed this uncertainty in the objects of the senses, and since the difficulty of distinguishing the waking state from dreams is commonly pointed out, I am sorry that the author, who is so outstanding in the field of original speculations, should be publishing this ancient material.

[*Third Objections*: CSM II 121]

The arguments for doubting, which the philosopher here accepts as valid, are ones that I was presenting as merely plausible. I was not trying to sell them as novelties, but had a threefold aim in mind when I used them. Partly I wanted to prepare my readers' minds for the study of the things 172 which are related to the intellect, and help them to distinguish these things from corporeal things; and such arguments seem to be wholly necessary for this purpose. Partly I introduced the arguments so that I could reply to them in the subsequent Meditations. And partly I wanted to show the firmness of the truths which I propound later on, in the light of the fact that they cannot be shaken by these metaphysical doubts. Thus I was not looking for praise when I set out these arguments; but I think I could not have left them out, any more than a medical writer can leave out the description of a disease when he wants to explain how it can be cured.

[*Third Replies*: CSM II 121]

[CERTAINTY IN DREAMS]

Has it never happened to you, as it has to many people, that things seemed clear and certain to you while you were dreaming, but that afterwards you discovered that they were doubtful or false? It is indeed 'prudent never to trust completely those who have deceived you even once'.[1] 'But', 457 you reply, 'matters of the utmost certainty are quite different. They are such that they cannot appear doubtful even to those who are dreaming or mad.' But are you really serious in what you say? Can you pretend that matters of the utmost certainty cannot appear doubtful even to dreamers or madmen? What are these utterly certain matters? If things which are ridiculous or absurd sometimes appear certain, even utterly

---

[1] Above, p. 25.

et summe certa, quidni etiam certa, et summe certa, falsa videantur et dubia? Novi ego, qui dormitabundus aliquando pulsari horam quartam audiverit, et sic numeravit: Una, Una, Una, Una; ac tum prae rei absurditate, quam animo concipiebat, exclamavit: Nae delirat horologium! quater pulsavit horam primam. Et vero quid adeo est absurdum et a ratione alienum, quod dormienti, quod deliro venire non possit in mentem? Quod non probet somnians, non credat, et de eo tanquam a se praeclare invento excogitatoque non gratuletur?

[*Objectiones Septimae*]

Concludere quidem potuisset ex meis, id omne quod ab aliquo clare et distincte percipitur esse verum, quamvis ille aliquis possit interim dubitare somnietne an vigilet, imo etiam, si lubet, quamvis somniet, quamvis sit delirus: quia nihil potest clare ac distincte percipi, a quocunque demum percipiatur, quod non sit tale quale percipitur, hoc est, quod non sit verum. Sed quia soli prudentes recte distinguunt inter id quod ita percipitur, et id quod tantum videtur vel apparet, nolo mirari quod vir bonus unum pro altero hic sumat.

[*Septimae Responsiones*]

certain, to people who are asleep or insane, then why should not things which are certain, even utterly certain, appear false and doubtful? I know a man who once, when falling asleep, heard the clock strike four, and counted the strokes as 'one, one, one, one'. It then seemed to him that there was something absurd about this, and he shouted out: 'That clock must be going mad; it has struck one o'clock four times!' Is there really anything so absurd or irrational that it could not come into the mind of someone who is asleep or raving? There are no limits to what a dreamer may not 'prove' or believe, and indeed congratulate himself on, as if he had managed to invent some splendid thought.

[*Seventh Objections*: CSM II 306]

My critic could have concluded from my writings that everything that anyone clearly and distinctly perceives is true, although the person in question may from time to time doubt whether he is dreaming or awake, and may even, if you like, be dreaming or mad. For no matter who the perceiver is, nothing can be clearly and distinctly perceived without its being just as we perceive it to be, i.e. without being true. But because it 462 requires some care to make a proper distinction between what is clearly and distinctly perceived and what merely seems or appears to be, I am not surprised that my worthy critic should here mistake the one for the other.

[*Seventh Replies*: CSM II 310]

Video te... statuere illud pronunciatum: *Ego sum, Ego existo*, quoties
259   a te profertur, vel mente concipitur, esse verum. Attamen non video
tibi opus fuisse tanto apparatu, quando aliunde certus eras, et verum
erat, te esse; poterasque idem vel ex quavis alia tua actione colligere,
cum lumine naturali notum sit, quicquid agit, esse.

[*Objectiones Quintae*]

(352)   Cum... ais *me idem potuisse ex quavis alia mea actione colligere*,
multum a vero aberras, quia nullius meae actionis omnino certus sum
(nempe certitudine illa Metaphysica, de qua sola hic quaestio est),
praeterquam solius cogitationis. Nec licet inferre, exempli causa: *ego
ambulo, ergo sum*, nisi quatenus ambulandi conscientia cogitatio est,
de qua sola haec illatio est certa, non de motu corporis, qui aliquando
nullus est in somnis, cum tamen etiam mihi videor ambulare; adeo ut
ex hoc quod putem me ambulare, optime inferam existentiam mentis
quae hoc putat, non autem corporis quod ambulet. Atque idem est de
caeteris.   [*Quintae Responsiones*]

*   *   *

[N]eque etiam, cum quis dicit, *ego cogito, ergo sum, sive existo*,
existentiam ex cogitatione per syllogismum deducit, sed tanquam
rem per se notam simplici mentis intuitu agnoscit, ut patet
ex eo quod, si eam per syllogismum deduceret, novisse prius
debuisset istam majorem, *illud omne, quod cogitat, est sive existit*; atqui profecto ipsam potius discit, ex eo quod apud se expe-
riatur, fieri non posse ut cogitet, nisi existat. Ea enim est natura

[ON THE SECOND MEDITATION]

[*COGITO ERGO SUM* ('I AM THINKING, THEREFORE I EXIST')]

I see that you conclude that this proposition, *I am, I exist*, is true whenever it is put forward by you or conceived in your mind.[1] But I do not see that 259 you needed all this apparatus, when on other grounds you were certain, and it was true, that you existed. You could have made the same inference from any one of your other actions, since it is known by the natural light that whatever acts exists. [*Fifth Objections*: CSM II 180]

When you say that I 'could have made the same inference from any one of (352) my other actions' you are far from the truth, since I am not wholly certain of any of my actions, with the sole exception of thought (in using the word 'certain' I am referring to metaphysical certainty, which is the sole issue at this point). I may not, for example, make the inference 'I am walking, therefore I exist', except in so far as the awareness of walking is a thought. The inference is certain only if applied to this awareness, and not to the movement of the body which sometimes – in the case of dreams – is not occurring at all, despite the fact that I seem to myself to be walking. Hence from the fact that I think I am walking I can very well infer the existence of a mind which has this thought, but not the existence of a body that walks. And the same applies in other cases. [*Fifth Replies*: CSM II 244]

*   *   *

When someone says 'I am thinking, therefore I am, or I exist', he does not deduce existence from thought by means of a syllogism, but recognizes it as something self-evident by a simple intuition of the mind. This is clear from the fact that if he were deducing it by means of a syllogism, he would have to have had previous knowledge of the major premiss 'Everything which thinks is, or exists'; yet in fact he learns it from experiencing in his own case that it is impossible that he should think without existing. It is

[1] Above, p. 35.

141 nostrae mentis, ut generales propositiones ex particularium cognitione efformet.

[*Secundae Responsiones*]

* * *

413 [N]on videri adeo certum nos esse, ex eo quod cogitemus. Ut enim certus sis te cogitare, debes scire quid sit cogitare seu cogitatio, quidve existentia tua; cumque necdum scias quid sint illa, qui nosse potes te cogitare vel existere? Cum igitur, dicens *cogito*, nescias quid dicas, cumque addens *sum igitur*, nescias etiam quid dicas, imo nequidem scias te dicere vel cogitare quidpiam, quoniam ad hoc necesse videtur ut scias te scire quid dicas, iterumque ut noveris quod scias te scire quid dicas, et sic in infinitum, constat te scire non posse an sis, vel etiam an cogites. [*Objectiones Sextae*]

(422) Verum quidem est neminem posse esse certum se cogitare, nec se existere, nisi sciat quid sit cogitatio, et quid existentia. Non quod ad hoc requiratur scientia reflexa, vel per demonstrationem acquisita, et multo minus scientia scientiae reflexae, per quam sciat se scire, iterumque se scire se scire, atque ita in infinitum, qualis de nulla unquam re haberi potest. Sed omnino sufficit ut id sciat cognitione illa interna, quae reflexam semper antecedit, et quae omnibus hominibus de cogitatione et existentia ita innata est, ut, quamvis forte praejudiciis obruti, et ad verba magis quam ad verborum significationes attenti, fingere possimus nos illam non habere, non possimus tamen revera non habere. Cum itaque quis advertit se cogitare, atque inde sequi se existere, quamvis forte nunquam antea quaesiverit quid sit cogitiatio, nec quid existentia, non potest tamen non utramque satis nosse, ut sibi in hac parte satisfaciat. [*Sextae Responsiones*]

Sum res cogitans; recte. Nam ex eo quod cogito, sive phantasma habeo, sive vigilans, sive somnians, colligitur quod sum cogitans; idem enim significant *cogito* et *sum cogitans*. Ex eo quod sum cogitans, sequitur, *Ego sum*, quia id quod cogitat non

in the nature of our mind to construct general propositions on the basis of 141
our knowledge of particular ones. *[Second Replies*: CSM II 100]

* * *

From the fact that we are thinking it does not seem to be entirely certain 413
that we exist. For in order to be certain that you are thinking you must
know what thought or thinking is, and what your existence is; but since
you do not yet know what these things are, how can you know that you are
thinking or that you exist? Thus neither when you say 'I am thinking' nor
when you add 'therefore, I exist' do you really know what you are saying.
Indeed, you do not even know that you are saying or thinking anything,
since this seems to require that you should know that you know what you
are saying; and this in turn requires that you be aware of knowing that you
know what you are saying, and so on *ad infinitum*. Hence it is clear that
you cannot know whether you exist or even whether you are thinking.
[Sixth Objections: CSM II 278]

It is true that no one can be certain that he is thinking or that he exists (422)
unless he knows what thought is and what existence is. But this does not
require reflective knowledge, or the kind of knowledge that is acquired by
means of demonstrations; still less does it require knowledge of reflective
knowledge, i.e. knowing that we know, and knowing that we know that
we know, and so on *ad infinitum*. This kind of knowledge cannot possibly
be obtained about anything. It is quite sufficient that we should know it by
that internal awareness which always precedes reflective knowledge. This
inner awareness of one's thought and existence is so innate in all men that,
although we may pretend that we do not have it if we are overwhelmed
by preconceived opinions and pay more attention to words than to their
meanings, we cannot in fact fail to have it. Thus when anyone notices that
he is thinking and that it follows from this that he exists, even though he
may never before have asked what thought is or what existence is, he still
cannot fail to have sufficient knowledge of them both to satisfy himself in
this regard. *[Sixth Replies*: CSM II 285]

[SUM RES COGITANS ('I AM A THINKING THING')]

I am a thinking thing: correct. For from the fact that I think, or have an
image (whether I am awake or dreaming), it can be inferred that I am
thinking; for 'I think' and 'I am thinking' mean the same thing. And
from the fact that I am thinking it follows that I exist, since that which

est nihil. Sed ubi subjungit, *hoc est mens, animus, intellectus, ratio,* oritur dubitatio. Non enim videtur recta argumentatio, dicere *ego sum cogitans,* ergo *sum cogitatio*; neque *ego sum intelligens,* ergo *sum intellectus.* Nam eodem modo possem dicere: *sum ambulans,* ergo *sum ambulatio.* Sumit ergo D. Cartesius idem esse rem intelligentem, et intellectionem, quae est actus intelligentis; vel saltem idem esse rem intelligentem, et intellectum, qui est potentia intelligentis. Omnes tamen Philosophi distinguunt subjectum a suis facultatibus

173 et actibus, hoc est a suis proprietatibus et essentiis; aliud enim est ipsum ens, aliud est ejus essentia; potest ergo esse ut res cogitans sit subjectum mentis, rationis, vel intellectus, ideoque corporeum aliquid: cujus contrarium sumitur, non probatur; est tamen haec illatio fundamentum conclusionis, quam videtur velle D. C. stabilire.

[*Objectiones Tertiae*]

(174) Ubi dixi *hoc est mens, animus, intellectus, ratio, etc.,* non intellexi per ista nomina solas facultates, sed res facultate cogitandi praeditas, ut per duo priora vulgo intelligitur ab omnibus, et per duo posteriora frequenter; hocque tam expresse, totque in locis explicui, ut nullus videatur fuisse dubitandi locus.

Neque hic est paritas inter ambulationem et cogitationem: quia ambulatio sumi tantum solet pro actione ipsa; cogitatio interdum pro actione, interdum pro facultate, interdum pro re in qua est facultas.

Nec dico idem esse rem intelligentem et intellectionem, nec quidem rem intelligentem et intellectum, si sumatur intellectus pro facultate, sed tantum quando sumitur pro re ipsa quae intelligit. Fateor autem ultro me ad rem, sive substantiam, quam volebam exuere omnibus iis quae ad ipsam non pertinent, significandam, usum fuisse verbis quammaxime potui abstractis, ut contra hic Philosophus utitur vocibus quammaxime concretis, nempe *subjecti, materiae,* et *corporis,* ad istam rem cogitantem significandam, ne patiatur ipsam a corpore divelli. [*Tertiae Responsiones*]

* * *

thinks is not nothing. But when the author adds 'that is, I am a mind, or intelligence, or intellect or reason',[1] a doubt arises. It does not seem to be a valid argument to say 'I am thinking, therefore I am thought' or 'I am using my intellect, hence I am an intellect.' I might just as well say 'I am walking, therefore I am a walk.' M. Descartes is identifying the thing which understands with intellection, which is an act of that which understands. Or at least he is identifying the thing which understands with the intellect, which is a power of that which understands. Yet all philosophers make a distinction between a subject and its faculties and acts, i.e. between a subject and its properties and its essences: an entity is one thing, its essence   173 is another. Hence it may be that the thing that thinks is the subject to which mind, reason or intellect belong; and this subject may thus be something corporeal. The contrary is assumed, not proved. Yet this inference is the basis of the conclusion which M. Descartes seems to want to establish.

[Third Objections: CSM II 122]

When I said 'that is, I am a mind, or intelligence, or intellect or reason', (174) what I meant by these terms was not mere faculties, but things endowed with the faculty of thought. This is what the first two terms are commonly taken to mean by everyone; and the second two are often understood in this sense. I stated this point so explicitly, and in so many places, that it seems to me there was no room for doubt.

There is no comparison here between 'a walk' and 'thought'. 'A walk' is usually taken to refer simply to the act of walking, whereas 'thought' is sometimes taken to refer to the act, sometimes to the faculty, and sometimes to the thing which possesses the faculty.

I do not say that the thing which understands is the same as intellection. Nor, indeed, do I identify the thing which understands with the intellect, if 'the intellect' is taken to refer to a faculty; they are identical only if 'the intellect' is taken to refer to the thing which understands. Now I freely admit that I used the most abstract terms I could in order to refer to the thing or substance in question, because I wanted to strip away from it everything that did not belong to it. This philosopher, by contrast, uses absolutely concrete words, namely 'subject', 'matter' and 'body', to refer to this thinking thing, because he wants to prevent its being separated from the body.

[Third Replies: CSM II 123]

*　　*　　*

---

[1] Above, p. 37.

[Q]uod fuerat ipso titulo Meditationis promissum, fore ut per ipsam mens humana efficeretur corpore notior, non video qui praestitum sit. Neque enim tuum institutum fuit, probare esse mentem humanam, ejusve existentiam esse existentia corporis notiorem, cum saltem, an sit existatve, controvertatur a nemine; sed voluisti haud dubie facere illius naturam notiorem natura corporea, et hoc tamen non praestitisti. De natura certa corporea recensuisti ipsa, o Mens,

276 quam multa noscamus, extensionem, figuram, occupationem spatii, etc. De te vero ecquidnam tandem? Non es compages corporea, non aër, non ventus, non res incedens, non sentiens, non alia. Haec ut concedantur (quorum tamen quaedam tu quoque refellisti), non ea sunt tamen, quae expectamus. Scilicet negationes sunt, et non postulatur quid non sis, sed quid tandem sis. Itaque refers nobis ad summum te esse *Rem cogitantem, id est dubitantem, affirmantem, etc.* Sed dicere primum te esse *Rem*, est nihil notum dicere. Haec enim vox est generalis, indiscreta, vaga, et te non magis attinens, quam quicquid in toto est mundo, quam quicquid non est prorsus nihil. Tu est *Res*? id es, nihil non es; seu, quod est idem, aliquid es. Sed lapis etiam nihil non est, seu aliquid est, et musca similiter, et cetera omnia. Deinde, quod te *cogitantem* dicis, rem quidem notam dicis, sed tamen non prius ignotam, neque requisitam a te. Quis dubitet enim quin sis cogitans? Quod nos latet, quod quaeritur, intima tua substantia est, cujus proprium est cogitare. Quocirca, ut inquirere, sic concludere oporteret, non quod sis res cogitans, sed qualis sis res, quae es cogitans. Annon, si quaeratur ex te Vini notitia supra vulgarem, non satis erit tibi dicere: Vinum est res liquida, ex uvis expressa, alba vel rubra, dulcis, inebrians, etc.; sed conabere explorare declarareque utcumque internam ejus substantiam, prout contexta observatur, ex spiritu, phlegmate, tartaro, caeterisque partibus, hac aliave quantitate temperationeque inter se commistis? Pari ergo modo, cum tui notitia supra vulgarem, hoc est hactenus habitam,

277 quaeratur, vides haud dubie non satis esse, si nobis renuncies te esse rem cogitantem, dubitantem, intelligentem, etc.; sed incumbere tibi, ut labore quodam quasi chymico teipsam ita examines, ut

What you promised in the title of this Meditation, namely that it would establish that the human mind is better known than the body, has not, so far as I can see, been achieved. Your aim was not to prove that the human mind exists, or that its existence is better known than the existence of the body, since its existence, at all events, is something which no one questions. Your intention was surely to establish that its nature is better known than the nature of the body, and this you have not managed to do. As regards the nature of the body, you have, O Mind, listed all the things we know: extension, shape, occupation of space, and so on. But 276 what, after all your efforts, have you told us about yourself? You are not a bodily structure, you are not air, not a wind, not a thing which walks or senses, you are not this and not that. Even if we grant these results (though some of them you did in fact reject), they are not what we are waiting for. They are simply negative results; but the question is not what you are not, but what you are. And so you refer us to your principal result, that you are a thing that thinks – i.e. a thing that doubts, affirms etc. But to say first of all that you are a 'thing' is not to give any information. This is a general, imprecise and vague word which applies no more to you than it does to anything in the entire world that is not simply a nothing. You are a 'thing'; that is, you are not nothing, or, what comes to the same thing, you are something. But a stone is something and not nothing, and so is a fly, and so is everything else. When you go on to say that you are a *thinking* thing, then we know what you are saying; but we knew it already, and it was not what we were asking you to tell us. Who doubts that you are thinking? What we are unclear about, what we are looking for, is that inner substance of yours whose property is to think. Your conclusion should be related to this inquiry, and should tell us not that you are a thinking thing, but what sort of thing this 'you' who thinks really is. If we are asking about wine, and looking for the kind of knowledge which is superior to common knowledge, it will hardly be enough for you to say 'wine is a liquid thing, which is compressed from grapes, white or red, sweet, intoxicating' and so on. You will have to attempt to investigate and somehow explain its internal substance, showing how it can be seen to be manufactured from spirits, tartar, the distillate, and other ingredients mixed together in such and such quantities and proportions. Similarly, given that you are looking for knowledge of yourself which is superior to common knowledge (that is, the kind of knowledge we have had up till now), you must see that it is certainly not enough for you to announce that you are a thing that thinks 277 and doubts and understands, etc. You should carefully scrutinize yourself and conduct, as it were, a kind of chemical investigation of yourself, if you

internam tuam substantiam et detegere et demonstrare nobis possis. Hoc certe si praestiteris, explorabimus ipsimet, sisne ipso corpore notior, quod anatomia, quod chymia, quod tot aliae artes, tot sensus, tot experimenta, cujusmodi sit, multum manifestant.

[*Objectiones Quintae*]

Miror te hic fateri, omnia illa quae in cera considero, demonstrare quidem me distincte cognoscere quod existam, non autem quis aut qualis sim, cum unum sine alio non demonstretur. Nec video quid amplius ea de re expectes, nisi ut dicatur cujus coloris, odori et saporis sit mens humana, vel ex quo sale, sulphure et mercurio sit conflata; vis enim ut ipsam, instar vini, labore quodam Chymico examinemus. Quod te profecto dignum est, o Caro,

360 et iis omnibus qui, cum nihil nisi admodum confuse concipiant, quid de quaque re quaerendum sit ignorant; sed quantum ad me, nihil unquam requiri putavi ad manifestandam substantiam, praeter varia ejus attributa, adeo ut, quo plura alicujus substantiae attributa cognoscamus, eo perfectius ejus naturam intelligamus. Atque, ut multa diversa attributa in cera distinguere possumus, unum quod sit alba, aliud quod sit dura, aliud quod ex dura fiat liquida etc.; ita etiam in mente totidem sunt, unum quod habeat vim cognoscendi albedinem cerae, aliud quod habeat vim cognoscendi ejus duritiem, aliud quod mutationem duritiei sive liquefactionem etc.; potest enim quis nosse duritiem, qui non ideo novit albedinem, nempe qui caecus natus est; et ita de caeteris. Unde clare colligur nullius rei tot attributa cognosci, quam nostrae mentis, quia, quotcunque cognoscuntur in qualibet alia re, tot etiam numerari possunt in mente, ex eo quod illa cognoscat; atque ideo ejus natura omnium est notissima.

[*Quintae Responsiones*]

*   *   *

(413) [C]um ais te cogitare et existere, contendet quispiam te decipi, neque cogitare, sed tantum moveri, teque nihil aliud esse quam motum corporeum, cum nullus dum tuam demonstrationem animo complecti potuerit, qua putas te demonstrasse nullum motum corporeum esse posse, quam vocas, cogitationem. An igitur

are to succeed in uncovering and explaining to us your internal substance. If you provide such an explanation, we shall ourselves doubtless be able to investigate whether or not you are better known than the body whose nature we know so much about through anatomy, chemistry, so many other sciences, so many senses and so many experiments.

[*Fifth Objections*: CSM II 192–3]

I am surprised that you should say here that all my considerations about the wax demonstrate that I distinctly know that I exist, but not that I know what I am or what my nature is; for one thing cannot be demonstrated without the other. Nor do I see what more you expect here, unless it is to be told what colour or smell or taste the human mind has, or the proportions of salt, sulphur and mercury from which it is compounded. You want us, you say, to conduct 'a kind of chemical investigation' of the mind, as we would of wine. This is indeed worthy of you, O Flesh, and of all those 360 who have only a very confused conception of everything, and so do not know the proper questions to ask about each thing. But as for me, I have never thought that anything more is required to reveal a substance than its various attributes; thus the more attributes of a given substance we know, the more perfectly we understand its nature. Now we can distinguish many different attributes in the wax: one, that it is white; two, that it is hard; three, that it can be melted; and so on. And there are correspondingly many attributes in the mind: one, that it has the power of knowing the whiteness of the wax; two, that it has the power of knowing its hardness; three, that it has the power of knowing that it can lose its hardness (i.e. melt); and so on. (Someone can have knowledge of the hardness without thereby having knowledge of the whiteness, e.g. a man born blind; and so on in other cases.) The clear inference from this is that we know more attributes in the case of our mind than we do in the case of anything else. For no matter how many attributes we recognize in any given thing, we can always list a corresponding number of attributes in the mind which it has in virtue of knowing the attributes of the thing; and hence the nature of the mind is the one we know best of all. [*Fifth Replies*: CSM II 248–9]

* * *

When you say you are thinking and that you exist, someone might maintain (413) that you are mistaken, and are not thinking but are merely in motion, and that you are nothing else but corporeal motion. For no one has yet been able to grasp that demonstration of yours by which you think you have proved that what you call thought cannot be a kind of corporeal motion.

ea qua uteris analysi motus omnes tuae materiae subtilis ita secuisti, ut certus sis, nobisque attentissimis et, ut putamus, satis perspicacibus ostendere possis, repugnare cogitationes nostras in illos motus corporeos refundi?

[*Objectiones Sextae*]

Nec etiam fieri potest, cum quis advertit se cogitare, intelligitque quid sit moveri, ut putet se decipi, seque non cogitare, sed tantum moveri. Cum enim plane aliam habet ideam sive notionem cogi-
423 tationis, quam motus corporei, necesse est ut unum tanquam ab alio diversum intelligat; etsi, propter consuetudinem plures diversas proprietates, et inter quas nulla connexio cognoscitur, uni et eidem subjecto tribuendi, fieri possit ut dubitet, vel etiam ut affirmet, se esse unum et eundem, qui cogitat et qui loco movetur. Notandumque est duobus modis ea, quorum diversas habemus ideas, pro una et eadem re sumi posse: nempe vel unitate et identitate naturae, vel tantum unitate compositionis. Ita, exempli causa, non eandem quidem habemus ideam figurae et motus; ut neque eandem habemus intellectionis et volitionis; neque etiam ossium et carnis, neque cogitationis et rei extensae. Atque nihilominus clare percipimus illi eidem substantiae, cui competit ut sit figurata, competere etiam ut possit moveri, adeo ut figuratum et mobile sit unum et idem unitate naturae; itemque rem intelligentem et volentem esse etiam unam et eandem unitate naturae. Non autem idem percipimus de re, quam consideramus sub forma ossis et de re, quam consideramus sub forma carnis; nec idcirco possumus illas pro una et eadem re sumere unitate naturae, sed tantum unitate compositionis, quatenus scilicet unum et idem est animal quod habet ossa et carnes. Iam vero quaestio est, an rem cogitantem et rem extensam percipiamus esse unam et eandem unitate naturae, ita scilicet ut inter cogitationem et extensionem aliquam talem affinitatem sive connexionem inveniamus, qualem inter figuram et motum, vel intellectionem et volitionem
424 advertimus; an potius dicantur tantum esse unum et idem unitate compositionis, quatenus in eodem homine reperiuntur, ut ossa et carnes in eodem animali. Quod ultimum affirmo, quia distinctionem

Have you used your method of analysis to separate off all the motions of that rarefied matter of yours? Is this what makes you so certain? And can you therefore show us (for we will give our closest attention and our powers of perception are, we think, reasonably keen) that it is self-contradictory that our thoughts should be reducible to these corporeal motions?

[*Sixth Objections*: CSM II 278]

When someone notices that he is thinking, then, given that he understands what motion is, it is quite impossible that he should believe that he is mistaken and is 'not thinking but merely in motion'. Since the idea or notion which he has of thought is quite different from his idea of corporeal 423 motion, he must necessarily understand the one as different from the other. Because, however, he is accustomed to attribute many different properties to one and the same subject without being aware of any connection between them, he may possibly be inclined to doubt, or may even affirm, that he is one and the same being who thinks and who moves from place to place. Notice that if we have different ideas of two things, there are two ways in which they can be taken to be one and the same thing: either in virtue of the unity or identity of their nature, or else merely in respect of unity of composition. For example, the ideas which we have of shape and of motion are not the same, nor are our ideas of understanding and volition, nor are those of bones and flesh, nor are those of thought and of an extended thing. But nevertheless we clearly perceive that the same substance which is such that it is capable of taking on a shape is also such that it is capable of being moved, and hence that that which has shape and that which is mobile are one and the same in virtue of a unity of nature. Similarly, the thing that understands and the thing that wills are one and the same in virtue of a unity of nature. But our perception is different in the case of the thing that we consider under the form of bone and that which we consider under the form of flesh; and hence we cannot take them as one and the same thing in virtue of a unity of nature but can regard them as the same only in respect of unity of composition – i.e. in so far as it is one and the same animal which has bones and flesh. But now the question is whether we perceive that a thinking thing and an extended thing are one and the same by a unity of nature. That is to say, do we find between thought and extension the same kind of affinity or connection that we find between shape and motion, or understanding and volition? Alternatively, when they are said to be 'one 424 and the same', is this not rather in respect of unity of composition, in so far as they are found in the same man, just as bones and flesh are found in the same animal? The latter view is the one I maintain, since I observe a

sive diversitatem omnimodam inter naturam rei extensae et rei cogitantis, non minus quam inter ossa et carnes, animadverto...

Ad id denique quod quaeritur: an ea qua utor Analysi motus
omnes meae materiae subtilis ita secuerim, ut certus sim, virisque
attentissimis atque, ut putant, satis perspicacibus ostendere possim, repugnare cogitationes in motus corporeos refundi, hoc est,
425 ut interpretor, cogitationes et motus corporeos esse unum et
idem, respondeo mihi quidem esse certissimum, sed non ideo
spondere aliis, quantumvis attentis et suo judicio perspicacibus,
idem posse persuaderi, saltem quandiu non ad res pure intelligibiles, sed tantum ad imaginabiles, attentionem suam conver-
tent, ut apparet illos fecisse, quid distinctionem cogitationis a
motu per dissectionem alicujus materiae subtilis intelligendam esse
finxerunt. Nam ex eo tantum intelligitur, quod notiones rei cogitantis et rei extensae sive mobilis sint plane diversae, atque a
se mutuo independentes, repugnetque ut illae res, quae a nobis
tanquam diversae et independentes clare intelliguntur, separatim,
saltem a Deo, poni non possint. Adeo ut quotiescunque illas
in uno et eodem subjecto reperimus, ut cogitationem et motum
corporeum in eodem homine, non debeamus idcirco existimare
ipsas ibi esse unum et idem unitate naturae, sed tantum unitate
compositionis.

[Sextae Responsiones]

(214) Addo quod exciderat, falsum mihi videri, quod pro certo affirmat
V.C., nihil in se, quatenus est res cogitans, esse posse, cujus conscius
non sit. Per se enim, quatenus est res cogitans, nihil aliud intelligit
quam mentem suam, quatenus a corpore distincta est. At quis non
videt, multa in mente esse posse, quorum mens conscia non sit? Mens
infantis in matris utero habet vim cogitandi; at ejus conscia non est.
Mitto innumera similia.   *[Objectiones Quartae]*

distinction or difference in every respect between the nature of an extended thing and that of a thinking thing, which is no less than that to be found between bones and flesh . . .

My critics ask whether I have used my method of analysis to separate off all the motions of that rarefied matter of mine. Is this (they ask) what makes me certain? And can I therefore show my critics, who are most attentive and (they think) reasonably perceptive men, that it is self-contradictory that our thought should be reduced to corporeal motions? By 'reduced' I take it that they mean that thoughts and corporeal motions are one and the same. 425 My reply is that I am very certain of this point, but I cannot guarantee that others can be convinced of it, however attentive they may be, and however keen, in their own judgement, their powers of perception may be. I cannot guarantee that they will be persuaded, at least so long as they focus their attention not on things which are objects of pure understanding but only on things which can be imagined. This mistake has obviously been made by those who have imagined that the distinction between thought and motion is to be understood by making divisions within some kind of rarefied matter. The only way of understanding the distinction is to realize that the notions of a thinking thing and an extended or mobile thing are completely different, and independent of each other; and it is self-contradictory to suppose that things that we clearly understand as different and independent could not be separated, at least by God. Thus, however often we find them in one and the same subject – e.g. when we find thought and corporeal motion in the same man – we should not therefore think that they are one and the same in virtue of a unity of nature, but should regard them as the same only in respect of unity of composition.

[*Sixth Replies*: CSM II 285–7]

[THE NATURE OF THOUGHT]

Let me add something which I forgot to include earlier. The author lays (214) it down as certain that there can be nothing in him, in so far as he is a thinking thing, of which he is not aware,[1] but it seems to me that this is false. For by 'himself, in so far as he is a thinking thing', he means simply his mind, in so far as it is distinct from the body. But all of us can surely see that there may be many things in our mind of which the mind is not aware. The mind of an infant in its mother's womb has the power of thought, but is not aware of it. And there are countless similar examples, which I will pass over.   [*Fourth Objections*: CSM II 150]

---

[1] Cf. Med. III, p. 69 above.

Quod autem nihil in mente, quatenus est res cogitans, esse possit, cujus
non sit conscia, per se notum mihi videtur, quia nihil in illa sic spectata
esse intelligimus, quod non sit cogitatio, vel a cogitatione dependens;
alioqui enim ad mentem, quatenus est res cogitans, non pertineret;
nec ulla potest in nobis esse cogitatio, cujus eodem illo momento, quo
in nobis est, conscii non simus. Quamobrem non dubito quin mens,
statim atque infantis corpori infusa est, incipiat cogitare, simulque sibi
suae cogitationis conscia sit, etsi postea ejus rei non recordetur, quia
species istarum cogitationum memoriae non inhaerent.

    Sed notandum est, actuum quidem, sive operationum, nostrae men-
tis nos semper actu conscios esse; facultatum, sive potentiarum, non
semper, nisi potentia; ita scilicet ut, cum ad utendum aliqua facultate
247 nos accingimus, statim, si facultas illa sit in mente, fiamus ejus actu
conscii; atque ideo negare possimus esse in mente, si ejus conscii fieri
nequeamus.   [*Quartae Responsiones*]

*   *   *

Cogitationis nomine complector illud omne quod sic in nobis est,
ut ejus immediate conscii simus. Ita omnes voluntatis, intellectus,
imaginationis et sensuum operationes sunt cogitationes. Sed addidi
immediate, ad excludenda ea quae ex iis consequuntur, ut motus vol-
untarius cogitationem quidem pro principio habet, sed ipse tamen
non est cogitatio.

    Ideae nomine intelligo cujuslibet cogitationis formam illam, per
cujus immediatam perceptionem ipsius ejusdem cogitationis conscius
sim; adeo ut nihil possim verbis exprimere, intelligendo id quod dico,
quin ex hoc ipso certum sit, in me esse ideam ejus quod verbis illis
significatur. Atque ita non solas imagines in phantasia depictas ideas
voco; imo ipsas hic nullo modo voco ideas, quatenus sunt in phantasia
161 corporea, hoc est in parte aliqua cerebri depictae, sed tantum quatenus
mentem ipsam in illam cerebri partem conversam informant.
[*Secundae Reponsiones*]

*   *   *

Si dicat se cogitare, hoc est se intelligere, velle, imaginari, sentire;
et sic cogitare, ut suam illam cogitationem actu reflexo intueatur
et consideret; adeoque cogitet, sive sciat et consideret se cogitare

As to the fact that there can be nothing in the mind, in so far as it is a thinking thing, of which it is not aware, this seems to me to be self-evident. For there is nothing that we can understand to be in the mind, regarded in this way, that is not a thought or dependent on a thought. If it were not a thought or dependent on a thought it would not belong to the mind *qua* thinking thing; and we cannot have any thought of which we are not aware at the very moment when it is in us. In view of this I do not doubt that the mind begins to think as soon as it is implanted in the body of an infant, and that it is immediately aware of its thoughts, even though it does not remember this afterwards because the impressions of these thoughts do not remain in the memory.

But it must be noted that, although we are always actually aware of the acts or operations of our minds, we are not always aware of the mind's faculties or powers, except potentially. By this I mean that when we concentrate on employing one of our faculties, then immediately, if the faculty in question resides in our mind, we become actually aware of it, and hence 247 we may deny that it is in the mind if we are not capable of becoming aware of it. [*Fourth Replies*: CSM II 171–2]

*   *   *

Thought. I use this term to include everything that is in us in such a way that we are immediately aware of it. Thus all the operations of the will, the intellect, the imagination and the senses are thoughts. I say 'immediately' so as to exclude the consequences of thoughts; a voluntary movement, for example, originates in a thought but it not itself a thought.

Idea. I understand this term to mean the form of any given thought, immediate perception of which makes me aware of the thought. Hence whenever I express something in words and understand what I am saying, this very fact makes it certain that there is within me an idea of what is signified by the words in question. Thus it is not only the images depicted in the corporeal imagination which I call 'ideas'. Indeed, in so far as these images are in the corporeal imagination, that is, are depicted in some part 161 of the brain, I do not call them 'ideas' at all; I call them 'ideas' only in so far as they give form to the mind itself, when it is directed towards that part of the brain. [*Second Replies*: CSM II 113]

*   *   *

By 'thinking' you may mean that you understand and will and imagine and have sensations, and that you think in such a way that you can contemplate and consider your thought by a reflexive act. This would mean that when

534 (quod vere est esse conscium, et actus alicujus habere conscientiam);
id vero esse proprium facultatis aut rei, quae sit posita supra materiam, quaeque sit plane spiritualis; eoque pacto se esse mentem, se
spiritum: dicet quod nondum dixit, et quod debuit dicere, et quod
expectabam ut diceret, et quod saepius saepe, ubi vidi parturien-
tem, sed inani conatu, volui suggerere: dicet, inquam, boni aliquid, sed novi nihil, cum illud nos a nostris olim praeceptoribus
acceperimus, et illi a suis, atque, opinor, alii ab aliis jam inde ab
Adamo.

[*Objectiones Septimae*]

Item cum ait non sufficere quod substantia aliqua sit cogitans, ut sit
posita supra materiam, et plane spiritualis, quam solam vult vocari
mentem, sed insuper requiri ut actu reflexo cogitet se cogitare, sive
habeat cogitationis suae conscientiam, aeque hallucinatur ac Cae-
mentarius, cum ait Architecturae peritum debere actu reflexo considerare se habere illam peritiam, priusquam esse possit architectus. Etsi enim revera nemo sit Architectus, qui non saepe consid-
erarit, aut saltem considerare potuerit, se habere aedificandi peritiam, manifestum tamen est istam considerationem non requiri ut
sit Architectus. Nec magis etiam similis consideratio sive reflexio
requiritur, ut substantia cogitans sit posita supra materiam. Etenim
prima quaevis cogitatio, per quam aliquid advertimus, non magis
differt a secunda per quam advertimus nos istud prius advertisse,
quam haec a tertia per quam advertimus nos advertisse nos advertisse: nec ulla vel minima ratio afferri potest, si prima concedatur
rei corporeae, cur non etiam secunda. Quapropter notandum est
Authorem nostrum multo periculosius errare hac in parte quam
Caementarium: tollendo enim veram et maxime intelligibilem differentiam, quae est inter res corporeas et incorporeas, quod nempe
hae cogitent, illae non item, et aliam in ejus locum substituendo,
quae nullo modo essentialis videri potest, quod nempe hae considerent se cogitare, illae non considerent, facit omne quod in se est ad
560 impediendum ne realis humanae mentis a corpore distinctio intelligatur.

[*Septimae Responsiones*]

you think, you know and consider that you are thinking (and this is really what it is to be conscious and to have conscious awareness of some activity). 534 Such consciousness, you claim, is a property of a faculty or thing that is superior to matter and is wholly spiritual, and it is in this sense that you are a mind or a spirit. This claim is one you have not made before, but which should have been made; indeed, I often wanted to suggest it when I saw your method struggling ineffectively to bring it forth. But the claim, although *sound*, is nothing *new*, since we all heard it from our teachers long ago, and they heard it from their teachers, and so on, I would think, right back to Adam. [*Seventh Objections*: CSM II 364]

My critic says that to enable a substance to be superior to matter and wholly spiritual (and he insists on using the term 'mind' only in this restricted sense), it is not sufficient for it to think: it is further required that it should think that it is thinking, by means of a reflexive act, or that it should have awareness of its own thought. This is as deluded as our bricklayer's saying that a person who is skilled in architecture must employ a reflexive act to ponder on the fact that he has this skill before he can be an architect. It may in fact be that all architects frequently reflect on the fact that they have this skill, or at least are capable of so reflecting. But it is obvious that an architect does not need to perform this reflexive act in order to be an architect. And equally, this kind of pondering or reflecting is not required in order for a thinking substance to be superior to matter. The initial thought by means of which we become aware of something does not differ from the second thought by means of which we become aware that we were aware of it, any more than this second thought differs from the third thought by means of which we become aware that we were aware that we were aware. And if it is conceded that a corporeal thing has the first kind of thought, then there is not the slightest reason to deny that it can have the second. Accordingly, it must be stressed that my critic commits a much more dangerous error in this respect than does the poor bricklayer. He removes the true and most clearly intelligible feature which differentiates corporeal things from incorporeal ones, viz. that the latter think, but not the former; and in its place he substitutes a feature which cannot in any way be regarded as essential, namely that incorporeal things reflect on their thinking, but corporeal ones do not. Hence he does everything he can to 560 hinder our understanding of the real distinction between the human mind and the body. [*Seventh Replies*: CSM II 382]

Adfers deinde exemplum cerae, ac circa illud plurima habes, ut significes aliud esse, quae vocant accidentia cerae, aliud ipsam ceram ejusve substantiam; ac opus esse solius mentis sive intellectus, non vero sensus aut imaginationis, ipsammet ceram ejusve substantiam distincte percipere. At primo, illud ipsum est, quod omnes vulgo profitentur, abstrahi posse conceptum cerae substantiaeve ejus a conceptibus accidentium. An vero propterea ipsa substantia seu natura cerae distincte concipitur? Concipimus quidem praeter colorem, figuram, liquabilitatem etc., esse aliquid, quod sit subjectum accidentium, mutationumque observatarum; sed quidnam aut quale illud sit, nescimus. Quippe latet semper, et solum, quasi conjiciendo, subesse debere aliquid putatur. Hinc miror qui dicas te, peracta illa detractione formarum
272 quasi vestium, perfectius atque evidentius percipere quid cera sit. Nam percipis quidem ceram ejusve substantiam debere esse aliquid praeter ejusmodi formas; at quid illud sit, non percipis, nisi nos fallis. Neque enim id tibi revelatur, ut revelari potest homo, cujus prius vestes pileumque solum conspeximus, dum ista illi detrahimus, ut quis, aut qualis sit, noscatur. Deinde, cum putes id te quomodocumque percipere, quomodo, quaeso, percipis? Annon ut aliquid fusum extensumque? Neque enim tanquam punctum concipis, tametsi hujusmodi sit, ut nunc latius nunc contractius extendatur. Et cum hujusmodi extensio infinita non sit, habeatque terminum, annon illud etiam concipis quadam ratione figuratum? Et cum videaris tibi illud quasi videre, nonne illi praeterea nescio quem, tametsi confusum, colorem affingis? Habes id certe, ut corpulentius, ita visibilius, quam merum inane. Quare et tua intellectio imaginatio quaedam est. Si dicas te absque ulla extensione, figura, coloreque concipere, dic, bona fide: qualenam ergo?

Illud, quod habes de hominibus visis, seu mente perceptis, quorum tamen non nisi pileos, aut vestes, conspicimus, non arguit mentem potius esse quam imaginatricem, quae dijudicet. Certe et canis, in quo parem tibi mentem non admittis, simili modo dijudicat, cum non herum suum, sed pileum solum aut vestes

[THE PIECE OF WAX]

Next you introduce the example of the wax, and you spend some time explaining that the so-called accidents of the wax are one thing, and the wax itself, or substance of the wax, is another. You say that in order to have a distinct perception of the wax itself or its substance we need only the mind or intellect, and not sensation or imagination.[1] But the first point is just what everyone commonly asserts, *viz.* that the concept of the wax or its substance can be abstracted from the concepts of its accidents. But does this really imply that the substance or nature of the wax is itself distinctly conceived? Besides the colour, the shape, the fact that it can melt, etc. we conceive that there is something which is the subject of the accidents and changes we observe; but what this subject is, or what its nature is, we do not know. This always eludes us; and it is only a kind of conjecture that leads us to think that there must be something underneath the accidents. So I am amazed at how you can say that once the forms have been stripped off like clothes, you perceive more perfectly and evidently what the wax is. 272 Admittedly, you perceive that the wax or its substance must be something over and above such forms; but what this something is you do not perceive, unless you are misleading us. For this 'something' is not revealed to you in the way in which a man can be revealed when, after first of all seeing just his hat and garments, we then remove the clothes so as to find out who and what he is. Moreover, when you think you somehow perceive this underlying 'something', how, may I ask, do you do so? Do you not perceive it as something spread out and extended? For you do not conceive of it as a point, although it is the kind of thing whose extension expands and contracts. And since this kind of extension is not infinite but has limits, do you not conceive of the thing as having some kind of shape? And when you seem as it were to see it, do you not attach to it some sort of colour, albeit not a distinct one? You certainly take it to be something more solid, and so more visible, than a mere void. Hence even your 'understanding' turns out to be some sort of imagination. If you say you conceive of the wax apart from any extension, shape or colour, then you must in all honesty tell us what sort of conception you do have of it.

What you have to say about 'men whom we see, or perceive with the mind, when we make out only their hats or cloaks' does not show that it is the mind rather than the imagination that makes judgements. A dog, which you will not allow to possess a mind like yours, certainly makes a similar kind of judgement when it sees not its master but simply his

---

[1] Cf. above, pp. 41–3.

videt. Quid, quod tametsi herus stet, sedeat, cubet, reclinetur, con-
trahatur, effundatur, agnoscit tamen semper herum, qui sub omnibus
273 illis formis esse potest, cum tamen non sub una potius quam sub alia,
sit eadem proportione, qua cera? Et cum leporem currentem venatur,
integrumque et mortuum, ac postea excoriatum discerptumque in
frusta, videt, putas, non existimat eundem semper leporem esse? Quod
proinde dicis, perceptionem coloris, duritiei, et similium, esse non
visionem, non tactionem, sed solius mentis inspectionem; esto: dum-
modo mens non differat ab imaginatrice reipsa. Cum vero addis, eam
inspectionem esse posse imperfectam et confusam, vel perfectam et
distinctam, prout minus vel magis ad illa, ex quibus constat cera, atten-
ditur; id sane arguit, non inspectionem mente factam illius nescio cujus
rei quae est praeter omnes formas, esse claram distinctamque cognitionem cerae, sed inspectionem per sensus factam omnium, quantum
fieri potest, accidentium mutationumque, quarum cera est capax. Ex
his certe concipere et explicare poterimus, quid nomine cerae intelligamus; at nudam illam vel potius occultatem substantiam, neque
ipsi concipere, neque explicare aliis valemus.   [*Objectiones Quintae*]

(359) Hic, ut saepe alibi, tantum ostendis te non satis intelligere illa quae
conaris reprehendere. Neque enim abstraxi conceptum cerae ab ejus
accidentium conceptu; sed potius indicare volui quo pacto ejus substantia per accidentia manifestetur, et quomodo ejus perceptio reflexa
et distincta, qualem nullam, o Caro, videris unquam habuisse, differat
a vulgari et confusa. Nec video quonam fretus argumento pro certo
affirmes canem simili modo atque nos dijudicare, nisi quia, cum videas
illum etiam carne constare, eadem omnia quae in te sunt, putas esse
etiam in illo; sed ego, qui nullam in eo mentem animadverto, nihil
simile iis quae in mente cognosco, in ipso reor inveniri.

[*Quintae Responsiones*]

hat or clothes. Indeed, even if the master is standing or sitting or lying down or reclining or crouching down or stretched out, the dog still always recognizes the master who can exist under all these forms, even though, like the wax, he does not keep the same proportions or always appear under one form rather than another. And when a dog chases a hare that 273 is running away, and sees it first intact, then dead, and afterwards skinned and chopped up, do you suppose that he does not think it is the same hare? When you go on to say that the perception of colour and hardness and so on is 'not vision or touch but is purely mental scrutiny', I accept this, provided the mind is not taken to be really distinct from the imaginative faculty. You add that this scrutiny 'can be imperfect and confused or perfect and distinct depending on how carefully we concentrate on what the wax consists in'. But this does not show that the scrutiny made by the mind, when it examines this mysterious something that exists over and above all the forms, constitutes clear and distinct knowledge of the wax; it shows, rather, that such knowledge is constituted by the scrutiny made by the senses of all the possible accidents and changes which the wax is capable of taking on. From these we shall certainly be able to arrive at a conception and explanation of what we mean by the term 'wax'; but the alleged naked, or rather hidden, substance is something that we can neither ourselves conceive nor explain to others.   [*Fifth Objections*: CSM II 189–91]

Here, as frequently elsewhere, you merely show that you do not have (359) an adequate understanding of what you are trying to criticize. I did not abstract the concept of the wax from the concept of its accidents. Rather, I wanted to show how the substance of the wax is revealed by means of its accidents, and how a reflective and distinct perception of it (the sort of perception which you, O Flesh, seem never to have had) differs from the ordinary confused perception. I do not see what argument you are relying on when you lay it down as certain that a dog makes discriminating judgements in the same way as we do. Seeing that a dog is made of flesh you perhaps think that everything which is in you also exists in the dog. But I observe no mind at all in the dog, and hence believe there is nothing to be found in a dog that resembles the things I recognize in a mind.
                    [*Fifth Replies*: CSM II 248]

Distinguis consequenter *Ideas* (quas vis esse cogitationes, prout sunt tanquam imagines) in innatas, adventitias, factitias. Et primi quidem generis statuis, quod intelligas quid sit res, quid veritas, quid cogitatio; secundi, quod strepitum audias, solem videas, ignem sentias; tertii, quod Sirenas et Hippogryphes fingas. Ac subdis posse forte omnes esse adventitias, vel omnes innatas, vel omnes factas, quatenus nondum originem illarum clare perspexisti. Porro, ne aliqua interea, donec perspexeris, fallacia subrepat, adnotare placet videri omnes Ideas esse adventitias, procedereve a rebus 280 extra ipsam mentem existentibus et cadentibus in aliquem sensum. Videlicet mens facultatem habet (vel ipsa potius facultas est) non perspiciendi modo ipsas Ideas adventitias, seu quas ex rebus per sensus trajectas accipit, perspiciendi, inquam, nudas et distinctas, et omnino quales in se recipit; sed praeterea illas varie componendi, dividendi, contrahendi, ampliandi, comparandi, et id genus similia.

Hinc tertium saltem Idearum genus distinctum non est a secundo: nam Idea chimaerae alia non est, quam Idea capitis leonis, ventris caprae, caudae serpentis, ex quidbus mens unam componit, cum illae seorsim, sive singulae, adventitiae sint. Sic Idea Gigantis, hominisve instar montis aut mundi totius concepti, non alia est, quam adventitia: Idea puta hominis magnitudinis vulgaris, quam mens ampliat pro libitu, tametsi tanto confusius, quanto amplius concipit illam. Sic idea Pyramidis, urbis, aut ulterius rei nunquam visae, non alia est, quam adventitia visae antea Pyramidis, urbis, aut alterius rei,

[ON THE THIRD MEDITATION]

[INNATE IDEAS]

You next distinguish ideas (by which you mean thoughts in so far as they are like images) into three classes: innate, adventitious and made up. In the first class you put 'your understanding of what a thing is, what truth is and what thought is'. In the second class you put 'your hearing a noise, seeing the sun and feeling a fire'. And in the third class you put 'your invented idea of sirens and hippogriffs'. You add that all your ideas may perhaps be adventitious or they may all be innate or all made up, since you have not as yet clearly perceived their origin.[1] But in case some fallacy should creep in before you have managed to perceive the origin of your ideas, I should like to go further and note that all ideas seem to be adventitious – 280 to proceed from things which exist outside the mind and come under one of our senses. The mind has the faculty (or rather is itself the faculty) of perceiving adventitious ideas – those which it receives through the senses and which are transmitted by things; these ideas, I say, are quite unadorned and distinct, and are received just exactly as they are. But in addition to this, the mind has the faculty of putting these ideas together and separating them in various ways, of enlarging them and diminishing them, of comparing them, and so on.

Hence the third class of ideas, at any rate, is not distinct from the second. For the idea of a chimera is simply the idea of the head of a lion, the body of a goat and the tail of a serpent, out of which the mind puts together one idea, although the individual elements are adventitious. Similarly the idea of a giant, or a man supposed to be as big as a mountain or the whole world, is merely adventitious. It is the idea of a man of ordinary size which the mind enlarges at will, although the more the idea is enlarged the more confused the conception becomes. Again the idea of a pyramid, or of a town, or of something else which we have not so far seen, is simply the adventitious idea of a pyramid or town or something else which we have

[1] Above, p. 53.

non nihil deformata, ac proinde confusa aliqua ratione multiplicata comparataque.

Quod spectat ad species quas dicis innatas, eae profecto nullae videntur, et quaecunque dicuntur tales, videntur originem quoque (283) habere adventitiam... [O]pponendum quoque et solvendum erat inter caetera, quamobrem in caeco nato nulla sit idea coloris, aut in surdo vocis, nisi quia istae res externae non potuerunt ex se immittere in infelicis illius mentem ullam sui speciem: quod fores nativitate conclusae, obicesque illis trajiciendis fuerint perpetuo positi.

[*Objectiones Quintae*]

(362) Miror vero ratiocinium quo probare vis omnes nostras ideas esse adventitias, nullasque a nobis factas, quia, inquis, mens facultatem habet non tantum percipiendi ipsas ideas adventitias, sed praeterea illas varie componendi, dividendi, contrahendi, ampliandi, comparandi, et id genus similia: unde concludis ideas Chimaerarum, quas mens facit componendo, dividendo etc., non esse ab ipsa factas, sed adventitias. Quo pacto etiam posses probare nec signa ulla facta fuisse a Praxitele, quoniam a se non habuit marmor ex quo illa exculperet, nec te has objectiones fecisse, quia ex verbis non a te inventis, sed ab aliis mutuatis, ipsas composuisti. At certe nec forma chimaerae in partibus caprae aut leonis, nec forma tuarum objectionum in singulis verbis quibus usus es, sed in sola compositione, consistit...

(363)   Et cum rationibus, quas mihi objeci et refutavi, unam vis addere, quamobrem in caeco nato nulla sit idea coloris, aut in surdo vocis, plane ostendis te nullam habere ullius momenti. Qui enim scis nullam esse ideam colorum in caeco? cum interdum in nobis, etsi claudamus oculos, nihilominus sensus lucis et colorum excitentur. Et, quamvis quod ais concedatur, nunquid eodem jure dici potest ab eo qui negat existentiam rerum materialium, caecum natum non habere ideas colorum, quia ejus mens facultate illas formandi est destituta, quo a te dicitur ipsum easdem non habere, quia oculis est privatus?

[*Quintae Responsiones*]

seen, with the form somewhat modified so that the idea is repeated and rearranged in a fairly confused way.

As for the forms which you say are innate, there do not seem to be any: whatever ideas are said to belong to this category also appear to have an external origin . . . [Y]ou should also have raised and answered, amongst (283) other things, the question of why a man born blind has no idea of colour, or a man born deaf has no idea of sound. Surely this is because external objects have not been able to transmit any images of themselves to the minds of such unfortunates, because the doors have been closed since birth, and there have always been barriers in place which have prevented these images from entering. [*Fifth Objections*: CSM II 195, 197]

I am amazed at the line of argument by which you try to prove that all our (362) ideas are adventitious and that none of them are constructed by us. You say that the mind has the faculty not just of perceiving adventitious ideas but also 'of putting them together and separating them in various ways, of enlarging them and diminishing them, of comparing them and so on'. Hence you conclude that the ideas of chimeras, which the mind makes up by the process of putting together and separating etc., are not constructed by the mind but are adventitious. By this argument you could prove that Praxiteles never made any statues on the grounds that he did not get from within himself the marble from which he sculpted them; or you could prove that you did not produce these objections on the grounds that you composed them out of words which you acquired from others rather than inventing them yourself. But in fact the form of a chimera does not consist in the parts of the goat or lion, nor does the form of your objections consist in the individual words you have used; they both consist simply in the fact that the elements are put together in a certain way . . .

In addition to the arguments which I put forward against myself and (363) refuted, you suggest the following: why is there no idea of colour in a man born blind, and no idea of sound in a man born deaf? Here you show plainly that you have no telling arguments to produce. How do you know that there is no idea of colour in a man born blind? From time to time we find in our own case that even though we close our eyes, sensations of light and colour are nevertheless aroused. And even if we grant what you say, those who deny the existence of material things may just as well attribute the absence of ideas of colour in the man born blind to the fact that his mind lacks the faculty for forming them; this is just as reasonable as your claim that he does not have the ideas because he is deprived of sight. [*Fifth Replies*: CSM II 250–1]

Cum hominem cogito, agnosco ideam, sive imaginem constitutam
ex figura et colore, de qua possum dubitare an sit hominis simili-
tudo vel non. Similiter cum cogito caelum. Cum Chimaeram cogito,
agnosco ideam, sive imaginem, de qua possum dubitare an sit simil-
itudo alicujus animalis, non existentis, sed quod existere possit, vel
extiterit alio tempore, vel non.

Caeterum, cogitanti Angelum obversatur animo aliquando imago
flammae, aliquando puelli formosi alati, de qua certus mihi videor esse,
quod non habet similitudinem Angeli; neque ergo esse eam Angeli
180 ideam. Sed credens esse creaturas aliquas Deo ministrantes, invisi-
biles et immateriales, rei creditae vel suppositae nomen imponimus
Angelum, cum tamen idea, sub qua Angelum imaginor, sit composita
ex ideis rerum visibilium.

Eodem modo ad nomen venerandum Dei, nullam Dei habemus
imaginem, sive ideam; ideoque prohibemur Deum sub imagine adorare, ne illum, qui inconceptibilis est, videamur nobis concipere.

Videtur ergo nullam esse in nobis Dei ideam. Sed sicut caecus
natus, saepius igni admotus, et sentiens se calere, agnoscit esse aliquid, a quo calefactus est, audiensque illud appelari ignem, concludit
ignem existere, nec tamen qualis figurae aut coloris ignis sit cognoscit,
vel ullam omnino ignis ideam, vel imaginem animo obversantem
habet; itaque homo cognoscens debere esse causam aliquam suarum
imaginum vel idearum, et causae illius aliam causam priorem, et sic
continuo, deducitur tandem ad finem, sive suppositionem alicujus
causae aeternae, quae, quia nunquam coepit esse, causam se habere
priorem non potest; necessario aliquid aeternum existere concludit.
Nec tamen ideam ullam habet, quam possit dicere esse ideam aeterni
illius, sed rem creditam vel agnitam nominat, sive appellat Deum.

Jam quoniam ex positione hac, quod habeamus ideam Dei in anima
nostra, procedit D. C. ad probationem hujus Theorematis, quod Deus
(id est summe potens, sapiens, mundi creator) existat, oportuit illam
ideam Dei melius explicare, et non modo inde deducere ipsius existentiam, sed etiam mundi creationem.   [*Objectiones Tertiae*]

181 Hic nomine ideae vult tantum intelligi imagines rerum materialium in phantasia corporea depictas, quod posito facile illi

[THE IDEA OF GOD]

When I think of a man, I am aware of an idea or image made up of a certain shape and colour; and I can doubt whether this image is the likeness of a man or not. And the same applies when I think of the sky. When I think of a chimera, I am aware of an idea or an image; and I can be in doubt as to whether it is the likeness of a non-existent animal which is capable of existing, or one which may or may not have existed at some previous time.

But when I think of an angel, what comes to mind is an image, now of a flame, now of a beautiful child with wings; I feel sure that this image has no likeness to an angel, and hence that it is not the idea of an angel. But I believe that there are invisible and immaterial creatures who serve God; 180 and we give the name 'angel' to this thing which we believe in, or suppose to exist. But the idea by means of which I imagine an angel is composed of the ideas of visible things.

In the same way we have no idea or image corresponding to the sacred name of God. And this is why we are forbidden to worship God in the form of an image; for otherwise we might think that we were conceiving of him who is incapable of being conceived.

It seems, then, that there is no idea of God in us. A man born blind, who has often approached fire and felt hot, recognizes that there is something which makes him hot; and when he hears that this is called 'fire' he concludes that fire exists. But he does not know what shape or colour fire has, and has absolutely no idea or image of fire that comes before his mind. The same applies to a man who recognizes that there must be some cause of his images or ideas, and that this cause must have a prior cause, and so on; he is finally led to the supposition of some eternal cause which never began to exist and hence cannot have a cause prior to itself, and he concludes that something eternal must necessarily exist. But he has no idea which he can say is the idea of that eternal being; he merely gives the name or label 'God' to the thing that he believes in, or acknowledges to exist.

Now from the premiss that we have an idea of God in our soul, M. Descartes proceeds to prove the theorem that God (that is, the supremely wise and powerful creator of the world) exists. But he ought to have given a better explanation of this 'idea' of God, and he should have gone on to deduce not only the existence of God but also the creation of the world.

[*Third Objections*: CSM II 126–7]

Here my critic wants the term 'idea' to be taken to refer simply to the 181 images of material things which are depicted in the corporeal imagination;

est probare, nullam Angeli nec Dei propriam ideam esse posse. Atqui ego passim ubique, ac praecipue hoc ipso in loco, ostendo me nomen ideae sumere pro omni eo quod immediate a mente percipitur, adeo ut, cum volo et timeo, quia simul percipio me velle et timere, ipsa volitio et timor inter ideas a me numerentur. Ususque sum hoc nomine, quia jam tritum erat a Philosophis ad formas perceptionum mentis divinae significandas, quamvis nullam in Deo phantasiam agnoscamus; et nullum aptius habebam. Satis autem puto me explicuisse ideam Dei pro iis quae ad meum sensum volunt attendere; sed pro iis qui mea verba malunt aliter quam ego intelligere, nunquam possem satis. Quod denique hic additur de mundi creatione, plane est a quaestione alienum. [*Tertiae Responsiones*]

*   *   *

(286) Dicis esse in idea Dei infiniti plus realitatis objectivae, quam in idea rei finitae. Sed primo, cum humanus intellectus non sit concipiendae infinitatis capax, ideo neque habet neque respicit ideam infinitae rei repraesentatricem. Quare et qui infinitum quid dicit, attribuit rei, quam non capit, nomen quod non intelligit; quoniam, ut res extenditur ultra omnem illius captum, ita finis negatio extensioni illi attributa, ab eo non intelligitur, cujus intelligentia fine aliquo semper coercetur. [*Objectiones Quintae*]

Cum autem addis, eum qui infinitum quid dicit, attribuere *rei, quam*
365 *non capit, nomen quod non intelligit,* non distinguis intellectionem modulo ingenii nostri conformem, qualem de infinito nos habere unusquisque apud se satis experitur, a conceptu rerum adaequato, qualem nemo habet, non modo de infinito, sed nec forte etiam de ulla alia re quantumvis parva. Nec verum est intelligi infinitum per finis sive limitationis negationem, cum e contra omnis limitatio negationem infiniti contineat. [*Quintae Responsiones*]

*   *   *

and if this is granted, it is easy for him to prove that there can be no proper idea of an angel or of God. But I make it quite clear in several places throughout the book, and in this passage in particular, that I am taking the word 'idea' to refer to whatever is immediately perceived by the mind. For example, when I want something, or am afraid of something, I simultaneously perceive that I want, or am afraid; and this is why I count volition and fear among my ideas. I used the word 'idea' because it was the standard philosophical term used to refer to the forms of perception belonging to the divine mind, even though we recognize that God does not possess any corporeal imagination. And besides, there was not any more appropriate term at my disposal. I think I did give a full enough explanation to the idea of God to satisfy those who are prepared to attend to my meaning; I cannot possibly satisfy those who prefer to attribute a different sense to my words than the one I intended. As for the comment at the end regarding the creation of the world, this is quite irrelevant.

[*Third Replies*: CSM II 127–8]

*   *   *

You claim that there is in the idea of an infinite God more objective reality (286) than in the idea of a finite thing[1] But first of all, the human intellect is not capable of conceiving of infinity, and hence it neither has nor can contemplate any idea representing an infinite thing. Hence if someone calls something 'infinite' he attributes to a thing which he does not grasp a label which he does not understand. For just as the thing extends beyond any grasp of it he can have, so the negation of a limit which he attributes to its extension is not understood by him, since his intelligence is always confined within some limit. [*Fifth Objections*: CSM II 200]

You say: 'If someone calls something "infinite", he attributes to a thing which he does not grasp a label which he does not understand.' Here 365 you fail to distinguish between, on the one hand, an understanding which is suited to the scale of our intellect (and each of us knows by his own experience quite well that he has this sort of understanding of the infinite) and, on the other hand, a fully adequate conception of things (and no one has this sort of conception either of the infinite or of anything else, however small it may be). Moreover, it is false that the infinite is understood through the negation of a boundary or limit; on the contrary, all limitation implies a negation of the infinite. [*Fifth Replies*: CSM II 252]

*   *   *

[1] Above, p. 57.

[E]x idea summi entis, quam a te minime produci posse contendis, audes concludere necessitatem existentiae summi entis, a quo solo possit esse illa idea, quae tuae menti obversatur. At vero in nobis ipsis sufficiens reperimus fundamentum, cui solum innixi praedictam ideam formare possumus, licet ens summum non existeret, aut illud existere nesciremus et nequidem de eo existente cogitaremus. Nunquid enim video me cogitantem gradum aliquem habere perfectionis? Igitur et aliquos praeter me habere similem gradum, unde fundamentum habeo cujuslibet numeri cogitandi, atque adeo gradum perfectionis alteri et alteri gradui superextrudendum usque in infinitum. Quemadmodum etiam, si unicus gradus lucis aut caloris existeret, novos semper gradus in infinitum usque fingere et addere possum: cur, simili ratione, alicui gradui entis, quem in me percipio, non possim addere quemlibet alium gradum, et ex omnibus addi possibilibus ideam entis perfecti formare? Sed, inquis, effectus nullum gradum perfectionis seu realitatis potest habere, qui non praecesserit in causa. Verum (praeterquam quod videmus muscas, et alia animalia, vel etiam plantas, produci a sole, pluvia, et terra, in quibus non est vita, quae nobilior est quolibet gradu mere corporeo, unde fit ut effectus aliquam realitatem habet a causa, quae tamen non sit in causa)

124 illa idea nil est aliud quam ens rationis, quod mente tua cogitante non est nobilius. Praeterea nisi doctos inter nutritus esses, sed solus in deserto quopiam tota vita degisses, unde scis tibi illam ideam adfuturam? quam ex praeconceptis animi meditationibus, libris, mutuis amicorum sermonibus etc., non a sola tua mente aut a summo ente existente, hausisti. Itaque clarius probandum est, istam ideam tibi adesse non posse, si non existat summum ens; quod ubi praestiteris, manus omnes damus. Quod autem illa idea veniat ab anticipatis notionibus, inde constare videtur, quod Canadenses, Hurones, et reliqui sylvestres homines, nullam prae se ferant hujuscemodi ideam; quam etiam efformare possis ex praevia rerum corporalium inspectione, adeo ut nil idea tua praeter mundum hunc corporeum referat, qui perfectionem omnimodam a te cogitabilem complectatur; ut nondum quidpiam concludas

[F]rom the idea of a supreme being, which you maintain is quite incapable of originating from you, you venture to infer that there must necessarily exist a supreme being who alone can be the origin of this idea which appears in your mind.[1] However, we can find simply within ourselves a sufficient basis for our ability to form the said idea, even supposing that the supreme being did not exist, or that we did not know that he exists and never thought about his existing. For surely I can see that, in so far as I think, I have some degree of perfection, and hence that others besides myself have a similar degree of perfection. And this gives me the basis for thinking of an indefinite number of degrees and thus positing higher and higher degrees of perfection up to infinity. Even if there were just one degree of heat or light, I could always imagine further degrees and continue the process of addition up to infinity. In the same way, I can surely take a given degree of being, which I perceive within myself, and add on a further degree, and thus construct the idea of a perfect being from all the degrees which are capable of being added on. You say, however, that an effect cannot possess any degree of reality or perfection that was not previously present in the cause. But we see that flies and other animals, and also plants, are produced from sun and rain and earth, which lack life. Now life is something nobler than any merely corporeal grade of being; and hence it does happen that an effect may derive from its cause some reality which is nevertheless not present in the cause. But leaving this aside, the idea of a perfect being is 124 nothing more than entity of reason, which has no more nobility than your own mind which is thinking. Moreover, if you had not grown up among educated people, but had spent your entire life alone in some deserted spot, how do you know that the idea would have come to you? You derived this idea from earlier preconceptions, or from books or from discussion with friends and so on, and not simply from your mind or from an existing supreme being. So a clearer proof needs to be provided that this idea could not be present within you if a supreme being did not exist, and when you have provided it, we shall all surrender. However, the fact that the natives of Canada, the Hurons and other primitive peoples, have no awareness of any idea of this sort seems to establish that the idea does come from previously held notions. It is even possible for you to form the idea from a previous examination of corporeal things, so that your idea would refer to nothing but this corporeal world, which includes every kind of perfection that can be thought of by you. In that case you could not infer the existence of

---

[1] Cf. above, p. 63.

praeter Ens corporeum perfectissimam, nisi quidpiam aliud addas
quod ad incorporeum seu spirituale nos evehat. Vis addamus te angeli
posse (quemadmodum et entis perfectissimi) formare ideam; sed illa
idea non efficietur in te ab angelo, quo tamen es imperfectior. Sed nec
ideam habes Dei, quemadmodum nec numeri infiniti, aut infinitae
lineae; quam si possis habere, est tamen numerus ille impossibilis.
Adde ideam illam unitatis et simplicitatis unius perfectionis, quae
omnes alias complectatur, fieri tantummodo ab operatione intellectus ratiocinantis, eo modo quo sunt unitates universales, quae non
sunt in re, sed tantum in intellectu, ut constat ex unitate generica,
transcendentali, etc.   [*Objectiones Secundae*]

[C]um dicitis in nobis ipsis sufficiens reperiri fundamentum ad ideam
Dei formandam, nihil a mea opinione diversum affertis. Ipse enim
expresse dixi, ad finem tertiae Meditationis, *hanc ideam mihi esse*
innatam, sive non aliunde quam a meipso mihi advenire. Concedo
etiam ipsam posse formari, *licet ens summum existere nesciremus*, sed
non *si revera non existeret*; nam contra monui omnem vim argumenti
in eo esse, quod fieri non posset ut facultas ideam istam formandi in
me sit, nisi a Deo sim creatus.

134   Nec urget id quod dicitis de muscis, plantis etc., ut probetis
aliquem gradum perfectionis esse posse in effectu, qui non prae-
cessit in causa. Certum enim est, vel nullam esse perfectionem in
animalibus ratione carentibus, quae non etiam sit in corporibus non
animatis; vel, si quae sit, illam ipsis aliunde advenire, nec solem, et
pluviam, et terram esse ipsorum causas adaequatas. Essetque a ratione
valde alienum, si quis, ex eo solo quod non agnoscat causam ullam,
quae ad generationem muscae concurrat habeatque tot gradus perfectionis quod habet musca, cum interim non sit certus nullam esse
praeter illas quas agnoscit, occasionem inde sumeret dubitandi de
re, quae, ut paulo post fusius dicam, ipso naturali lumine manifesta
est.
    Quibus addo istud de muscis, cum a rerum materialium con-
sideratione sit desumptum, non posse venire in mentem iis qui,

anything beyond an utterly perfect corporeal being, unless you were to add something further which lifts us up to an incorporeal or spiritual plane. We may add that you can form the idea of an angel just as you can form the idea of a supremely perfect being; but this idea is not produced in you by an angel, although the angel is more perfect than you. But in fact you do not have the idea of God, just as you do not have the idea of an infinite number or an infinite line (even if you may have the idea, the number is still impossible). Moreover, the idea of the unity and simplicity of one perfection that includes all others arises merely from an operation of the reasoning intellect, in the same way as those universal unities which do not exist in reality but merely in the intellect (as can be seen in the case of generic unity, transcendental unity, and so on).

[*Second Objections*: CSM II 88–9]

When you say that we can find simply within ourselves a sufficient basis for forming the idea of God, your claim in no way differs from my own view. I expressly said at the end of the Third Meditation that 'this idea is innate in me'[1] – in other words, that it comes to me from no other source than myself. I concede also that 'we could form this idea even supposing that we did not know that the supreme being exists'; but I do not agree that we could form the idea 'even supposing that the supreme being did not exist'. On the contrary, I pointed out that the whole force of the argument lies in the fact that it would be impossible for me to have the power of forming this idea unless I were created by God.

Your remarks about flies, plants etc. do not go to show that there can 134 be a degree of perfection in the effect which was not previously present in the cause. For, since animals lack reason, it is certain that they have no perfection which is not also present in inanimate bodies; or, if they do have any such perfections, it is certain that they derive them from some other source, and that the sun, the rain and the earth are not adequate causes of animals. Suppose someone does not discern any cause cooperating in the production of a fly which possesses all the degrees of perfection possessed by the fly; suppose further that he is not sure whether there is any additional cause beyond those which he does discern: it would be quite irrational for him to take this as a basis for doubting something which, as I shall shortly explain at length, is manifest by the very light of nature.

I would add that the claim regarding flies is based on a consideration of material things, and so it could not occur to those who follow my

---

[1] Above, p. 71.

Meditationes meas sequuti, cogitationem a rebus sensibilibus avo-
cabunt, ut ordine philosophentur.

Non magis urget, quod ideam Dei, quae in nobis est, *ens rationis*
appelletis. Neque enim hoc eo sensu verum est, quo per *ens rationis*
intelligitur id quod non est, sed eo tantum quo omnis operatio intellectus ens rationis, hoc est ens a ratione profectum; atque etiam totus hic
mundus ens rationis divinae, hoc est ens per simplicem actum mentis
divinae creatum, dici potest. Jamque satis variis in locis inculcavi, me
agere tantum de perfectione sive realitate ideae objectiva, quae, non
minus quam artificium objectivum quod est in idea machinae alicujus
135 valde ingeniose excogitatae, causam exigit, in qua revera contineatur
illud omne quod in ipsa continetur objective.

Nec sane video quid addi possit, ut clarius appareat ideam istam
mihi adesse non posse, nisi existat summum ens, praeterquam ex parte
lectoris, ita scilicet ut, ad ea quae jam scripsi diligentius attendendo,
liberet se praejudiciis, quibus forte lumen ejus naturale obruitur, et
primis notionibus, quibus nihil evidentius aut verius esse potest, potius
quam opinionibus obscuris et falsis, sed longo usu menti infixis,
credere assuescat.

Quod enim nihil sit in effectu, quod non vel simili vel eminentiori
aliquo modo praeextiterit in causa, prima notio est, qua nulla clarior
habetur; haecque vulgaris *a nihilo nihil fit*, ab eo non differt; quia si
concedatur aliquid esse in effectu, quod non fuerit in causa, conce-
dendum etiam est hoc aliquid a nihilo factum esse; nec patet cur nihil
non possit esse rei causa, nisi ex eo quod in tali causa non esset idem
quod in effectu.

Prima enim notio est, omnem realitatem sive perfectionem, quae
tantum est objective in ideis, vel formaliter vel eminenter esse debere
in earum causis; et huic soli innixa est omnis opinio, quam de rerum
extra mentem nostram positarum existentia unquam habuimus: unde
enim suspicati fuimus illas existere, nisi ex eo solo quod ipsarum ideae
per sensus ad mentem nostram pervenirent?

Meditations and direct their thought away from the things which are perceivable by the senses with the aim of philosophizing in an orderly manner.

As for your calling the idea of God which is in us an 'entity of reason', this is not a compelling objection. If by 'entity of reason' is meant something which does not exist, it is not true that the idea of God is an entity of reason in this sense. It is true only in the sense in which every operation of the intellect is an entity of reason, that is, an entity which has its origin in rational thought; and indeed this entire universe can be said to be an entity originating in God's reason, that is, an entity created by a simple act of the divine mind. Moreover I have already insisted in various places that I am dealing merely with the objective perfection or reality of an idea; and this, no less than the objective intricacy in the idea of a machine of very ingenious design, requires a cause which contains in reality whatever 135 is contained merely objectively in the idea.

I do not see what I can add to make it any clearer that the idea in question could not be present to my mind unless a supreme being existed. I can only say that it depends on the reader: if he attends carefully to what I have written he should be able to free himself from the preconceived opinions which may be eclipsing his natural light, and to accustom himself to believing in the primary notions, which are as evident and true as anything can be, in preference to opinions which are obscure and false, albeit fixed in the mind by long habit.

The fact that 'there is nothing in the effect which was not previously present in the cause, either in a similar or in a higher form' is a primary notion which is as clear as any that we have; it is just the same as the common notion 'Nothing comes from nothing.' For if we admit that there is something in the effect that was not previously present in the cause, we shall also have to admit that this something was produced by nothing. And the reason why nothing cannot be the cause of a thing is simply that such a cause would not contain the same features as are found in the effect.

It is also a primary notion that 'all the reality or perfection which is present in an idea merely objectively must be present in its cause either formally or eminently'.[1] This is the sole basis for all the beliefs we have ever had about the existence of things located outside our mind. For what could ever have led us to suspect that such things exist if not the simple fact that ideas of these things reach our mind by means of the senses?

---

[1] Cf. above, pp. 57–9.

Quod autem aliqua idea sit in nobis entis summe potentis et perfecti, ac etiam quod hujus ideae realitas objectiva nec formaliter, nec
eminenter in nobis reperitur, clarum fiet iis qui satis attendent, et diu
136 mecum meditabuntur. Neque enim id, quod ab alterius cogitatione
tantum pendet, possum ipsi oscitanti obtruere.

[*Secundae Responsiones*]

[Q]uid est esse objective in intellectu? Olim didici: est ipsum
actum intellectus per modum objecti terminare. Quod sane extrinseca denominatio est, et nihil rei. Sicut enim videri nihil aliud est
quam actum visionis in me tendere, ita cogitari, aut objective esse in
intellectu, est mentis cogitationem in se sistere et terminare; quod, re
immota immutataque, quin et non existente, fieri potest. Quid ergo
causam ejus inquiro, quod actu non est, quod nuda denominatio et
nihil est?

Et tamen, inquit magnum istud ingenium, quod haec idea realitatem objectivam hanc vel illam contineat potius quam aliam, hoc
profecto habere debet ab aliqua causa. Imo a nulla: realitas enim
objectiva pura denominatio est, actu non est. Causa autem realem
93 influxum donat et actualem; illam istud quod actu non est non recipit,
ac proinde actualem causae effluxum non patitur, neque requirit. Ergo
ideas habeo, causam earum non habeo, tantum abest ut me majorem
et infinitam.   [*Objectiones Primae*]

Scripsi autem: ideam esse ipsam rem cogitatam, quatenus est objective in intellectu; quae verba plane aliter quam a me dicantur, fin-
git a se intelligi, ut occasionem det illa clarius explicandi. Esse,
inquit, objective in intellectu, est ipsum actum intellectus per modum
objecti terminare, quod tantum extrinseca denominatio est, et nihil
rei, etc. Ubi advertendum, illum respicere ad rem ipsam tanquam
extra intellectum positam, ratione cujus est sane extrinseca denominatio quod sit objective in intellectu; me autem loqui de idea,
quae nunquam est extra intellectum, et ratione cujus esse objective

Those who give the matter their careful attention and spend time meditating with me will clearly see that there is within us an idea of a supremely powerful and perfect being, and also that the objective reality of this idea cannot be found in us, either formally or eminently. I cannot force this truth on my readers if they are lazy, since it depends solely on their exercising 136 their own powers of thought.   [*Second Replies*: CSM II 96–7]

[OBJECTIVE REALITY]

[W]hat is 'objective being in the intellect'? According to what I was taught, this is simply the determination of an act of the intellect by means of an object. And this is merely an extraneous label which adds nothing to the thing itself. Just as 'being seen' is nothing other than an act of vision attributable to myself, so 'being thought of', or having objective being in the intellect, is simply a thought of the mind which stops and terminates in the mind. And this can occur without any movement or change in the thing itself, and indeed without the thing in question existing at all. So why should I look for a cause of something which is not actual, and which is simply an empty label, a non-entity?

'Nevertheless', says our ingenious author, 'in order for a given idea to contain such and such objective reality it must surely derive it from some cause.'[1] On the contrary, this requires no cause; for objective reality is a pure label, not anything actual. A cause imparts some real and actual 93 influence; but what does not actually exist cannot take on anything, and so does not receive or require any actual causal influence. Hence, though I have ideas, there is no cause for these ideas, let alone some cause which is greater than I am, or which is infinite.   [*First Objections*: CSM II 66–7]

Now I wrote that an idea is the thing which is thought of in so far as it has objective being in the intellect. But to give me an opportunity of explaining these words more clearly the objector pretends to understand them in quite a different way from that in which I used them. 'Objective being in the intellect', he says, 'is simply the determination of an act of the intellect by means of an object, and this is merely an extraneous label which adds nothing to the thing itself.' Notice here that he is referring to the thing itself as if it were located outside the intellect, and in this sense 'objective being in the intellect' is certainly an extraneous label; but I was speaking of the idea, which is never outside the intellect, and in this sense

[1] Above, p. 59.

non aliud significat quam esse in intellectu eo modo quo objecta in illa esse solent. Ita, exempli gratia, si quis quaerat quid Soli accidat, ex eo quod sit objective in meo intellectu, optime respondetur nihil ei accidere nisi extrinsecam denominationem, quod nempe operationem intellectus per modum objecti terminet. Si autem de idea Solis quaeratur quid sit, et respondeatur illam esse rem cogitatam, quatenus est objective in intellectu, nemo intelliget illam esse ipsum solem quatenus in eo extrinseca ista denominatio est; neque ibi, *objective esse in intellectu*, significabit ejus operationem per modum objecti terminare, sed in intellectu eo modo esse quo solent ejus objecta, adeo ut idea solis sit sol ipse in intellectu existens, non quidem formaliter, 103 ut in caelo, sed objective, hoc est eo modo quo objecta in intellectu esse solent; qui sane essendi modus longe imperfectior est quam ille quo res extra intellectum existunt, sed non idcirco plane nihil est, ut jam ante scripsi. [*Primae Responsiones*]

Sed ulterius quaerere libet, an ego ipse, habens illam ideam, esse posse, si tale ens nullum existeret, nempe a quo idea entis me perfectioris procedat, ut immediate ante dicit. Nempe, inquit, a quo essem? A me scilicet, vel a parentibus, vel ab aliis, etc. Atqui, si a me essem, nec dubitarem, nec optarem, nec omnino quicquam mihi deesset; omnes enim perfectiones, quarum idea aliqua in me est, mihi dedissem, atque ita ipsemet Deus essem. Si vero ab alio sum, tandem ad illud deveniam quod a se est, et ita de illo, idem quod de me, est argumentum. Illa demum ipsa illa via est, quam et S. Thomas ingreditur, quam vocat viam a causalitate causae efficientis, eamque desumpsit ex Philosopho; nisi quod isti de causis idearum non sint soliciti. Et forte opus non erat;

'objective being' simply means being in the intellect in the way in which objects are normally there. For example, if anyone asks what happens to the sun through its being objectively in my intellect, the best answer is that nothing happens to it beyond the application of an extraneous label which does indeed 'determine an act of the intellect by means of an object'. But if the question is about what the *idea* of the sun is, and we answer that it is the thing which is thought of, in so far as it has objective being in the intellect, no one will take this to be the sun itself with this extraneous label applied to it. 'Objective being in the intellect' will not here mean 'the determination of an act of the intellect by means of an object', but will signify the object's being in the intellect in the way in which its objects are normally there. By this I mean that the idea of the sun is the sun itself existing in the intellect – not of course formally existing, as it does in the heavens, but objectively existing, i.e. in the way in which objects normally are in the intellect. Now this mode of being is of course much less perfect 103 than that possessed by things which exist outside the intellect; but, as I did explain, it is not therefore simply nothing.[1]   [*First Replies*: CSM II 74–5]

[GOD, AUTHOR OF MY EXISTENCE]

He goes on: 'I should like to go further and inquire whether I myself who have this idea could exist if no such being existed' (that is, as he says just before this, if there did not exist a being from whom my idea of a being more perfect than myself proceeds). He goes on: 'From whom, in that case, would I derive my existence? From myself, presumably, or from my parents or from others etc. Yet if I derived my existence from myself, then I should neither doubt nor want, nor lack anything at all; for I should have given myself all the perfections of which I have any idea, and thus I should myself be God.'[2] But if I derive my existence from some other, then if I trace the series back I will eventually come to a being which derives its existence from itself; and so the argument here becomes the same as the argument based on the supposition that I derive my existence from myself.[3] This is exactly the same approach as that taken by St Thomas: he called this way 'the way based on the causality of the efficient cause'.[4] He took the argument from Aristotle, although neither he nor Aristotle was bothered about the causes of ideas. And perhaps they had no need to be;

[1] Above, p. 59.   [2] Above, p. 67.   [3] Cf. above, p. 71.
[4] This is the second of Aquinas' 'Five Ways': *Summa Theologiae*, Pars 1, Quaestio 2, art. 3. Cf. Aristotle, *Physics* VIII 2651ff.; *Metaphysics* A 1072ff.

quidni enim stricte rectaque incedam? Cogito, ergo sum, imo ipsa mens et cogitatio sum. Illa autem mens et cogitatio aut a seipsa est, aut ab alio. Si hoc, istud porro a quo? Si a se est, ergo Deus est: quod enim a se est, omnia sibi ipsi facile dederit.

95   Rogo virum obsecroque, ut avidum Lectorem et forte minus intelligentem, se non celat. Accipitur enim *a se* duplici modo. Primo, positive, nempe a seipso ut a causa; atque ita, quod a se esset, sibique ipsi daret esse suum, si praevio delectu sibi daret quod vellet, haud dubie sibi omnia daret, atque adeo Deus esset. Secundo, accipitur *a se* negative, ut sit idem quod *seipso*, aut *non ab alio*; atque hoc modo, quantum memini, ab omnibus accipitur.

    Nunc vero, si aliquid a se est, id est non ab alio, quomodo probem istud omnia complecti et esse infinitum? Jam enim non audio, si dicas: si a se est, sibi facile omnia dedisset. Nec enim a se est ut a causa, nec sibi praevium fuit, ut ante deligeret quod esset postmodum.

[Objectiones Primae]

Hic vero vir nimis officiosus in locum invidiosum me adducit; confert enim meum argumentum cum alio quodam ex S. Thoma et Aristotele desumptum, ut ita veluti rationem exigat, cur, cum eandam quam illi viam essem ingressus, non tamen in omnibus eandem sim secutus; sed permittat, quaeso, de aliis me tacere, atque eorum tantum, quae ipse scripsi, reddere rationem.

    Primo itaque, non desumpsi meum argumentum ex eo quod viderem in sensibilibus esse ordinem sive successionem quandam causarum efficientium; tum quia Deum existere multo evidentius esse putavi, quam ullas res sensibiles; tum etiam quia per istam causarum successionem non videbar alio posse devenire, quam ad imperfectionem mei intellectus agnoscendam, quod nempe non possim comprehendere quomodo infinitae tales causae sibi mutuo ab aeterno ita successerint, ut nulla fuerit prima. Nam certe, ex eo quod istud non possim comprehendere, non sequitur aliquam primam esse debere, ut neque ex eo quod non possim

for can I not take a much shorter and more direct line of argument? 'I am thinking, therefore I exist; indeed, I am thought itself, I am a mind. But this mind and thought derives its existence either from itself, or from another. If the latter, then we continue to repeat the question – where does this other being derive its existence from? And if the former, if it derives its existence from itself, it is God. For what derives existence from itself will without difficulty have endowed itself with all things.'

I beg and beseech our author not to hide his meaning from a reader 95 who, though perhaps less intelligent, is eager to follow. The phrase 'from itself' has two senses. In the first, positive, sense, it means 'from itself as from a cause'. What derives existence from itself in this sense bestows its own existence on itself; so if by an act of premeditated choice it were to give itself what it desired, it would undoubtedly give itself all things, and so would be God. But in the second, negative, sense, 'from itself' simply means 'not from another'; and this, as far as I remember, is the way in which everyone takes the phrase.

But now, if something derives its existence from itself in the sense of 'not from another', how can we prove that this being embraces all things and is infinite? This time I shall not listen if you say 'If it derives its existence from itself it could easily have given itself all things.' For it does not derive existence from itself as a cause, nor did it exist prior to itself so that it could choose in advance what it should subsequently be.

[*First Objections*: CSM II 68–9]

At this point my critic has, through his excessive desire to be kind to me, put me in an unfortunate position. For in comparing my argument with one taken from St Thomas and Aristotle, he seems to be demanding an explanation for the fact that, after starting on the same road as they do, I have not kept to it in all respects. However, I hope he will allow me to avoid commenting on what others have said, and simply give an account of what I have written myself.

Firstly, then, I did not base my argument on the fact that I observed there to be an order or succession of efficient causes among the objects perceived by the senses. For one thing, I regarded the existence of God as much more evident than the existence of anything that can be perceived by the senses; and for another thing, I did not think that such a succession of causes could lead me anywhere except to a recognition of the imperfection of my intellect, since an infinite chain of such successive causes from eternity without any first cause is beyond my grasp. And my inability to grasp it certainly does not entail that there must be a first cause, any more than

etiam comprehendere infinitas divisiones in quantitate finita, sequitur aliquam dari ultimam, ita ut ulterius dividi non possit; sed tantum
107 sequitur intellectum meum, qui est finitus, non capere infinitum. Itaque malui uti pro fundamento meae rationis existentia meiipsius, quae a nulla causarum serie dependet, mihique tam nota est ut nihil notius esse possit; et de me non tam quaesivi a qua causa olim essem productus, quam a qua tempore praesenti conserver, ut ita me ab omni causarum successione liberarem.

Deinde non quaesivi quae sit causa mei, quatenus consto mente et corpore, sed praecise tantum quatenus sum res cogitans. Quod puto non parum ad rem pertinere: nam sic potui longe melius a praejudiciis me liberare, ad naturae lumen attendere, interrogare meipsum, ac pro certo affirmare nihil in me, cujus nullo modo sim conscius, esse posse; quod plane aliud est quam si, ex eo quod videam me a patre genitum esse, patrem etiam ab avo esse considerarem; et quia, in parentum parentes inquirendo, non possem progredi in infinitum, ideo ad finem quaerendi faciendum statuerem aliquam esse causam primam.

Praeterea non tantum quaesivi quae sit causa mei, quatenus sum res cogitans, sed maxime etiam et praecipue quatenus inter caeteras cogitationes ideam entis summe perfecti in me esse animadverto. Ex hoc enim uno tota vis demonstrationis meae dependet: primo, quia in illa idea continetur quid sit Deus, saltem quantum a me potest intelligi; et, juxta leges verae Logicae, de nulla unquam re quaeri debet
108 *an sit*, nisi prius *quid sit* intelligatur; secundo, quia illa ipsa est quae mihi dat occasionem examinandi an sim a me, vel ab alio, et defectus meos agnoscendi; ac postremo, illa est quae docet non modo aliquam esse mei causam, sed praeterea etiam in causa illa contineri omnes perfectiones, ac proinde illam Deum esse . . .
(109)   Etsi enim ii qui, non nisi ad propriam et strictam efficientis signi-ficationem attendentes, cogitant impossibile esse, ut aliquid sit causa efficiens sui ipsius, nullumque hic aliud causae genus efficienti ana-
110 logum locum habere animadvertunt, non soleant aliud intelligere,

my inability to grasp the infinite number of divisions in a finite quantity entails that there is an ultimate division beyond which any further division is impossible. All that follows is that my intellect, which is finite, does 107 not encompass the infinite. Hence I preferred to use my own existence as the basis of my argument, since it does not depend on any chain of causes and is better known to me than anything else could possibly be. And the question I asked concerning myself was not what was the cause that originally produced me, but what is the cause that preserves me at present. In this way I aimed to escape the whole issue of the succession of causes.

Next, in inquiring about what caused me, I was asking about myself, not in so far as I consist of mind and body, but only and precisely in so far as I am a thinking thing. This point is, I think, of considerable relevance. For such a procedure made it much easier for me to free myself from my preconceived opinions, to attend to the light of nature, to ask myself questions, and to affirm with certainty that there can be nothing within me of which I am not in some way aware. This is plainly a quite different approach from observing that my father begot me, inferring that my grandfather begot my father, and in view of the impossibility of going on *ad infinitum* in the search for parents of parents, bringing the inquiry to a close by deciding that there is a first cause.

Moreover, in inquiring about what caused me I was not simply asking about myself as a thinking thing; principally and most importantly I was asking about myself in so far as I observe, amongst my other thoughts, that there is within me the idea of a supremely perfect being. The whole force of my proof depends on this one fact. For, firstly, this idea contains the essence of God, at least in so far as I am capable of understanding it; and according to the laws of true logic, we must never ask about the existence of anything until we first understand its essence.[1] Secondly, it is this idea 108 which provides me with the opportunity of inquiring whether I derive my existence from myself, or from another, and of recognizing my defects. And, lastly, it is this same idea which shows me not just that I have a cause, but that this cause contains every perfection, and hence that it is God . . .

There are some who attend only to the literal and strict meaning of the (109) phrase 'efficient cause' and thus think it is impossible for anything to be the cause of itself. They do not see that there is any place for another kind of cause analogous to an efficient cause, and hence when they say that 110

---

[1] Literally: 'we must never ask *if* it is (*an est*) until we first understand *what* it is (*quid est*)'.

cum dicunt aliquid *a se* esse, quam quod nullam habeat causam,
si tamen iidem ipsi ad rem potius quam ad verba velint attendere,
facile advertent negativam verbi *a se* acceptionem a sola intellectus humani imperfectione procedere, nullumque in rebus habere
fundamentum: quandam vero aliam esse positivam, quae a rerum
veritate petita est, et de qua sola meum argumentum processit.
Nam si, exempli gratia, quis putet corpus aliquod a se esse, forte
non aliud intelligit quam nullam causam habere: neque hoc ob
positivam ullam rationem affirmat, sed negative tantum, quia nullum ejus causam agnoscit. Atqui hoc imperfectio quaedam in eo
est, ut facile experietur postea, si consideret partes temporis unas
ab aliis non pendere, nec proinde ex eo quod illud corpus supponatur ad hoc usque tempus a se fuisse, id est sine causa, hoc
sufficere ut etiam in posterum sit futurum, nisi aliqua potentia
in eo sit ipsum continuo veluti reproducens; tunc enim, videns
talem potentiam in idea corporis nullam reperiri, statim inde col-
liget istud a se non esse, sumetque hoc verbum *a se* positive. Simili modo, cum dicimus Deum a se esse, possumus quidem etiam
intelligere istud negative, ita scilicet ut tantum sensus sit, nullam esse ejus causam; sed, si prius de causa cur sit, sive cur esse
perseveret, inquisivimus, attendentesque ad immensam et incomprehensibilem potentiam quae in ejus idea continetur, tam exu-
perantem illam agnovimus, ut plane sit causa cur ille esse perseveret nec alia praeter ipsam esse possit, dicimus Deum a se esse,
non amplius negative, sed quammaxime positive. Quamvis enim
111 dicere non opus sit illum esse causam efficientem sui ipsius, ne
forte de verbis disputetur, quia tamen hoc, quod a se sit, sive
quod nullum a se diversam habeat causam, non a nihilo, sed a
reali ejus potentiae immensitate esse percipimus, nobis omnino
licet cogitare illum quodammodo idem praestare respectu sui ipsius
quod causa efficiens respectu sui effectus, ac proinde esse a seipso
positive; licetque etiam unicuique seipsum interrogare, an eodem
sensu sit a se; cumque nullam in se invenit potentiam, quae sufficiat ad ipsum vel per momentum temporis conservandum, merito concludit se esse ab alio, et quidem ab alio qui sit a se, quia

something derives its existence 'from itself' they normally mean simply that it has no cause. But if they would look at the facts rather than the words, they would readily observe that the negative sense of the phrase 'from itself' comes merely from the imperfection of the human intellect and has no basis in reality. But there is a positive sense of the phrase which is derived from the true nature of things, and it is this sense alone which is employed in my argument. For example, if we think that a given body derives its existence from itself, we may simply mean that it has no cause; but our claim here is not based on any positive reason, but merely arises in a negative way from our ignorance of any cause. Yet this is a kind of imperfection in us, as we will easily see if we consider the following. The separate divisions of time do not depend on each other; hence the fact that the body in question is supposed to have existed up till now 'from itself', that is, without a cause, is not sufficient to make it continue to exist in future, unless there is some power in it that as it were recreates it continuously. But when we see that no such power is to be found in the idea of a body, and immediately conclude that the body does not derive its existence from itself, we shall then be taking the phrase 'from itself' in the positive sense. Similarly, when we say that God derives his existence 'from himself', we can understand the phrase in the negative sense, in which case the meaning will simply be that he has no cause. But if we have previously inquired into the cause of God's existing or continuing to exist, and we attend to the immense and incomprehensible power that is contained within the idea of God, then we will have recognized that this power is so exceedingly great that it is plainly the cause of his continuing existence, and nothing but this can be the cause. And if we say as a result that God derives his existence from himself, we will not be using the phrase in its negative sense but in an absolutely positive sense. There is no need to say that God is the efficient cause of himself, for this might give rise to 111 a verbal dispute. But the fact that God derives his existence from himself, or has no cause apart from himself, depends not on nothing but on the real immensity of his power; hence, when we perceive this, we are quite entitled to think that in a sense he stands in the same relation to himself as an efficient cause does to its effect, and hence that he derives his existence from himself in the positive sense. And each one of us may ask himself whether he derives his existence from himself in this same sense. Since he will find no power within himself which suffices to preserve him even for one moment of time, he will be right to conclude that he derives his existence from another being, and indeed that this other being derives its existence from itself (there is no possibility of an infinite regress here, since

cum de tempore praesenti, non de praeterito vel futuro, quaestio sit, non potest hic procedi in infinitum; quinimo etiam hic addam, quod tamen ante non scripsi, nequidem ad secundam ullam causam devenire, sed omnino illam, in qua tantum potentiae est ut rem extra se positam conservet, tanto magis seipsam sua propria potentia conservare, atque adeo a se esse.   [*Primae Responsiones*]

the question concerns the present, not the past or the future). Indeed, I will now add something which I have not put down in writing before, namely that the cause we arrive at cannot merely be a secondary cause; for a cause which possesses such great power that it can preserve something situated outside itself must, *a fortiori*, preserve itself by its own power, and hence derive its existence from itself.   [*First Replies*: CSM II 77–8, 79–80]

Dicis: tametsi non valeas ab erroribus abstinere ex evidenti perceptione rerum, posse tamen ex instituto, quod firmiter tibi proponas nulli
313 rei assentire, quam evidenter non perceperis. Sed, utcumque possis ea
semper attentione esse, nonne semper est imperfectio, ea, quae dijudicare est opus, non percipere evidenter ac errandi periculo esse perpetuo
obnoxium?

Dicis: errorem inesse in ipsa operatione, quatenus a te procedit et privatio quaedam est, non in facultate quam a Deo accepisti, neque etiam
ab operatione, quatenus ab illo dependet. Sed, non sit error in facultate
a Deo accepta proxime, est tamen remote, quatenus cum ea imperfectione creata est, ut errare possit. Quare non est quidem, ut ais, quod conquerare de Deo, qui revera tibi nihil debuit, et tamen illa bona tribuit,
ob quae debes illi gratias agere; sed est semper quod admiremur, cur
perfectiora non dederit, si scivit quidem, si potuit, si livore ductus non
fuit.

Addis: neque esse cur conquerare, quod tecum concurrat ad errandi
actum: cum actus omnes sint veri et boni, quatenus a Deo dependent,
majorque quoddammodo perfectio in te sit, elicere illos posse, quam
non posse; et privatio, in qua sola falsitatis et culpae est ratio formalis,
concursu Dei nullo indigeat, quia neque sit res, neque ad eum relata.
Verum, cum sit illa subtilis distinctio, non tamen plane satisfacit. Siquidem non concurrat Deus ad privationem quae est in actu falsitasque et
error est, concurrit tamen ad actum; ad quem si non concurreret, privatio

[ON THE FOURTH MEDITATION]

[THE CAUSE OF ERROR]

You say that although you have no power to avoid error through having a clear perception of things, you can still avoid it by firmly resolving to adhere to the rule of not assenting to anything which you do not clearly perceive.[1] But although you can always keep this rule carefully in mind, is it not still an imperfection not to perceive clearly matters which you need to decide upon, and hence to be perpetually liable to the risk of error? 313

You say that error resides in the mental operation itself in so far as it proceeds from you and is a kind of privation, but not in the faculty God gave you, nor in its operation in so far as it depends on him.[2] But although the error does not immediately reside in the faculty God gave you, it does indirectly attach to it, since it was created with the kind of imperfection which makes error possible. Admittedly, as you say, you have no cause for complaint against God who, despite owing you nothing, bestowed on you the good gifts which you should thank him for. But there is still cause to wonder why he did not bestow more perfect gifts on you, given that he had the knowledge and the power and was not malevolent.

You go on to say that you have no cause to complain that God's concurrence is involved in your action when you go wrong. For in so far as these acts depend on God, they are all true and good; and your ability to perform them means that there is, in a sense, more perfection in you than would be the case if you lacked this ability. You continue: 'As for the privation involved – which is all that the essential definition of falsity and wrong consists in – this does not in any way require the concurrence of God, since it is not a thing and should not be referred to him.'[3] But although this is a subtle distinction it is not quite enough to resolve the problem. For even if God does not concur in the privation in which the falsity and error of the act consists, he nonetheless concurs in the act itself; and if he

---

[1] Cf. p. 87 above.   [2] Cf. p. 85 above.   [3] Above, p. 85.

185

non esset. Et aliunde ipse est Author potentiae quae fallitur aut errat, atque adeo, ut ita dicam, impotentis potentiae. Sicque defectus, qui est in actu, non tam ad illam, quae impotens est, quam ad Authorem, qui impotentiam fecit, nec potentem potentioremve, cum posset, voluit facere, videtur esse referendus. Certe, ut fabro non vertitur vitio, quod aperiendo scriniolo praegrandem clavim non elaboret, sed quod, pusillam fabricatus, formam aperiendo aut inhabilem aut difficilem tribuat: ita non est quidem culpa in Deo, quod facultatem judicatricem tribuens homuncioni, non tantam illi dederit, quantam rebus vel omnibus vel plurimis vel maximis suffecturam arbitraretur; sed permirum est, cur ad pauca illa, quae dijudicari ab homine voluit, imparem, implicitam incertamque tribuerit.

Requiris proinde quaenam sit in te falsitas vel erroris causa. Ac primum quidem hic non disputo, cur intellectum voces solam facultatem noscendi ideas, seu res ipsas simpliciter et absque ulla affirmatione aut negatione apprehendendi, voluntatem vero ac liberum arbitrium voces facultatem judicandi, cujus sit affirmare aut negare, assentiri aut dissentire. Propono solum: quare voluntas libertasve arbitrii limitibus nullis circumscribatur per te, circumscribatur intellectus? Sane etiam videntur hae duae facultates aeque late patere, et non intellectus saltem minus quam voluntas, cum in nullam rem voluntas feratur, quam intellectus non praeviderit.

Dixi non saltem minus; quippe videtur intellectus etiam latius quam voluntas patere. Siquidem non modo voluntas, sive arbitrium, judicium, et consequenter electio, prosequutio, fuga, de nulla re est, quam non apprehenderimus, seu cujus idea percepta et proposita ab intellectu non fuerit; sed etiam multa obscure intelligimus, de quibus nullum judicium, prosequutio, aut fuga est. Et facultas judicandi ita saepe est anceps, ut, paribus rationum momentis, nullisve existentibus, nullum sequatur judicium, cum intellectus interim apprehendat ea quae remanent injudicata.

Quod porro dicis: te posse semper majora majoraque intelligere, ac nominatim facultatem ipsam intellectus, cujus ideam etiam

did not concur in it, there would be no privation. In any case, he is the author of that power in you which is subject to deception and error; and hence he is the author of a power which is, so to speak, ineffective. Thus the defect in the act should not, it seems, be referred so much to the power 314 which is ineffective as to the author who made it ineffective and did not choose to make it effective, or more effective, though he was able to do so. It is certainly no fault in a workman if he does not trouble to make an enormous key to open a tiny box; but it is a fault if, in making the key small, he gives it a shape which makes it difficult or impossible to open the box. Similarly, God is admittedly not to be blamed for giving puny man a faculty of judging that is too small to cope with everything, or even with most things or the most important things; but this still leaves room to wonder why he gave man a faculty which is uncertain, confused and inadequate even for the few matters which he did want us to decide upon.

You next ask what is the cause of error or falsity in you.[1] First of all, I do not question your basis for saying the intellect is simply the faculty of being aware of ideas, or of apprehending things simply and without any affirmation or negation; nor do I dispute your calling the will or freedom of choice a faculty of judging whose function is to affirm or deny, to give or withhold assent. My only question concerns why, on your account, our will or freedom of choice is not restricted by any limits, whereas the intellect is restricted. In fact it seems that these two faculties have an equally broad scope; certainly the scope of the intellect is at the very least no narrower than that of the will, since the will never aims at anything which the intellect has not already perceived.

I said that the scope of the intellect was 'at the very least no narrower'; in fact its scope seems to be even wider than that of the will. For the will or choice or judgement, and hence our selection or pursuit or avoidance of something, never occurs unless we have previously apprehended that thing, or unless the idea of that thing has been previously perceived and set before us by the intellect. What is more, there are many things which we understand only obscurely, so that no judgement or pursuit or avoidance 315 occurs in respect of them. Also, the faculty of judgement is often undecided, and if there are reasons of equal weight on either side, or no reasons at all, no judgement follows; but the intellect still continues to apprehend the matters on which no judgement has been passed.

You say that you can always understand the possibility of your understanding more and more, including the intellectual faculty itself, of which

---

[1] Above, pp. 81–3.

infinitam formare valeas, hoc ipsum arguit intellectum non esse magis
limitatum quam voluntatem, quando sese extendere ad usque objectum infinitum potest. Quod vero agnoscis voluntatem tuam exaequari
voluntati divinae, non extensive quidem, sed formaliter, vide quorsum
idem non possit de intellectu quoque dici, ubi formalem intellectus
non secus atque voluntatis notionem definiveris. Sed, paucis, dic nobis,
ad quid se voluntas extendere possit, quod intellectum effugiat?

[*Objectiones Quintae*]

Vis ut hic paucis dicam ad quid se voluntas possit extendere, quod
intellectum effugiat. Nempe ad id omne in quo contingit nos errare. Ita
cum judicas mentem esse tenue quoddam corpus, intelligere quidem
potes, ipsam esse mentem, hoc est, rem cogitantem, itemque tenue
corpus esse rem extensam; unam autem et eandem esse rem quae
377 cogitet et quae sit extensa, profecto non intelligis, sed tantummodo
vis credere, quia jam antea credidisti, nec libenter de sententia decedis.
Ita cum pomum, quod forte venenatum est, judicas tibi in alimentum
convenire, intelligis quidem ejus odorem, colorem, et talia grata esse,
non autem ideo ipsum pomum tibi esse utile in alimentum; sed quia
ita vis, ita judicas. Atque sic fateor quidem nihil nos velle de quo
non aliquid aliquo modo intelligamus; sed nego nos aeque intelligere
ac velle; possumus enim de eadem re velle permulta, et perpauca
tantum cognoscere. Cum autem prave judicamus, non ideo prave
volumus, sed forte pravum quid; nec quidquam prave intelligimus,
sed tantum dicimur prave intelligere, quando judicamus nos aliquid
amplius intelligere quam revera intelligamus.

[*Quintae Responsiones*]

[S]crupulus oritur ex indifferentia judicii, seu libertatis, quam negas
ad arbitrii perfectionem attinere, sed ad solam imperfectionem,
adeo ut indifferentia tollatur, quoties mens clare perspicit quae

you can form an infinite idea. But this itself shows that the intellect is not any more limited than the will, since it can extend itself even to an infinite object. You say that you recognize your will to be equal to that of God – not, indeed, in respect of its extent, but essentially. But surely the same could be said of the intellect too, since you have defined the essential notion of the intellect in just the same way as you have defined that of the will. In short, will you please tell us if the will can extend to anything that escapes the intellect? [*Fifth Objections*: CSM II 217–19]

You here ask me to say briefly whether the will can extend to anything that escapes the intellect. The answer is that this occurs whenever we happen to go wrong. Thus when you judge that the mind is a kind of rarefied body, you can understand that the mind is itself, i.e. a thinking thing, and that a rarefied body is an extended thing; but the proposition that it is one and the same thing that thinks and is extended is one which you certainly do 377 not understand. You simply want to believe it, because you have believed it before and do not want to change your view. It is the same when you judge that an apple, which may in fact be poisoned, is nutritious: you understand that its smell, colour and so on are pleasant, but this does not mean that you understand that this particular apple will be beneficial to eat; you judge that it will because you want to believe it. So, while I do admit that when we direct our will towards something, we always have some sort of understanding of some aspect of it, I deny that our understanding and our will are of equal scope. In the case of any given object, there may be many things about it that we desire but very few things of which we have knowledge. And when we make a bad judgement, it is not that we exercise our will in a bad fashion, but that the object of our will happens to be bad. Again, we never understand anything in a bad fashion; when we are said to 'understand in a bad fashion', all that happens is that we judge that our understanding is more extensive than it in fact is.

[*Fifth Replies*: CSM II 259]

[THE INDIFFERENCE OF THE WILL]

[T]he difficulty arises in connection with the indifference that belongs to our judgement, or liberty. This indifference, you claim, does not belong to the perfection of the will but has to do merely with its imperfection; thus, according to you, indifference is removed whenever the mind clearly

credenda, vel facienda, vel omittenda sunt. Quibus positis, numquid
417 vides te Dei libertatem destruere, a qua tollis indifferentiam, dum
creat mundum hunc potius quam alium aut nullum condit? Cum
sit tamen de fide Deum ab aeterno fuisse indifferentem, ut con-
deret unum, vel innumeros, vel etiam nullum. Quis vero dubitat
Deum omnia, tam agenda quam omittenda, semper clarissimo intuitu perspexisse? Non igitur clarissima rerum visio atque perceptio
tollit arbitrii indifferentiam; quae, si non possit humanae libertati
convenire, neque divinae congruet, quandoquidem essentiae rerum
sunt, instar numerorum, indivisibiles et immutabiles. Quapropter non
minus includitur indifferentia in divini quam in humani arbitrii libertate.

[*Objectiones Sextae*]

Quantum ad arbitrii libertatem, longe alia ejus ratio est in Deo, quam
in nobis. Repugnat enim Dei voluntatem non fuisse ab aeterno indif-
432 ferentiam ad omnia quae facta sunt aut unquam fient, quia nullum bonum, vel verum, nullumve credendum, vel faciendum, vel
omittendum fingi potest, cujus idea in intellectu divino prius fuerit,
quam ejus voluntas se determinarit ad efficiendum ut id tale esset.
Neque hic loquor de prioritate temporis, sed ne quidem prius fuit
ordine, vel natura, vel ratione ratiocinata, ut vocant, ita scilicet ut
ista boni idea impulerit Deum ad unum potius quam aliud eligendum. Nempe, exempli causa, non ideo voluit mundum creare in
tempore, quia vidit melius sic fore, quam si creasset ab aeterno; nec
voluit tres angulos trianguli aequales esse duobus rectis, quia cognovit aliter fieri non posse etc. Sed contra, quia voluit mundum
creare in tempore, ideo sic melius est, quam si creatus fuisset ab
aeterno; et quia voluit tres angulos trianguli necessario aequales esse
duobus rectis, idcirco jam hoc verum est, et fieri aliter non potest;
atque ita de reliquis. Nec obstat quod dici possit, merita sancto-
rum esse causam cur vitam aeternam consequantur; neque enim
ita ejus sunt causa, ut Deum determinent ad aliquid volendum,
sed tantum sunt causa effectus, cujus Deus voluit ab aeterno ut
causa essent. Et ita summa indifferentia in Deo summum est ejus

perceives what it should believe or do or refrain from doing.[1] But do you
not see that by adopting this position you are destroying God's freedom,   417
since you are removing from his will the indifference as to whether he shall
create this world rather than another world or no world at all? Yet it is
an article of faith that God was from eternity indifferent as to whether
he should create one world, or innumerable worlds, or none at all. But
who doubts that God has always perceived with the clearest vision what he
should do or refrain from doing? Thus, a very clear vision and perception
of things does not remove indifference of choice; and if indifference cannot
be a proper part of human freedom, neither will it find a place in divine
freedom, since the essences of things are, like the essences of numbers,
indivisible and immutable. Therefore indifference is involved in God's
freedom of choice no less than it is in the case of human freedom of choice.

[*Sixth Objections*: CSM II 280–1]

As for the freedom of the will, the way in which it exists in God is quite
different from the way in which it exists in us. It is self-contradictory to
suppose that the will of God was not indifferent from eternity with respect
to everything which has happened or will ever happen; for it is impossible   432
to imagine that anything is thought of in the divine intellect as good or
true, or worthy of belief or action or omission, prior to the decision of the
divine will to make it so. I am not speaking here of temporal priority: I
mean that there is not even any priority of order, or nature, or of 'rationally
determined reason' as they call it, such that God's idea of the good impelled
him to choose one thing rather than another. For example, God did not
will the creation of the world in time because he saw that it would be better
this way than if he had created it from eternity; nor did he will that the
three angles of a triangle should be equal to two right angles because he
recognized that it could not be otherwise; and so on. On the contrary, it
is because he willed to create the world in time that it is better this way
than if he had created it from eternity; and it is because he willed that
the three angles of a triangle should necessarily equal two right angles that
this is true and cannot be otherwise; and so on in other cases. There is no
problem in the fact that the merit of the saints may be said to be the cause
of their obtaining eternal life; for it is not the cause of this reward in the
sense that it determines God to will anything, but is merely the cause of an
effect of which God willed from eternity that it should be the cause. Thus
the supreme indifference to be found in God is the supreme indication

---

[1] Above, p. 81.

omnipotentiae argumentum. Sed quantum ad hominem, cum naturam omnis boni et veri jam a Deo determinatam inveniat, nec in aliud ejus voluntas ferri possit, evidens est ipsum eo libentius, ac proinde etiam liberius, bonum et verum amplecti, quo illud clarius videt, nunquamque esse indifferentem, nisi quando quidnam sit melius aut

433 verius ignorat, vel certe quando tam perspicue non videt, quin de eo possit dubitare. Atque ita longe alia indifferentia humanae libertati convenit quam divinae. Neque hic refert quod essentiae rerum dicantur esse indivisibiles: nam primo, nulla essentia potest univoce Deo et creaturae convenire; ac denique indifferentia non pertinet ad essentiam humanae libertatis, cum non modo simus liberi, quando ignorantia recti nos reddit indifferentes, sed maxime quando clara perceptio ad aliquid prosequendum impellit.

[*Sextae Responsiones*]

of his omnipotence. But as for man, since he finds that the nature of all goodness and truth is already determined by God, and his will cannot tend towards anything else, it is evident that he will embrace what is good and true all the more willingly, and hence more freely, in proportion as he sees it more clearly. He is never indifferent except when he does not know which of the two alternatives is the better or truer, or at least when he does 433 not see this clearly enough to rule out any possibility of doubt. Hence the indifference which belongs to human freedom is very different from that which belongs to divine freedom. The fact that the essences of things are said to be indivisible is not relevant here. For, firstly, no essence can belong univocally to both God and his creatures; and, secondly, indifference does not belong to the essence of human freedom, since not only are we free when ignorance of what is right makes us indifferent, but we are also free – indeed at our freest – when a clear perception impels us to pursue some object.   [*Sixth Replies*: CSM II 291–2]

Aggrederis consequenter demonstrare Dei existentiam, visque argumenti est in illis verbis:

attendenti fit manifestum, non magis posse existentiam ab essentia Dei separari, quam ab essentia trianguli magnitudinem trium ejus angulorum aequalium duobus rectis, sive ab idea montis ideam vallis: adeo ut non magis repugnet cogitare Deum (hoc est ens summe perfectum) cui desit existentia (hoc est, cui desit aliqua perfectio), quam cogitare montem cui desit vallis.

Etenim vero attendendum est, videri tuam hujusmodi comparationem non satis justam.

Nam rite quidem comparas essentiam cum essentia; verum non comparas deinde aut existentiam cum existentia, aut proprietatem cum proprietate, sed existentiam cum proprietate. Hinc vel dicendum fuisse videtur, non posse magis separari omnipotentiam ... a Dei essentia, quam ab essentia trianguli illam magnitudinis angulorum aequalitatem; vel certe, non posse magis separari Dei existentiam ab ejus essentia, quam ab essentia trianguli ejus existentiam. Sic enim bene processisset utravis comparatio, et non modo prior fuisset concessa, verum etiam posterior, quanquam non proterea evicisses Deum necessario existere, quia neque triangulus necessario existit, tametsi illius essentia existentiaque separari reipsa non valeant, quantumcumque mente separentur sive seorsim cogitentur, ut cogitari etiam essentia existentiaque divina possunt.

You next attempt to demonstrate the existence of God, and the thrust of your argument is contained in the following passage:

> When I concentrate, it is quite evident that existence can no more be separated from the essence of God than the fact that its three angles equal two right angles can be separated from the essence of a triangle, or than the idea of a mountain can be separated from the idea of a valley. Hence it is just as much of a contradiction to think of God (that is, a supremely perfect being) lacking existence (that is, lacking a perfection) as it is to think of a mountain without a valley.[1]

But we must note here that the kind of comparison you make is not wholly fair.

It is quite all right for you to compare essence with essence, but instead of going on to compare existence with existence or a property with a property, you compare existence with a property. It seems that you should have said that omnipotence, for example, can no more be separated from the essence 323 of God than the fact that its angles equal two right angles can be separated from the essence of a triangle. Or, at any rate, you should have said that the existence of God can no more be separated from his essence than the existence of a triangle can be separated from its essence. If you had done this, both your comparisons would have been satisfactory, and I would have granted you not only the first one but the second one as well. But you would not for all that have established that God necessarily exists, since a triangle does not necessarily exist either, even though its essence and existence cannot in actual fact be separated. Real separation is impossible no matter how much the mind may separate them or think of them apart from each other – as indeed it can even in the case of God's essence and existence.

[1] Above, p. 93.

Deinde attendendum est te collocare existentiam inter divinas perfectiones, et non collocare tamen inter perfectiones trianguli aut montis, cum perinde tamen, et suo cujusque modo, perfectio dici valeat.
Sed nimirum, neque in Deo, neque in ulla alia re existentia perfectio
est, sed id, sine quo non sunt perfectiones.

Siquidem id, quod non existit, neque perfectionem neque imperfectionem habet; et quod existit pluresque perfectiones habet, non habet
existentiam ut perfectionem singularem unamque ex eo numero, sed ut
illud, quo tam ipsum quam perfectiones existentes sunt, et sine quo nec
ipsum habere, nec perfectiones haberi dicuntur. Hinc neque existentia
perfectionum instar existere in re dicitur, neque, si res careat existentia,
tam imperfecta (sive privata perfectione) dicitur quam nulla.

Quamobrem, ut enumerando perfectiones trianguli non recenses
existentiam, neque proinde concludis existere triangulum: ita, enumerando perfectiones Dei, non debuisti in illis ponere existentiam, ut
concluderes Deum existere, nisi principium petere velles . . .

(324)   Dicis: liberum non esse cogitare Deum absque existentia, h.e.
ens summe perfectum absque summa perfectione, ut liberum est
equum cum alis vel sine alis imaginari. Sed nihil addendum, nisi
quod, ut liberum est cogitare equum non habentem alas, non cogitata existentia, quae si advenerit, perfectio, per te, in eo fuerit:
ita liberum est cogitare Deum habentem scientiam, potentiam et
325 perfectiones ceteras, non cogitata existentia, quam si habuerit, tum
consummatae sit perfectionis. Quare, ut ex eo quod equus, cogi-
tatus perfectionem alarum habens, non propterea colligitur habere
existentiam, perfectionum, per te, praecipuam: ita neque ex eo
quod Deus cogitatur habens scientiam perfectionesque ceteras, colligitur propterea ejus existentia, sed ea demum probanda est. Et
quamvis dicas: tam existentiam quam perfectiones caeteras in idea
entis summe perfecti comprehendi, id dicis, quod probandum est,
et conclusionem pro principio assumis. Nam etiam alioquin dicerem
in idea Pegasi perfecti contineri, non tantum perfectionem illam,
quod habeat alas, sed etiam illam, quod existat. Ut enim Deus
cogitatur perfectus in omni genere perfectionis, ita Pegasus cogitatur perfectus in suo genere; nihilque hic posse instari videtur,

Next we must note that you place existence among the divine perfections, but do not place it among the perfections of a triangle or mountain, though it could be said that in its own way it is just as much a perfection of each of these things. In fact, however, existence is not a perfection either in God or in anything else; it is that without which no perfections can be present.

For surely, what does not exist has no perfections or imperfections, and what does exist and has several perfections does not have existence as one of its individual perfections; rather, its existence is that in virtue of which both the thing itself and its perfections are existent, and that without which we cannot say that the thing possesses the perfections or that the perfections are possessed by it. Hence we do not say that existence 'exists in a thing' in the way perfections do; and if a thing lacks existence, we do not say it is imperfect, or deprived of a perfection, but say instead that it is nothing at all.

Thus, just as when you listed the perfections of the triangle you did not include existence or conclude that the triangle existed, so when you listed the perfections of God you should not have included existence among them so as to reach the conclusion that God exists, unless you wanted to beg the question . . .

You say that you are not free to think of God without existence (that is, (324) a supremely perfect being without a supreme perfection) as you are free to imagine a horse with or without wings. The only comment to be added to this is as follows. You are free to think of a horse not having wings without thinking of the existence which would, according to you, be a perfection in the horse if it were present; but, in the same way, you are free to think of God as having knowledge and power and other perfections without thinking of him as having the existence which would complete his 325 perfection, if he had it. Just as the horse which is thought of as having the perfection of wings is not therefore deemed to have the existence which is, according to you, a principal perfection, so the fact that God is thought of as having knowledge and other perfections does not therefore imply that he has existence. This remains to be proved. And although you say that both existence and all the other perfections are included in the idea of a supremely perfect being, here you simply assert what should be proved, and assume the conclusion as a premiss. Otherwise I could say that the idea of a perfect Pegasus contains not just the perfection of his having wings but also the perfection of existence. For just as God is thought of as perfect in every kind of perfection, so Pegasus is thought of as perfect in his own kind. It seems that there is no point that you can raise in this connection

quod, proportione servata, usurpari utrimque non valeat.

[Objectiones Quintae]

383 Hic non video cujus generis rerum velis esse existentiam, nec quare non aeque proprietas atque omnipotentia dici possit, sumendo scilicet nomen proprietatis pro quolibet attributo, sive pro omni eo quod de re potest praedicari, ut hic omnino sumi debet. Quin etiam existentia necessaria est revera in Deo proprietas strictissimo modo sumpta, quia illi soli competit, et in eo solo essentiae partem facit. Nec proinde existentia trianguli cum existentia Dei debet conferri, quia manifeste aliam habet relationem ad essentiam in Deo quam in triangulo.

Nec magis est petitio principii, quod existentia inter ea, quae ad essentiam Dei pertinent, numeretur, quam quod aequalitas trium angulorum cum duobus rectis inter trianguli proprietates recenseatur.

Nec verum est essentiam et existentiam in Deo, quemadmodum in triangulo, unam absque alia posse cogitari, quia Deus est suum esse, non autem triangulus. Nec tamen inficior quin existentia possibilis sit perfectio in idea trianguli, ut existentia necessaria est perfectio in idea Dei; efficit enim illam praestantiorem quam sint ideae illarum Chimaerarum, quarum existentia nulla esse posse supponitur. Nec proinde vel minimum ulla in re argumenti mei vires infregisti...

[Quintae Responsiones]

*   *   *

Itaque permittamus, aliquis claram distinctamque ideam habeat entis summi et perfectissimi; quid inde promoves ulterius? Nempe istud infinitum ens existere, idque ita certo ut in eodem ad minimum certitudinis gradu Dei existentia apud me esse debeat, in quo fuerunt hactenus mathematicae veritates: adeo ut non magis repugnat cogitare Deum (hoc est summe perfectum) cui desit existentia (hoc est aliqua perfectio), quam cogitare montem cui desit vallis. Ibi totius rei cardo est; qui nunc cedit, victum se fateatur oportet: mihi, quia cum

which, if we preserve the analogy, will not apply to Pegasus if it applies to God, and vice versa. [*Fifth Objections*: CSM II 224–6]

Here I do not see what sort of thing you want existence to be, nor why it cannot be said to be a property just like omnipotence – provided, of course, that we take the word 'property' to stand for any attribute, or for whatever can be predicated of a thing; and this is exactly how it should be taken in this context. Moreover, in the case of God necessary existence is in fact a property in the strictest sense of the term, since it applies to him alone and forms a part of his essence as it does of no other thing. Hence the existence of a triangle should not be compared with the existence of God, since the relation between existence and essence is manifestly quite different in the case of God from what it is in the case of the triangle.

To list existence among the properties which belong to the nature of God is no more 'begging the question' than listing among the properties of a triangle the fact that its angles are equal to two right angles.

Again, it is not true to say that in the case of God, just as in the case of a triangle, existence and essence can be thought of apart from one another; for God is his own existence, but this is not true of the triangle. I do not, however, deny that possible existence is a perfection in the idea of a triangle, just as necessary existence is a perfection in the idea of God; for this fact makes the idea of a triangle superior to the ideas of chimeras, which cannot possibly be supposed to have existence. Thus at no point have you weakened the force of my argument in the slightest...

[*Fifth Replies*: CSM II 262–3]

* * *

Let us then concede that someone does possess a clear and distinct idea of a supreme and utterly perfect being. What is the next step you will take from here? You will say that this infinite being exists, and that his existence is so certain that 'I ought to regard the existence of God as having at least the same level of certainty as I have hitherto attributed to the truths of mathematics. Hence it is just as much of a contradiction to think of God (that is, a supremely perfect being) lacking existence (that is, lacking a perfection), as it is to think of a mountain without a valley.'[1] This is the lynchpin of the whole structure; to give in on this point is to be obliged to admit defeat. But since I am taking on an opponent whose strength is

---

[1] Above p. 91.

98 fortiori ago, libet paululum velitari, ut, cum vincendus sim, nonnihil
tamen differam quod vitare non possum.

Ac in primis, etsi modo authoritate non agimus, sed ratione tantum,
tamen ne ex libidine maximo ingenio videar reluctari, ipsum potius
S. Thomam audite. Objicit sibi:

Intellecto quid significet hoc nomen *Deus*, statim habetur quod Deus est;
significatur enim hoc nomine id quo majus significari non potest. Majus
autem est quod est in re et in intellectu, quam quod est in intellectu tantum;
unde cum intellecto hoc nomine *Deus* statim sit in intellectu, sequitur etiam
quod sit in re.

Quod argumentum in forma ita reddo: Deus est quo majus significari non potest; sed illud, quo majus significari non potest, includit existentiam; ergo Deus ipso nomine vel conceptu suo includit
existentiam, ac proinde sine existentia nec concipi, nec esse potest.
Nunc, amabo vos, nunquid ipsum hoc argumentum est D. Carte-
sii? S. Thomas Deum ita definit: quo majus significari non potest.
D. C. vocat eum Ens summe perfectum; illo sane majus significari non potest. S. Thomas subsumit: id quo majus significari non
potest, includit existentiam; alioqui eo majus aliquid significari potest,
nempe id quod etiam existentiam significatur includere. At nunquid
D. C. idem subsumere videtur? Deus est ens summe perfectum, atqui
ens summe perfectum existentiam includit, alioqui summe perfectum non esset. Infert S. Thomas: ergo cum intellecto hoc nomine
Deus statim in ipso intellectu sit, sequitur etiam quod sit in re; hoc
est, eo ipso quod in ipso conceptu essentiali entis, quo majus significari non potest, involvatur existentia, sequitur illud ipsum ens
99 esse. Idem Dominus Cartesius infert: atqui, inquit, ex eo quod
non possum cogitare Deum nisi existentem, sequitur existentiam
ab eo esse inseparabilem, ac proinde illum revera existere. Nunc

greater than my own, I should like to have a preliminary skirmish with him, so that, although I am sure to be beaten in the end, I may at least put 98 off the inevitable for a while.

I know we are basing our argument on reason alone and not on appeals to authority. But to avoid giving the impression that I am wilfully taking issue with such an outstanding thinker as M. Descartes, let me nevertheless begin by asking you to listen to what St Thomas says. He raises the following objection to his own position:

> As soon as we understand the meaning of the word 'God', we immediately grasp that God exists. For the word 'God' means 'that than which nothing greater can be conceived'. Now that which exists in reality as well as in the intellect is greater than that which exists in the intellect alone. Hence, since God immediately exists in the intellect as soon as we have understood the word 'God', it follows that he also exists in reality.[1]

This argument may be set out formally as follows. 'God is that than which nothing greater can be conceived. But that than which nothing greater can be conceived includes existence. Hence God, in virtue of the very word or concept of "God", contains existence; and hence he cannot lack, or be conceived of as lacking, existence.' But now please tell me if this is not the selfsame argument as that produced by M. Descartes? St Thomas defines God as 'that than which nothing greater can be conceived'. M. Descartes calls him 'a supremely perfect being'; but of course nothing greater than this can be conceived. St Thomas's next step is to say 'that than which nothing greater can be conceived includes existence', for otherwise something greater could be conceived, namely a being conceived of as also including existence. Yet surely M. Descartes's next step is identical to this. God, he says, is a supremely perfect being; and a supremely perfect being includes existence, for otherwise it would not be a supremely perfect being. St Thomas's conclusion is that 'since God immediately exists in the intellect as soon as we have understood the word "God", it follows that he also exists in reality'. In other words, since the very concept or essence of 'a being than which nothing greater can be conceived' implies existence, it follows that this very being exists. M. Descartes's conclusion is the same: 'From the very fact that I cannot think of God except as existing it follows 99 that existence is inseparable from God and hence that he really exists.'[2] But

---

[1] *Summa theologiae*, P1, Q2, art. 1. Aquinas is in fact criticizing St Anselm's version of the ontological argument.
[2] Above, pp. 91–3.

vero S. Thomas et sibi et D. Cartesio respondeat: Dato, inquit,

quod quilibet intelligat hoc nomine *Deus* significari hoc quod dicitur, scilicet illud quo majus cogitari non potest, non tamen propter hoc sequitur quod intelligat, id quod significatur per nomen, esse in rerum natura, sed in apprehensione intellectus tantum. Nec potest argui quod sit in re, nisi daretur quod sit in re aliquid, quo majus cogitari non potest, quod non est datum a ponentibus Deum non esse.

Ex quo ego quoque breviter respondeo: etiamsi detur ens summe perfectum ipso nomine suo importare existentiam, tamen non sequitur ipsammet illam existentiam in rerum natura actu quid esse, sed tantum cum conceptu entis summi conceptum existentiae inseparabiliter esse conjunctum. Ex quo non inferas existentiam Dei actu quid esse, nisi supponas illud ens summum actu existere; tunc enim et omnes perfectiones, et hanc quoque realis existentiae, actu includet.

Ignoscite, Viri clarissimi, lassus sum; ludam paululum. Complexum hoc, *Leo existens*, utrumque includit, et quidem essentialiter, nempe leonem et modum existentiae; si enim alterutrum demas, idem hoc complexum non erit. Nunc autem, nunquid ab aeterno Deus hoc compositum clare distincteque cognovit? Et nunquid idea hujus compositi, ut compositum, utramque ejus partem essentialiter involvit? 100 Hoc est, nunquid existentia de essentia hujus compositi est, *Leo existens*? Et tamen distincta cognitio Dei, distincta, inquam, cognitio Dei ab aeterno non necessario urget alterutram partem hujus compositi esse, nisi supponas ipsum compositum esse: tunc enim essentiales suas perfectiones omnes, ac proinde etiam actualem existentiam involvet. Ita quoque, etiamsi distincte cognoscam ens summum, et licet ens summe perfectum in conceptu suo essentiali existentiam includat, non tamen sequitur existentiam modo actu quid esse, nisi supponas ens illud summum esse; tunc enim, ut omnes sui perfectiones, ita etiam hanc existentiam actu includet. Atque ita ens illud summe perfectum existere aliunde probandum erit.

[*Objectiones Primae*]

Confert hic rursus unum ex meis argumentis cum alio ex S. Thoma, ut me veluti cogat ostendere quae major vis in uno quam in altero

now let St Thomas reply both to himself and to M. Descartes. 'Let it be granted', he says,

that we all understand that the word 'God' means what it is claimed to mean, namely 'that than which nothing greater can be thought of'. However, it does not follow that we all understand that what is signified by this word exists in the real world. All that follows is that it exists in the apprehension of the intellect. Nor can it be shown that this being really exists unless it is conceded that there really is something such that nothing greater can be thought of; and this premiss is denied by those who maintain that God does not exist.

My own answer to M. Descartes, which is based on this passage, is briefly this. Even if it is granted that a supremely perfect being carries the implication of existence in virtue of its very title, it still does not follow that the existence in question is anything actual in the real world; all that follows is that the concept of existence is inseparably linked to the concept of a supreme being. So you cannot infer that the existence of God is anything actual unless you suppose that the supreme being actually exists; for then it will actually contain all perfections, including the perfection of real existence.

Pardon me, gentlemen: I am now rather tired and propose to have a little fun. The complex 'existing lion' includes both 'lion' and 'existence', and it includes them essentially, for if you take away either element it will not be the same complex. But now, has not God had clear and distinct knowledge of this composite from all eternity? And does not the idea of this composite, as a composite, involve both elements essentially? In other words, does not existence belong to the essence of the composite 'existing lion'? Nevertheless 100 the distinct knowledge of God, the distinct knowledge he has from eternity, does not compel either element in the composite to exist, unless we assume that the composite itself exists (in which case it will contain all its essential perfections including actual existence). Similarly even if I have distinct knowledge of a supreme being, and even if the supremely perfect being includes existence as an essential part of the concept, it still does not follow that the existence in question is anything actual, unless we suppose that the supreme being exists (for in that case it will include actual existence along with all its other perfections). Accordingly we must look elsewhere for a proof that the supremely perfect being exists.

[*First Objections*: CSM II 70–2]

The author of the objections here again compares one of my arguments with one of St Thomas's, thus as it were forcing me to explain how one

reperiatur. Atque hoc videor sine magna invidia facere posse, quia nec S. Thomas argumento illo usus est tanquam suo, nec idem concludit quod meum, nec denique ulla hic in re ab Angelico doctore dissentio. Quaeritur enim ab ipso, an Deum esse sit per se notum secundum nos, hoc est an unicuique sit obvium; quod negat, et merito. Argumentum autem, quod sibi objicit, ita potest proponi: Intellecto quid significet hoc nomen *Deus*, intelligitur id quo majus significari non potest; sed est majus esse in re, et in intellectu, quam esse in intellectu tantum; ergo intellecto quid significet hoc nomen *Deus*, intelligitur Deum esse in re et in intellectu. Ubi est manifestum vitium in forma; concludi enim tantum debuisset: ergo, intellecto quid significet hoc nomen *Deus*, intelligitur significari Deum esse in re et in intellectu; atqui quod verbo significatur, non ideo apparet esse verum. Meum autem argumentum fuit tale. Quod clare et distincte intelligimus pertinere ad alicujus rei veram et immutabilem naturam, sive essentiam, 116 sive formam, id potest de ea re cum veritate affirmari; sed postquam satis accurate investigavimus quid sit Deus, clare et distincte intelligimus ad ejus veram et immutabilem naturam pertinere ut existat; ergo tunc cum veritate possumus de Deo affirmare, quod existat. Ubi saltem conclusio recte procedit. Sed neque etiam major potest negari, quia jam ante concessum est illud omne quod clare et distincte intelligimus esse verum. Sola minor restat, in qua fateor esse difficultatem non parvam: primo, quia sumus tam assueti in reliquis omnibus existentiam ab essentia distinguere, ut non satis advertamus quo pacto ad essentiam Dei potius quam aliarum rerum pertineat; ac deinde, quia non distinguentes ea quae ad veram et immutabilem alicujus rei essentiam pertinent, ab iis quae non nisi per figmentum intellectus illi tribuuntur, etiamsi satis advertamus existentiam ad Dei essentiam pertinere, non tamen inde concludimus Deum existere, quia nescimus an ejus essentia sit immutabilis et vera, an tantum a nobis efficta.

Sed, ut prima hujus difficultatis pars tollatur, est distinguendum inter existentiam possibilem et necessariam, notandumque in eorum quidem omnium, quae clare et distincte intelliguntur,

argument can have any greater force than the other. I think I can do this without too much unpleasantness. For, first, St Thomas did not put forward the argument as his own; second, he did not arrive at the same conclusion as I do; and lastly, on this issue I do not differ from the Angelic Doctor in any respect. St Thomas asks whether the existence of God is self-evident as far as we are concerned, that is, whether it is obvious to everyone; and he answers, correctly, that it is not. The argument which he then puts forward as an objection to his own position can be stated as follows. 'Once we have understood the meaning of the word "God", we understand it to mean "that than which nothing greater can be conceived". But to exist in reality as well as in the intellect is greater than to exist in the intellect alone. Therefore, once we have understood the meaning of the word "God" we understand that God exists in reality as well as in the understanding.' In this form the argument is manifestly invalid, for the only conclusion that should have been drawn is: 'Therefore, once we have understood the meaning of the word "God", we understand that what is conveyed is that God exists in reality as well as in the understanding.' Yet because a word conveys something, that thing is not therefore shown to be true. My argument however was as follows: 'That which we clearly and distinctly understand to belong to the true and immutable nature, or essence, or form of something, can truly be asserted of that thing. But once 116 we have made a sufficiently careful investigation of what God is, we clearly and distinctly understand that existence belongs to his true and immutable nature. Hence we can now truly assert of God that he does exist.' Here at least the conclusion does follow from the premisses. But, what is more, the major premiss cannot be denied, because it has already been conceded that whatever we clearly and distinctly understand is true. Hence only the minor premiss remains, and here I confess that there is considerable difficulty. In the first place we are so accustomed to distinguishing existence from essence in the case of all other things that we fail to notice how closely existence belongs to essence in the case of God as compared with that of other things. Next, we do not distinguish what belongs to the true and immutable essence of a thing from what is attributed to it merely by a fiction of the intellect. So, even if we observe clearly enough that existence belongs to the essence of God, we do not draw the conclusion that God exists, because we do not know whether his essence is immutable and true, or merely invented by us.

But to remove the first part of the difficulty we must distinguish between possible and necessary existence. It must be noted that possible existence is contained in the concept or idea of everything that we clearly and

conceptu sive idea existentiam possibilem contineri, sed nullibi necessariam, nisi in sola idea Dei. Qui enim ad hanc diversitatem quae
est inter ideam Dei et reliquas omnes diligenter attendent, non dubito
117 quin sint percepturi, etiamsi caeteras quidem res nunquam intelligamus nisi tanquam existentes, non tamen inde sequi illas existere, sed
tantummodo posse existere, quia non intelligimus necesse esse ut actualis existentia cum aliis ipsarum proprietatibus conjuncta sit; ex hoc
autem quod intelligamus existentiam actualem necessario et semper
cum reliquis Dei attributis esse conjunctam, sequi omnino Deum
existere.

Deinde, ut altera pars difficultatis tollatur, advertendum est illas
ideas, quae non continent veras et immutabiles naturas, sed tantum fictitias et ab intellectu compositas, ab eodem intellectu non
per abstractionem tantum, sed per claram et distinctam operationem
dividi posse, adeo ut illa, quae intellectus sic dividere non potest,
procul dubio ab ipso non fuerint composita. Ut, exempli causa,
cum cogito equum alatum, vel leonem actu existentem, vel triangulum quadrato inscriptum, facile intelligo me etiam ex adverso
posse cogitare equum non alatum, leonem non existentem, triangulum sine quadrato, et talia, nec proinde illas veras et immutabiles
naturas habere. Si vero cogito triangulum, vel quadratum (de leone
aut equo hic non loquor, quia eorum naturae nobis non sint plane
perspicuae), tunc certe quaecunque in idea trianguli contineri dep-
rehendam, ut quod ejus tres anguli sunt aequales duobus rectis
etc., de triangulo cum veritate affirmabo, et de quadrato quaecunque in idea quadrati reperiam; etsi enim possim intelligere triangulum, abstrahendo ab eo quod ejus tres anguli sint aequales
118 duobus rectis, non possum tamen de eo id negare per claram et
distinctam operationem, hoc est recte intelligendo hoc quod dico.
Praeterea, si considerem triangulum quadrado inscriptum, non ut
ea quae pertinent ad solum triangulum quadrato tribuam, vel triangulo ea quae pertinent ad quadratum, sed ut ea tantum examinem quae ex utriusque conjunctione exurgunt, non minus vera et
immutabilis erit ejus natura, quam solius quadrati vel trianguli; atque
ideo affirmare licebit quadratum non esse minus duplo trianguli
illi inscripti, et similia, quae ad compositae hujus figurae naturam
pertinent.

distinctly understand; but in no case is necessary existence so contained, except in the case of the idea of God. Those who carefully attend to this difference between the idea of God and every other idea will undoubtedly perceive that even though our understanding of other things always involves 117 understanding them as if they were existing things, it does not follow that they do exist, but merely that they are capable of existing. For our understanding does not show us that it is necessary for actual existence to be conjoined with their other properties. But, from the fact that we understand that actual existence is necessarily and always conjoined with the other attributes of God, it certainly does follow that God exists.

To remove the second part of the difficulty, we must notice a point about ideas which do not contain true and immutable natures but merely ones which are invented and put together by the intellect. Such ideas can always be split up by the same intellect, not simply by an abstraction but by a clear and distinct intellectual operation, so that any ideas which the intellect cannot split up in this way were clearly not put together by the intellect. When, for example, I think of a winged horse or an actually existing lion, or a triangle inscribed in a square, I readily understand that I am also able to think of a horse without wings, or a lion which does not exist, or a triangle apart from a square, and so on; hence these things do not have true and immutable natures. But if I think of a triangle or a square (I will not now include the lion or the horse, since their natures are not transparently clear to us), then whatever I apprehend as being contained in the idea of a triangle – for example that its three angles are equal to two right angles – I can with truth assert of the triangle. And the same applies to the square with respect to whatever I apprehend as being contained in the idea of a square. For even if I can understand what a triangle is if I abstract the fact that its three angles are equal to two right angles, I cannot deny that this property applies to the triangle by a clear and distinct intellectual 118 operation – that is, while at the same time understanding what I mean by my denial. Moreover, if I consider a triangle inscribed in a square, with a view not to attributing to the square properties that belong only to the triangle, or attributing to the triangle properties that belong to the square, but with a view to examining only the properties which arise out of the conjunction of the two, then the nature of this composite will be just as true and immutable as the nature of the triangle alone or the square alone. And hence it will be quite in order to maintain that the square is not less than double the area of the triangle inscribed within it, and to affirm other similar properties that belong to the nature of this composite figure.

Si vero considerem in idea corporis summe perfecti contineri existentiam, quia nempe major perfectio est esse in re et in intellectu, quam tantum esse in intellectu, non inde possum concludere corpus illud summe perfectum existere, sed tantummodo posse existere; satis enim animadverto ideam istam ab ipsomet meo intellectu omnes corporeas perfectiones simul jungente fuisse conflatam; existentiamque ex aliis corporeis perfectionibus non exurgere, quia de illis aeque potest negari atque afirmari; quinimo ex eo quod, ideam corporis examinando, nullam in eo vim esse percipio, per quam seipsum producat sive conservet, recte concludo existentiam necessariam, de qua sola hic est quaestio, non magis ad naturam corporis, quantumvis summe perfecti, pertinere, quam ad naturam montis pertinet ut vallem non habeat, vel ad naturam trianguli ut angulos habeat majores duobus rectis. Nunc autem si quaeramus, non de corpore, sed de re, qualiscunque
119　tandem illa sit, quae habeat omnes eas perfectiones quae simul esse possunt, an existentia inter illas sit numeranda, prima quidem fronte dubitabimus; quia cum mens nostra quae finita est non soleat illas nisi separatas considerare, non statim fortasse advertet quam necessario inter se conjunctae sint. Atqui, si attente examinemus an enti summe potenti competat existentia, et qualis, poterimus clare et distincte percipere primo illi saltem competere possibilem existentiam, quemadmodum reliquis omnibus aliis rebus, quarum distincta idea in nobis est, etiam iis quae per figmentum intellectus componuntur. Deinde, quia cogitare non possumus ejus existentiam esse possibilem quin simul etiam, ad immensam ejus potentiam attendentes, agnoscamus illud propria sua via posse existere, hinc concludemus ipsum revera existere, atque ab aeterno extitisse; est enim lumine naturali notissimum, id, quod propria sua vi potest existere, semper existere. Atque ita intelligemus existentiam necessariam in idea entis summe potentis contineri, non per figmentum intellectus, sed quia pertinet ad veram et immutabilem naturam talis entis, ut existat: nec non etiam facile percipiemus illud ens summe potens non posse non habere in se omnes alias perfectiones quae in idea Dei continentur, adeo ut illae, absque ullo figmento intellectus et ex natura sua, simul junctae sint, atque in Deo existant.　　　　　　　[*Primae Responsiones*]

But if I were to think that the idea of a supremely perfect body contained existence, on the grounds that it is a greater perfection to exist both in reality and in the intellect than it is to exist in the intellect alone, I could not infer from this that the supremely perfect body exists, but only that it is capable of existing. For I can see quite well that this idea has been put together by my own intellect which has linked together all bodily perfections; and existence does not arise out of the other bodily perfections because it can equally well be affirmed or denied of them. Indeed, when I examine the idea of a body, I perceive that a body has no power to create itself or maintain itself in existence; and I rightly conclude that necessary existence – and it is only necessary existence that is at issue here – no more belongs to the nature of a body, however perfect, than it belongs to the nature of a mountain to be without a valley, or to the nature of a triangle to have angles whose sum is greater than two right angles. But instead of a body, let us now take a thing – whatever this thing turns out to be – which possesses all the perfections which can exist together. If we ask whether 119 existence should be included among these perfections, we will admittedly be in some doubt at first. For our mind, which is finite, normally thinks of these perfections only separately, and hence may not immediately notice the necessity of their being joined together. Yet if we attentively examine whether existence belongs to a supremely powerful being, and what sort of existence it is, we shall be able to perceive clearly and distinctly the following facts. First, possible existence, at the very least, belongs to such a being, just as it belongs to all the other things of which we have a distinct idea, even to those which are put together through a fiction of the intellect. Next, when we attend to the immense power of this being, we shall be unable to think of its existence as possible without also recognizing that it can exist by its own power; and we shall infer from this that this being does really exist and has existed from eternity, since it is quite evident by the natural light that what can exist by its own power always exists. So we shall come to understand that necessary existence is contained in the idea of a supremely powerful being, not by any fiction of the intellect, but because it belongs to the true and immutable nature of such a being that it exists. And we shall also easily perceive that this supremely powerful being cannot but possess within it all the other perfections that are contained in the idea of God; and hence these perfections exist in God and are joined together not by any fiction of the intellect but by their very nature.

[*First Replies*: CSM II 82–5]

125 [C]um nondum certus sis de illa Dei existentia, neque tamen te de ulla re certum esse, vel clare et distincte aliquid te cognoscere, posse dicas, nisi prius certo et clare Deum noveris existere, sequitur te nondum clare et distincte scire quod sis res cogitans, cum ex te illa cognitio pendeat a clara Dei existentis cognitione, quam nondum probasti locis illis, ubi concludis te clare nosse quod sis.

Adde Atheum clare et distincte cognoscere trianguli tres angulos aequales esse duobus rectis; quamvis tantum absit ut supponat existentiam Dei, quam plane negat, ex eo quod, si existeret, inquit, esset summum ens, summumque bonum, hoc est infinitum; at infinitum in omni genere perfectionis excludit quodlibet aliud, nempe quodlibet ens et bonum, imo et quodlibet non ens et malum, cum tamen plura, entia bona, non entia et mala, sint; cui objectioni te satisfacere debere judicamus, ne quid impiis supersit quod obtendant.

[*Objectiones Secundae*]

(140) [U]bi dixi nihil nos certo posse scire, nisi prius Deum existere cognoscamus, expressis verbis testatus sum me non loqui nisi de scientia earum conclusionum, quarum memoria potest recurrere, cum non amplius attendimus ad rationes ex quibus ipsas deduximus. Principiorum enim notitia non solet a dialecticis scientia appellari . . .

(141)   Quod autem Atheus possit clare cognoscere trianguli tres angulos aequales esse duobus rectis, non nego; sed tantum istam ejus cognitionem non esse veram scientiam affirmo, quia nulla cognitio, quae dubia reddi potest, videtur scientia appellanda; cumque ille supponatur esse atheus, non potest esse certus se non decipi in iis ipsis quae illi evidentissima videntur, ut satis ostensum est; et quamvis forte dubium istud ipsi non occurrat, potest tamen occurrere, si examinet,

[CLEAR AND DISTINCT PERCEPTION AND THE 'CARTESIAN CIRCLE']

[Y]ou are not yet certain of the existence of God, and you say that you are not certain of anything, and cannot know anything clearly and distinctly 125 until you have achieved clear and certain knowledge of the existence of God.[1] It follows from this that you do not yet clearly and distinctly know that you are a thinking thing, since, on your own admission, that knowledge depends on the clear knowledge of an existing God; and this you have not yet proved in the passage where you draw the conclusion that you clearly know what you are.

Moreover, an atheist is clearly and distinctly aware that the three angles of a triangle are equal to two right angles; but so far is he from supposing the existence of God that he completely denies it. According to the atheist, if God existed there would be a supreme being and a supreme good; that is to say, the infinite would exist. But the infinite in every category of perfection excludes everything else whatsoever – every kind of being and goodness, as well as every kind of non-being and evil. Yet in fact there are many kinds of being and goodness, and many kinds of non-being and evil. We think you should deal with this objection, so that the impious have no arguments left to put forward.

[*Second Objections*: CSM II 89]

[W]hen I said that we can know nothing for certain until we are aware that (140) God exists, I expressly declared that I was speaking only of knowledge of those conclusions which can be recalled when we are no longer attending to the arguments by means of which we deduced them.[2] Now awareness of first principles is not normally called 'knowledge' by dialecticians...

The fact that an atheist can be 'clearly aware that the three angles of a (141) triangle are equal to two right angles' is something I do not dispute. But I maintain that this awareness of his is not true knowledge, since no act of awareness that can be rendered doubtful seems fit to be called knowledge.[3] Now since we are supposing that this individual is an atheist, he cannot be certain that he is not being deceived on matters which seem to him to be very evident (as I fully explained). And although this doubt may not occur to him, it can still crop up if someone else raises the point or if he

---

[1] Cf. Med. III, p. 51 above; Med. V, p. 99 above.   [2] Cf. above, p. 97.
[3] Descartes seems to distinguish here between an isolated cognition or act of awareness (*cognitio*) and systematic, properly grounded knowledge (*scientia*). Compare the remarks in *The Search for Truth* about the need to acquire 'a body of knowledge firm and certain enough to deserve the name "science"' (AT X 513: CSM II 408).

vel ab alio proponatur; nec unquam ab eo erit tutus, nisi prius Deum agnoscat.

Nec refert quod forte existimet se habere demonstrationes ad probandum nullum Deum esse. Cum enim nullo modo sint verae, semper illi earum vitia ostendi possunt; et cum hoc fiet, ab opinione dejicietur. [*Secundae Reponsiones*]

* * *

(126) Quanquam non est necessarium Deum fingere deceptorem, ut in iis quae te clare et distincte nosse putas decipiaris, cum deceptionis istius causa in te possit esse, licet de ea nequidem cogites. Quid enim, si tua natura sit ejuscemodi ut semper decipiatur, vel saltem saepe saepius? Sed unde habes quod in iis, quae clare et distincte putas te cognoscere, certum sit te neque decipi, neque posse decipi? Quoties enim quempiam experti sumus deceptum fuisse in iis, quae sole clarius se scire credebat? Hoc igitur principium clarae et distinctae cognitionis ita clare et distincte debet explicari, ut nullus probae mentis possit unquam decipi in iis, quae se clare et distincte scire crediderit; alioqui nullum adhuc certitudinis gradum penes homines, seu apud te, possibilem cernimus. [*Objectiones Secundae*]

[I]n maxime claris et accuratis nostris judiciis, quae, si falsa essent, 144 per nulla clariora, nec ope ullius alterius naturalis facultatis, possent emendari, plane affirmo nos falli non posse. Cum enim Deus sit summum ens, non potest non esse etiam summum bonum et verum, atque idcirco repugnat, ut quid ab eo sit, quod positive tendat in falsum. Atqui, cum nihil reale in nobis esse possit, quod non ab ipso sit datum (ut simul cum ejus existentia demonstratum est), realem autem habeamus facultatem ad verum agnoscendum, illudque a falso distinguendum (ut patet vel ex hoc solo quod nobis insint ideae falsi et veri), nisi haec facultas in verum tenderet, saltem cum ipsa recte utimur (hoc est cum nullis nisi clare et distincte perceptis assentimur, nullus enim alius rectus ipsius usus fingi potest), merito Deus ejus dator pro deceptore haberetur.

looks into the matter himself. So he will never be free of this doubt until he acknowledges that God exists.

It does not matter that the atheist may think he has demonstrations to prove that there is no God. For, since these proofs are quite unsound, it will always be possible to point out their flaws to him, and when this happens he will have to abandon his view.   [*Second Replies*: CSM II 100–1]

* * *

It is not, however, necessary to suppose that God is a deceiver in order to (126) explain your being deceived about matters which you think you clearly and distinctly know. The cause of this deception could lie in you, though you are wholly unaware of it. Why should it not be in your nature to be subject to constant – or at least very frequent – deception? How can you establish with certainty that you are not deceived, or capable of being deceived, in matters which you think you know clearly and distinctly? Have we not often seen people turn out to have been deceived in matters where they thought their knowledge was as clear as the sunlight? Your principle of clear and distinct knowledge thus requires a clear and distinct explanation, in such a way as to rule out the possibility that anyone of sound mind may be deceived on matters which he thinks he knows clearly and distinctly. Failing this, we do not see that any degree of certainty can possibly be within your reach or that of mankind in general.

[*Second Objections*: CSM II 90]

[I]n the case of our clearest and most careful judgements, if such judgements were false they could not be corrected by any clearer judgements or by 144 means of any other natural faculty. In such cases I simply assert that it is impossible for us to be deceived. Since God is the supreme being, he must also be supremely good and true, and it would therefore be a contradiction that anything should be created by him which positively tends towards falsehood. Now everything real which is in us must have been bestowed on us by God (this was proved when his existence was proved); moreover, we have a real faculty for recognizing the truth and distinguishing it from falsehood, as is clear merely from the fact that we have within us ideas of truth and falsehood. Hence this faculty must tend towards the truth, at least when we use it correctly (that is, by assenting only to what we clearly and distinctly perceive, for no other correct method of employing this faculty can be imagined). For if it did not so tend then, since God gave it to us, he would rightly have to be regarded as a deceiver.

Atque ita videtis, postquam Deum existere cognitum est, necesse esse ut illum fingamus esse deceptorem, si ea, quae clare et distincte percipimus, in dubium revocare velimus; et quia deceptor fingi non potest, illa omnino pro veris et certis esse admittenda.

Sed quia hic adverto vos adhuc haerere in dubiis quae, a me in prima Meditatione proposita, satis accurate in sequentibus putabam fuisse sublata, exponam hic iterum fundamentum, cui omnis humana certitudo niti posse mihi videtur.

Imprimis, statim atque aliquid a nobis recte percipi putamus, sponte nobis persuademus illud esse verum. Haec autem persuasio si tam firma sit ut nullam unquam possimus habere causam dubitandi de eo quod nobis ita persuademus, nihil est quod ulterius inquiramus; habemus omne quod cum ratione licet optare. Quid enim ad nos, si forte quis fingat illud ipsum, de cujus veritate tam firmiter sumus persuasi, Deo vel Angelo falsum apparere, atque ideo, absolute loquendo, falsum esse? Quid curamus istam falsitatem absolutam, cum illam nullo modo credamus, nec vel minimum suspicemur? Supponimus enim persuasionem tam firmam ut nullo modo tolli possit; quae proinde persuasio idem plane est quod perfectissima certitudo.

Sed dubitari potest an habeatur aliqua talis certitudo, sive firma et immutabilis persuasio.

Et quidem perspicuum est illam non haberi de iis quae vel minimum obscure aut confuse perspicimus: haec enim qualiscumque obscuritas satis est causae, ut de ipsis dubitemus. Non habetur etiam de iis quae, quantumvis clare, solo sensu percipiuntur, quia saepe notavimus in sensu errorem posse reperiri, ut cum hydropicus sitit, vel cum ictericus nivem videt ut flavam: non enim minus clare et distincte illam sic videt, quam nos ut albam. Superest itaque ut, si quae habeatur, sit tantum de iis quae clare ab intellectu percipiuntur.

Ex his autem quaedam sunt tam perspicua, simulque tam simplicia, ut nunquam possimus de iis cogitare, quin vera esse credamus: ut quod ego, dum cogito, existam; quod ea, quae semel facta sunt, infecta esse non possint; et talia, de quibus manifestum est hanc

Hence you see that once we have become aware that God exists it is necessary for us to imagine that he is a deceiver if we wish to cast doubt on what we clearly and distinctly perceive. And since it is impossible to imagine that he is a deceiver, whatever we clearly and distinctly perceive must be completely accepted as true and certain.

But since I see that you are still stuck fast in the doubts which I put forward in the First Meditation, and which I thought I had very carefully removed in the succeeding Meditations, I shall now expound for a second time the basis on which it seems to me that all human certainty can be founded.

First of all, as soon as we think that we correctly perceive something, we are spontaneously convinced that it is true. Now if this conviction is so firm that it is impossible for us ever to have any reason for doubting what we are convinced of, then there are no further questions for us to ask: we have everything that we could reasonably want. What is it to us that someone may make out that the perception whose truth we are so firmly convinced of may appear false to God or an angel, so that it is, absolutely speaking, false? Why should this 'absolute falsity' bother us, since we neither believe in it nor have even the smallest suspicion of it? For the supposition which we are making here is of a conviction so firm that it is quite incapable of being destroyed; and such a conviction is clearly the same as the most perfect certainty.

But it may be doubted whether any such certainty, or firm and immutable conviction, is in fact to be had.

It is clear that we do not have this kind of certainty in cases where our perception is even the slightest bit obscure or confused, for such obscurity, whatever its degree, is quite sufficient to make us have doubts in such cases. Again, we do not have the required kind of certainty with regard to matters which we perceive solely by means of the senses, however clear such perception may be. For we have often noted that error can be detected in the senses, as when someone with dropsy feels thirsty or when someone with jaundice sees snow as yellow; for when he sees it as yellow he sees it just as clearly and distinctly as we do when we see it as white. Accordingly, if there is any certainty to be had, the only remaining alternative is that it occurs in matters that are clearly perceived by the intellect and nowhere else.

Now some of these are so transparently clear and at the same time so simple that we cannot ever think of them without believing them to be true. The fact that I exist so long as I am thinking, or that what is done cannot be undone, are examples of truths in respect of which we manifestly possess

certitudinem haberi. Non possumus enim de iis dubitare, nisi de ipsis
146 cogitemus; sed non possumus de iisdem cogitare, quin simul credamus
vera esse, ut assumptum est; ergo non possumus de iis dubitare, quin
simul credamus vera esse, hoc est, non possumus unquam dubitare.

Nec obstat, quod saepe simus experti alios deceptos fuisse in iis quae
sole clarius se scire credebant. Neque enim unquam advertimus, vel
ab ullo adverti potest, id contigisse iis qui claritatem suae perceptionis
a solo intellectu petierunt, sed iis tantum qui vel a sensibus, vel a falso
aliquo praejudicio, ipsam desumpserunt.

Nec obstat etiam, si quis fingat illa Deo vel Angelo apparere esse
falsa, quia evidentia nostrae perceptionis non permittet ut talia fin-
gentem audiamus.

Alia sunt, quae quidem etiam clarissime ab intellectu nostro percipiuntur, cum ad rationes ex quibus pendet ipsorum cognitio satis
attendimus, atque ideo tunc temporis non possumus de iis dubitare;
sed quia istarum rationum possumus oblivisci, et interim recordari
conclusionum ex ipsis deductarum, quaeritur an de his conclusionibus
habeatur etiam firma et immutabilis persuasio, quandiu recordamur
ipsas ab evidentibus principiis fuisse deductas; haec enim recordatio
supponi debet, ut dici possint conclusiones. Et respondeo haberi quidem ab iis qui Deum sic norunt ut intelligant fieri non posse quin
facultas intelligendi ab eo ipsis data tendat in verum; non autem haberi
ab aliis. Hocque in fine quintae Meditationis tam clare explicatum est,
ut nihil hic addendum videatur.   [*Secundae Responsiones*]

*   *   *

(214) Unicus mihi restat scrupulus, quomodo circulus ab eo non commit-
tatur, dum ait, non aliter nobis constare, quae a nobis clare et distincte
percipiuntur, vera esse, quam quia Deus est.

At nobis constare non potest Deum esse, nisi quia id a nobis clare et
evidenter percipitur; ergo, priusquam nobis constet Deum esse, nobis
constare debet, verum esse quodcunque a nobis clare et evidenter
percipitur.   [*Objectiones Quartae*]

this kind of certainty. For we cannot doubt them unless we think of them; but we cannot think of them without at the same time believing they are 146 true, as was supposed. Hence we cannot doubt them without at the same time believing they are true; that is, we can never doubt them.

It is no objection to this to say that we have often seen people 'turn out to have been deceived in matters where they thought their knowledge was as clear as the sunlight'. For we have never seen, indeed no one could possibly see, this happening to those who have relied solely on the intellect in their quest for clarity in their perceptions; we have seen it happen only to those who tried to derive such clarity from the senses or from some false preconceived opinion.

It is also no objection for someone to make out that such items might appear false to God or to an angel. For the evident clarity of our perceptions does not allow us to listen to anyone who makes up this kind of story.

There are other matters which are perceived very clearly by our intellect so long as we attend to the arguments on which our knowledge of them depends; and we are therefore incapable of doubting them during this time. But we may forget the arguments in question and later remember simply the conclusions which were deduced from them. The question will now arise as to whether we possess the same firm and immutable conviction concerning these conclusions, when we simply recollect that they were previously deduced from quite evident principles (our ability to call them 'conclusions' presupposes such a recollection). My reply is that the required certainty is indeed possessed by those whose knowledge of God enables them to understand that the intellectual faculty which he gave them cannot but tend towards the truth; but the required certainty is not possessed by others. This point was explained so clearly at the end of the Fifth Meditation[1] that it does not seem necessary to add anything further here.   [*Second Replies*: CSM II 102–5]

*   *   *

I have one further worry, namely how the author avoids reasoning in a (214) circle when he says that we are sure that what we clearly and distinctly perceive is true only because God exists.[2]

But we can be sure that God exists only because we clearly and distinctly perceive this. Hence, before we can be sure that God exists, we ought to be able to be sure that whatever we perceive clearly and evidently is true.

[*Fourth Objections*: CSM II 150]

[1] Above, p. 97.   [2] Cf. above, p. 97.

Denique, quod circulum non commiserim, cum dixi non aliter nobis constare, quae clare et distincte percipiuntur vera esse, quam quia 246 Deus est; et nobis non constare Deum esse, nisi quia id clare percipitur; jam satis in responsione ad secundas Objectiones . . . explicui, distinguendo scilicet id quo reipsa clare percipimus, ab eo quod recordamur nos antea clare percepisse. Primum etiam, nobis constat Deum existere, quoniam ad rationes quae id probant attendimus; postea vero, sufficit ut recordemur nos aliquam rem clare percepisse, ut ipsam veram esse simus certi; quod non sufficeret, nisi Deum esse et non fallere sciremus. [*Quartae Responsiones*]

Lastly, as to the fact that I was not guilty of circularity when I said that the only reason we have for being sure that what we clearly and distinctly perceive is true is the fact that God exists, but that we are sure that God 246 exists only because we perceive this clearly: I have already given an adequate explanation of this point in my reply to the Second Objections . . . where I made a distinction between what we in fact perceive clearly and what we remember having perceived clearly on a previous occasion.[1] To begin with, we are sure that God exists because we attend to the arguments which prove this; but subsequently it is enough for us to remember that we perceived something clearly in order for us to be certain that it is true. This would not be sufficient if we did not know that God exists and is not a deceiver.

[*Fourth Replies*: CSM II 171]

[1] See above, p. 217.

[P]atet... integram restare quaestionem quam se soluturum spondet: quo pacto, ex eo quod nihil aliud ad essentiam suam pertinere cognoscat, sequatur nihil etiam aliud revera ad illam pertinere. Quod tamen ab illo praestitum esse tota Meditatione 2, ut fatear tarditatem meam, deprehendere non potui. Sed quantum conjicere possum, hujus rei probationem aggreditur in Meditatione 6, eo quod illam dependere judicarit a clara Dei notitia, quam Meditatione 2 sibi nondum compararat. Sic ergo rem istam probat:

quoniam... scio omnia quae clare et distincte intelligo, talia a Deo fieri posse qualia illa intelligo, satis est quod possim unam rem absque altera clare et distincte intelligere, ut certus sim unam ab altera esse diversam, quia potest saltem a Deo seorsim poni; et non refert a qua potentia id fiat, ut diversa existimetur. Quia ergo ex una parte claram et distinctam habeo ideam mei ipsius, quatenus sum tantum res cogitans, non extensa, et ex alia parte distinctam ideam corporis, quatenus est tantum res extensa, non cogitans, 200 certum est me a corpore meo revera esse distinctum, et absque illo posse existere.

Hic paulisper subsistendum; in his enim paucis verbis totius difficultatis cardo versari mihi videtur.

Ac primum quidem, ut vera sit illius syllogismi propositio, non de quacunque, etiam clara et distincta, sed tantummodo de adaequata rei cognitione, intelligi debet. Fatetur enim V.C., in responsione ad Theologum, sufficere distinctionem formalem, nec requiri

[ON THE SIXTH MEDITATION]

[THE REAL DISTINCTION BETWEEN MIND AND BODY]

[I]t is clear that . . . the question he promised to answer still remains outstanding: how does it follow, from the fact that he is aware of nothing else belonging to his essence, that nothing else does in fact belong to it?[1] I must confess that I am somewhat slow, but I have been unable to find anywhere in the Second Meditation an answer to this question. As far as I can gather, however, the author does attempt a proof of this claim in the Sixth Meditation, since he takes it to depend on his having clear knowledge of God, which he had not yet arrived at in the Second Meditation. This is how the proof goes:

I know . . . that everything which I clearly and distinctly understand is capable of being created by God so as to correspond exactly with my understanding of it. Hence the fact that I can clearly and distinctly understand one thing apart from another is enough to make me certain that the two things are distinct, since they are capable of being separated, at least by God. The question of what kind of power is required to bring about such a separation does not affect the judgement that the two things are distinct < . . . > Now on the one hand I have a clear and distinct idea of myself, in so far as I am simply a thinking, non-extended thing; and on the other hand I have a distinct idea of body, in so far as this is simply an extended, non-thinking thing. And accordingly, it is certain that I am really distinct from my body, and can exist without it.[2]   200

We must pause a little here, for it seems to me that in these few words lies the crux of the whole difficulty.

First of all, if the major premiss of this syllogism is to be true, it must be taken to apply not to any kind of knowledge of a thing, nor even to clear and distinct knowledge; it must apply solely to knowledge which is adequate. For our distinguished author admits in his reply to the theologian that if one thing can be conceived distinctly and separately from another

---

[1] See Preface, p. 11 above.   [2] Above, p. 109.

221

realem, ut unum ab alio distincte et seorsim concipiatur per abstractionem intellectus rem inadaequate concipientis; unde in eodem loco
subsumit:

Atqui complete intelligo quid sit corpus, putando tantum illud esse extensum, figuratum, mobile etc., deque illo negando ea omnia quae ad mentis
naturam pertinent: et vice versa intelligo mentem esse rem completam, quae
dubitat, quae intelligit, quae vult etc., quamvis negem in ea quidquam esse
ex iis quae in corporis idea continentur. Ergo inter corpus et mentem est
distinctio realis.

Sed si quis hanc sumptionem in dubium revocet, contendatque
inadaequatam tantum esse tui conceptionem, dum te concipis tanquam rem cogitantem, non extensam, similiterque cum te concipis
tanquam rem extensam, non cogitantem, videndumque quomodo id
in superioribus probatum sit. Non enim arbitror rem istam ita claram
esse, ut tanquam principium indemonstrabile assumi debeat, non
probari.

201 Et quidem, quod ad illius primam partem attinet, quod scilicet
complete intelligas quid sit corpus, putando tantum illud esse extensum, figuratum, mobile etc., deque illo negando ea omnia quae ad
mentis naturam pertinent, parum ad rem facit. Qui enim contenderet
mentem nostram esse corpoream, non ideo existimaret corpus omne
mentem esse. Corpus ergo se haberet ad mentem, sicut genus ad
speciem. At genus potest intelligi sine specie, et de illo negando
quidquid speciei proprium et peculiare est; unde vulgo Logici ajunt,
negata specie, non negari genus: sic possum intelligere figuram absque
eo quod intelligam ullam ex iis affectionibus quae circulo propriae
sunt. Probandum ergo superest, mentem complete et adaequate posse
intelligi sine corpore.

Non aliud in toto opere idoneum video ad hanc probationem argumentum, praeter illud quod initio propositum est: possum negare
ullum esse corpus, ullam rem extensam et tamen certum mihi est me
esse, quandiu hoc nego, seu cogito; sum ergo res cogitans, non corpus,
et ad mei notitiam non pertinet corpus.

'by an abstraction of the intellect which conceives the thing inadequately', then this is sufficient for there to be a formal distinction between the two, but it does not require that there be a real distinction. And in the same passage he draws the following conclusion:

By contrast, I have a complete understanding of what a body is when I think that it is merely something having extension, shape and motion, and I deny that it has anything which belongs to the nature of a mind. Conversely, I understand the mind to be a complete thing, which doubts, understands, wills, and so on, even though I deny that it has any of the attributes which are contained in the idea of a body. Hence there is a real distinction between the body and the mind.[1]

But someone may call this minor premiss into doubt and maintain that the conception you have of yourself when you conceive of yourself as a thinking, non-extended thing is an inadequate one; and the same may be true of your conception of yourself[2] as an extended, non-thinking thing. Hence we must look at how this is proved in the earlier part of the argument. For I do not think that this matter is so clear that it should be assumed without proof as a first principle that is not susceptible of demonstration.

As to the first part of your claim, namely that you have a complete understanding of what a body is when you think that it is merely something 201 having extension, shape, motion etc., and you deny that it has anything which belongs to the nature of a mind, this proves little. For those who maintain that our mind is corporeal do not on that account suppose that every body is a mind. On their view, body would be related to mind as a genus is related to a species. Now a genus can be understood apart from a species, even if we deny of the genus what is proper and peculiar to the species – hence the common maxim of logicians, 'The negation of the species does not negate the genus.' Thus I can understand the genus 'figure' apart from my understanding of any of the properties which are peculiar to a circle. It therefore remains to be proved that the mind can be completely and adequately understood apart from the body.

I cannot see anywhere in the entire work an argument which could serve to prove this claim, apart from what is suggested at the beginning: 'I can deny that any body exists, or that there is any extended thing at all, yet it remains certain to me that I exist, so long as I am making this denial or thinking it. Hence I am a thinking thing, not a body, and the body does not belong to the knowledge I have of myself.'[3]

---

[1] First Replies (AT VII 121: CSM II 86).   [2] '. . . i.e. your body' (supplied in French version).
[3] Not an exact quotation. Cf. Med. II, p. 37 above.

At ex eo confici tantum video, aliquam mei notitiam parari posse absque notitia corporis; sed notitiam illam esse completam et adaequatam, ita ut certus sim me non falli, dum ab essentia mea corpus excludo, mihi nondum plane perspicuum est. Rem exemplo declarabo.

Certo noverit aliquis angulum in semicirculo rectum esse, et proinde triangulum ex illo angulo et diametro circuli rectangulum esse; dubitet vero, necdum certo deprehenderit, imo sophismate aliquo delusus neget, quadratum basis rectanguli aequale esse quadratis laterum: eadem ratione quam vir clarissimus proponit, videtur se in falsa sua persuasione confirmaturus: Ut enim, inquit, clare et distincte percipio triangulum illum esse rectangulum, dubito tamen utrum illius basis quadratum aequale sit quadratis laterum; non ergo ad illius essentiam pertinet, quod illius basis quadratum aequale sit quadratis laterum.

Deinde, etiamsi negavero quod illius basis quadratum sit aequale quadratis laterum, certus tamen remaneo quod sit rectangulus, et clara distinctaque remanet in mea mente notitia, quod unus ex illius angulis sit rectus; quo salvo, ne Deus quidem efficere possit ut non sit rectangulus.

Non ergo id de quo dubito, immo quo sublato, ea mihi remanet idea, ad illius essentiam pertinet.

Praeterea, quoniam scio omnia quae clare et distincte intelligo, talia a Deo fieri posse qualia illa intelligo, satis est quod possim rem unam absque altera clare et distincte intelligere, ut certus sim unam ab altera esse diversam, quia potest a Deo seorsim poni. At clare et distincte intelligo hunc triangulum esse rectangulum, absque eo quod intelligam quadratum illius basis aequale esse quadratis laterum; ergo saltem a Dei fieri potest triangulus rectangulus, cujus basis quadratum aequale non sit quadratis laterum.

Non video quid hic responderi possit, nisi illum hominem clare et distincte non percipere triangulum rectangulum. At unde

But so far as I can see, the only result that follows from this is that I can obtain some knowledge of myself without knowledge of the body. But it is not yet transparently clear to me that this knowledge is complete and adequate, so as to enable me to be certain that I am not mistaken in excluding body from my essence. I shall explain the point by means of an example.

Suppose someone knows for certain that the angle in a semi-circle is a right angle, and hence that the triangle formed by this angle and the diameter of the circle is right-angled. In spite of this, he may doubt, or not yet have grasped for certain, that the square on the hypotenuse is equal to the squares on the other two sides; indeed he may even deny this if he is misled by some fallacy. But now, if he uses the same argument as that proposed by our illustrious author, he may appear to have confirmation of his false belief, as follows: 'I clearly and distinctly perceive', he may say, 'that the triangle is right-angled; but I doubt that the square on the hypotenuse 202 is equal to the squares on the other two sides; therefore it does not belong to the essence of the triangle that the square on its hypotenuse is equal to the squares on the other sides.'

Again, even if I deny that the square on the hypotenuse is equal to the square on the other two sides, I still remain sure that the triangle is right-angled, and my mind retains the clear and distinct knowledge that one of its angles is a right angle. And given that this is so, not even God could bring it about that the triangle is not right-angled.

I might argue from this that the property which I doubt, or which can be removed while leaving my idea intact, does not belong to the essence of the triangle.

Moreover, 'I know', says M. Descartes, 'that everything which I clearly and distinctly understand is capable of being created by God as to correspond exactly with my understanding of it. And hence the fact that I can clearly and distinctly understand one thing apart from another is enough to make me certain that the two things are distinct, since they are capable of being separated by God.'[1] Yet I clearly and distinctly understand that this triangle is right-angled, without understanding that the square on the hypotenuse is equal to the squares on the other sides. It follows on this reasoning that God, at least, could create a right-angled triangle with the square on its hypotenuse not equal to the squares on the other sides.

I do not see any possible reply here, except that the person in this example does not clearly and distinctly perceive that the triangle is

[1] Above, p. 109.

habeo me clarius percipere naturam mentis meae, quam ille percipiat
naturam trianguli? Aeque enim certus est ille triangulum in semicirculo habere unum angulum rectum, quae est notio trianguli rectanguli,
ac ego certus sum me existere, ex eo quod cogitem.

Quemadmodum ergo ille in eo fallitur quod ad illius trianguli
naturam, quem clare et distincte novit esse rectangulum, pertinere
203　non arbitretur quod illius basis quadratum sit etc.; ita cur in eo fortasse
non fallor, quod ad mei naturam, quam certe et distincte novi esse rem
cogitantem, nihil aliud pertinere arbitrer, quam quod sim res cogitans?
cum etiam forte ad illam pertineat, quod sim res extensa.

[Objectiones Quartae]

Hic tamen urget Vir C.: etsi aliqua mei notitia parari possit absque
notitia corporis, non tamen inde confici, notitiam illam esse completam et adaequatam, ita ut certus sim me non falli, dum ab essentia
224　mea corpus excludo. Remque declarat exemplo trianguli semicirculo
inscripti, quam possumus clare et distincte intelligere esse rectangulum, quamvis ignoremus, vel etiam negemus, illius basis quadratum
aequale esse quadratis laterum; nec tamen inde licet inferre, dari posse
triangulum, cujus basis quadratum aequale non sit quadratis laterum.

Sed quantum ad hoc exemplum, multis modis differt a re proposita.

Nam primo, quamvis forte triangulus sumi possit in concreto pro
substantia figuram habente triangularem, certe proprietas habendi
quadratum basis aequale quadratis laterum non est substantia; nec
proinde unumquodque ex his duobus potest intelligi ut res completa,
quemadmodum intelliguntur Mens et Corpus; nec quidem potest *res*
vocari, eo sensu quo dixi satis esse quod possim unam rem (nempe rem
completam) absque altera intelligere, etc., ut sit manifestum ex verbis
quae sequebantur: Praeterea invenio in me facultates etc. Neque enim
istas facultates dixi esse *res*, sed ipsas accurate a rebus sive substantiis
distinxi.

Secundo, quamvis clare et distincte possimus intelligere triangulum in semicirculo esse rectangulum, absque eo quod advertamus

right-angled. But how is my perception of the nature of my mind any clearer than his perception of the nature of the triangle? He is just as certain that the triangle in the semi-circle has one right angle (which is the criterion of a right-angled triangle) as I am certain that I exist because I am thinking.

Now although the man in the example clearly and distinctly knows that the triangle is right-angled, he is wrong in thinking that the aforesaid relationship between the squares on the sides does not belong to the nature 203 of the triangle. Similarly, although I clearly and distinctly know my nature to be something that thinks, may I, too, not perhaps be wrong in thinking that nothing else belongs to my nature apart from the fact that I am a thinking thing? Perhaps the fact that I am an extended thing may also belong to my nature. [*Fourth Objections*: CSM II 140–3]

Here my distinguished critic argues that although I can obtain some knowledge of myself without knowledge of the body, it does not follow that this knowledge is complete and adequate, so as to enable me to be certain that I am not mistaken in excluding body from my essence. He explains the 224 point by using the example of a triangle inscribed in a semi-circle, which we can clearly and distinctly understand to be right-angled although we do not know, or may even deny, that the square on the hypotenuse is equal to the squares on the other sides. But we cannot infer from this that there could be a right-angled triangle such that the square on the hypotenuse is not equal to the squares on the other sides.

But this example differs in many respects from the case under discussion.

First of all, though a triangle can perhaps be taken concretely as a substance having a triangular shape, it is certain that the property of having the square on the hypotenuse equal to the squares on the other sides is not a substance. So neither the triangle nor the property can be understood as a complete thing in the way in which mind and body can be so understood; nor can either item be called a 'thing' in the sense in which I said 'it is enough that I can understand one thing (that is, a complete thing) apart from another' etc.[1] This is clear from the passage which comes next: 'Besides I find in myself faculties' etc. I did not say that these faculties were *things*, but carefully distinguished them from things or substances.

Secondly, although we can clearly and distinctly understand that a triangle in a semi-circle is right-angled without being aware that the square on

---

[1] Cf. above, p. 109.

ejus basis quadratum aequale esse quadratis laterum, non tamen ita
225 possumus clare intelligere triangulum in quo basis quadratum sit
aequale quadratis laterum, quin simul advertamus esse rectangulum.
Atqui et mentem sine corpore, et corpus sine mente, clare et distincte
percipimus.

Tertio, quamvis conceptus trianguli semicirculo inscripti talis haberi
possit, ut in eo aequalitas inter quadratum basis et quadrata laterum
non contineatur, non potest tamen haberi talis ut nulla proportio inter
basis quadratum et quadrata laterum ad hunc triangulum pertinere
intelligatur; ac proinde, quamdiu ignoratur qualis sit ista proportio,
nulla de eo potest negari, nisi quam clare intelligamus ad ipsum non
pertinere; quod de proportione aequalitatis nunquam potest intelligi.
Sed nihil plane in corporis conceptu includitur, quod pertineat ad
mentem; nihilque in conceptu mentis, quod pertineat ad corpus.

Itaque, quamvis dixerim satis esse quod possim unam rem absque
altera clare et distincte intelligere etc., non ideo potest subsumi: at
clare et distincte intelligo hunc triangulum etc. Primo, quia proportio inter quadratum basis et quadrata laterum non est res completa.
Secundo, quia non clare intelligitur ista proportio aequalitatis, nisi in
triangulo rectangulo. Tertio, quia nequidem triangulus distincte potest
intelligi, si negetur proportio quae est inter quadrata ejus laterum et
basis.

226 Sed jam dicendum est quo pacto ex hoc solo quod unam substantiam absque altera clare et distincte intelligam, certus sim unam ab
alia excludi.

Nempe haec ipsa est notio *substantiae*, quod per se, hoc est absque
ope ullius alterius substantiae, possit existere; nec ullus unquam qui
duas substantias per duos diversos conceptus percepit, non judicavit
illas esse realiter distinctas.

Ideoque, nisi certitudinem vulgari majorem quaesivissem, contenus
fuissem ostendisse, in secunda Meditatione, *Mentem* ut rem subsistentem intelligi, quamvis nihil plane illi tribuatur quod pertineat ad corpus, et vice versa etiam *Corpus* intelligi ut rem subsistentem, etsi nihil

the hypotenuse is equal to the squares on the other two sides, we cannot have a clear understanding of a triangle having the square on its hypotenuse equal to the squares on the other sides without at the same time being aware 225 that it is right-angled. And yet we can clearly and distinctly perceive the mind without the body and the body without the mind.

Thirdly, although it is possible to have a concept of a triangle inscribed in a semi-circle which does not include the fact that the square on the hypotenuse is equal to the squares on the other sides, it is not possible to have a concept of the triangle such that no ratio at all is understood to hold between the square on the hypotenuse and the squares on the other sides. Hence, though we may be unaware of what that ratio is, we cannot say that any given ratio does not hold unless we clearly understand that it does not belong to the triangle; and where the ratio is one of equality, this can never be understood. Yet the concept of body includes nothing at all which belongs to the mind, and the concept of mind includes nothing at all which belongs to the body.

So although I said 'it is enough that I can clearly and distinctly understand one thing apart from another' etc., one cannot go on to argue 'yet I clearly and distinctly understand that this triangle is right-angled without understanding that the square on the hypotenuse' etc. There are three reasons for this. First, the ratio between the square on the hypotenuse and the squares on the other sides is not a complete thing. Secondly, we do not clearly understand the ratio to be equal except in the case of a right-angled triangle. And thirdly, there is no way in which the triangle can be distinctly understood if the ratio which obtains between the square on the hypotenuse and the squares on the other sides is said not to hold.

But now I must explain how the mere fact that I can clearly and distinctly 226 understand one substance apart from another is enough to make me certain that one excludes the other.[1]

The answer is that the notion of a *substance* is just this – that it can exist by itself, that is without the aid of any other substance. And there is no one who has ever perceived two substances by means of two different concepts without judging that they are really distinct.

Hence, had I not been looking for greater than ordinary certainty, I should have been content to have shown in the Second Meditation that the mind can be understood as a subsisting thing despite the fact that nothing belonging to the body is attributed to it, and that, conversely, the body can be understood as a subsisting thing despite the fact that nothing

---

[1] Cf. above, p. 109.

illi tribuatur quod pertineat ad mentem. Nihilque amplius addidissem ad demonstrandum mentem realiter a corpore distingui: quia vulgo res omnes eodem modo se habere judicamus in ordine ad ipsam veritatem, quo se habent in ordine ad nostram perceptionem. Sed, quia inter hyperbolicas illas dubitationes, quas in prima Meditatione proposui, una eousque processit ut de hoc ipso (nempe quod res juxta veritatem sint tales quales ipsas percipimus) certus esse non possem, quandiu authorem meae originis ignorare me supponebam, idcirco omnia quae de Deo et de veritate in tertia, quarta et quinta Meditatione scripsi, conferunt ad conclusionem de reali mentis a corpore distinctione, quam demum in sexta Meditatione perfeci.

227   Atqui, ait Vir C., intelligo triangulum semicirculo inscriptum absque eo quod sciam ejus basis quadratum aequale esse quadratis laterum. Imo, potest quidem ille triangulus intelligi, etsi de proportione quae est inter quadrata ejus basis et laterum non cogitetur; sed non potest intelligi ipsam de eo esse negandam. Contra vero de mente, non modo intelligimus illam esse sine corpore, sed etiam omnia illa quae ad corpus pertinent, de ipsa posse negari; haec enim est natura substantiarum, quod sese mutuo excludant.   [*Quartae Responsiones*]

*   *   *

[S]ubjungas certam rationem, certosque characteres, qui nos certissimos reddant, quandonam rem aliquam ita complete absque alia intelligimus, ut certum sit unam ab alia ita distingui, ut seorsim possint, saltem Dei virtute, subsistere: hoc est, quomodo possimus certo, clare distincteque cognoscere illam intellectionis distinctionem non ab ipso fieri intellectu, sed ab ipsis rebus procedere. Enimvero cum immensitatem Dei contemplamur, non cogitantes de illius justitia; vel cum de illius existentia, non cogitantes de Filio vel Spiritu sancto; numquid complete percipimus illam existentiam, vel Deum existentem, absque illis personis, quas peraeque possit

419

belonging to the mind is attributed to it. I should have added nothing more in order to demonstrate that there is a real distinction between the mind and the body, since we commonly judge that the order in which things are mutually related in our perception of them corresponds to the order in which they are related in actual reality. But one of the exaggerated doubts which I put forward in the First Meditation went so far as to make it impossible for me to be certain of this very point (namely whether things do in reality correspond to our perception of them), so long as I was supposing myself to be ignorant of the author of my being. And this is why everything I wrote on the subject of God and truth in the Third, Fourth and Fifth Meditations contributes to the conclusion that there is a real distinction between the mind and the body, which I finally established in the Sixth Meditation.

And yet, says M. Arnauld, 'I have a clear understanding of a trian- 227 gle inscribed in a semi-circle without knowing that the square on the hypotenuse is equal to the squares on the other sides.' It is true that the triangle is intelligible even though we do not think of the ratio which obtains between the square on the hypotenuse and the squares on the other sides; but it is not intelligible that this ratio should be denied of the triangle. In the case of the mind, by contrast, not only do we understand it to exist without the body, but, what is more, all the attributes which belong to a body can be denied of it. For it is of the nature of substances that they should mutually exclude one another.   [*Fourth Replies*: CSM II 157–9]

*   *   *

[W]e ask you to provide in addition a reliable rule and some firm criteria which will make us utterly sure of the following point: when we understand something entirely apart from some other thing, in the way you describe, is it indeed certain that the one is so distinct from the other that they could subsist apart – at least through the power of God?[1] That is, how can we know for sure, clearly and distinctly, that when our intellect makes 419 this distinction, the distinction does not arise solely from the intellect but arises from the nature of the things themselves? For when we contemplate the immensity of God while not thinking of his justice, or when we contemplate his existence when not thinking of the Son or the Holy Spirit, do we not have a complete perception of that existence, or of God as existing, entirely apart from the other Persons of the Trinity? So could not

---

[1] Cf. above, p. 109.

aliquis infidelis negare, atque negas mentem vel cogitationem de corpore? Quemadmodum igitur male quis concludet, Filium et Spiritum
sanctum a Deo Patre essentialiter esse distinctos, aut ab eo separari
posse, ita neque tibi concesserit quispiam, cogitationem vel mentem
humanam a corpore distingui, licet unum absque alio concipias, et
unum de alio perneges, neque putes id fieri per ullam tuae mentis
abstractionem.   [*Objectiones Sextae*]

440 Cum primum ex rationibus in his Meditationibus expositis mentem
humanam realiter a corpore distingui, et notiorem esse quam corpus,
et reliqua collegissem, cogebar quidem ad assensionem, quia nihil in
ipsis non cohaerens, atque ex evidentibus principiis juxta Logicae reg-
ulas conclusum, advertebam. Sed fateor me non idcirco fuisse plane
persuasum, idemque fere contigisse quod Astronomis, qui, postquam
Solem esse aliquoties Terra majorem rationibus evicerunt, non possunt tamen a se impetrare, dum in illum oculos convertunt, ut judi-
cent non esse minorem. Postquam autem ulterius perrexi, et iisdem
innixus fundamentis, ad rerum Physicarum considerationem transivi,
primo attendendo ad ideas, sive notiones, quas de unaquaque re apud
me inveniebam, et unas ab aliis diligenter distinguendo, ut judicia
omnia mea cum ipsis consentirent, adverti nihil plane ad rationem
corporis pertinere, nisi tantum quod sit res longa, lata et profunda,
variarum figurarum, variorumque motuum capax; ejusque figuras ac
motus esse tantum modos, qui per nullam potentiam sine ipso possunt existere; colores vero, odores, sapores, et talia, esse tantum sensus
quosdam in cogitatione mea existentes, nec minus a corporibus dif-
ferentes, quam dolor differt a figura et motu teli dolorem incutientis;
ac denique gravitatem, duritiem, vires calefaciendi, attrahendi, pur-
gandi, aliasque omnes qualitates, quas in corporibus experimur, in solo
motu motusve privatione, partiumque configuratione ac situ consistere.

441   Quae opiniones cum plurimum different ab iis, quas prius de iisdem
rebus habueram, coepi deinde considerare quas ob causas aliter antea
credidissem; praecipuamque esse animadverti, quod primum ab infantia varia de rebus Physicis, utpote quae ad vitae, quam ingrediebar,
conservationem conferebant, judicia tulissem, easdemque postea

an unbeliever deny that these Persons belong to God on the same reasoning that leads you to deny that the mind or thought belongs to the body? If anyone concludes that the Son and the Holy Spirit are essentially distinct from God the Father or that they can be separated from him, this will be an unsound inference; and in the same way, no one will grant you that thought, or the human mind, is distinct from the body, despite the fact that you conceive one apart from the other and deny the one of the other, and despite your belief that this does not come about simply through an abstraction of your mind. [*Sixth Objections*: CSM II 282]

When, on the basis of the arguments set out in these Meditations, I first 440 drew the conclusion that the human mind is really distinct from the body, better known than the body, and so on, I was compelled to accept these results because everything in the reasoning was coherent and was inferred from quite evident principles in accordance with the rules of logic. But I confess that for all that I was not entirely convinced; I was in the same plight as astronomers who have established by argument that the sun is several times larger than the earth, and yet still cannot prevent themselves judging that it is smaller, when they actually look at it. However, I went on from here, and proceeded to apply the same fundamental principles to the consideration of physical things. First I attended to the ideas or notions of each particular thing which I found within myself, and I carefully distinguished them one from the other so that all my judgements should match them. I observed as a result that nothing whatever belongs to the concept of body except the fact that it is something which has length, breadth and depth and is capable of various shapes and motions; moreover, these shapes and motions are merely modes which no power whatever can cause to exist apart from body. But colours, smells, tastes and so on are, I observed, merely certain sensations which exist in my thought, and are as different from bodies as pain is different from the shape and motion of the weapon which produces it. And lastly, I observed that heaviness and hardness and the power to heat or to attract, or to purge, and all the other qualities which we experience in bodies, consist solely in the motion of bodies, or its absence, and the configuration and situation of their parts.

Since these opinions were completely different from those which I had 441 previously held regarding physical things, I next began to consider what had led me to take a different view before. The principal cause, I discovered, was this. From infancy I had made a variety of judgements about physical things in so far as they contributed to preserving the life which I was embarking

opiniones, quas tunc de ipsis praeconceperam, retinuissem. Cumque mens, illa aetate, minus recte organis corporeis uteretur, iisque firmius affixa nihil absque ipsis cogitaret, res tantum confusas advertebat; et quamvis propriae suae naturae sibi conscia esset, nec minus apud se ideam cogitationis quam extensionis haberet, quia tamen nihil intelligebat, quin simul etiam aliquid imaginaretur, utrumque pro uno et eodem sumebat, notionesque omnes, quas de rebus intellectualibus habebat, ad corpus referebat. Et cum deinde in reliqua vita nunquam me illis praejudiciis liberassem, nihil omnino satis distincte cognoscebam, nihilque quod non supponerem esse corporeum; etiamsi earum rerum, quas corporeas esse supponebam, tales saepe ideas sive conceptus effingerem, ut mentes potius quam corpora referrent.

Nam cum, exempli causa, concipiebam gravitatem instar qualitatis cujusdam realis, quae crassis corporibus inesset, etsi vocarem illam *qualitatem*, quatenus scilicet ad corpora, quibus inerat, ipsam referebam, quia tamen addebam esse *realem*, revera putabam esse substantiam: eodem modo quo vestis, in se spectata, substantia est, etsi, cum ad hominem vestitum refertur, sit qualitas; atque etiam mens, etsi revera substantia sit, nihilominus tamen corporis, cui adjuncta est, qualitas dici potest. Et quamvis gravitatem per totum corpus, quod grave est, sparsam esse imaginarer, non tamen ipsi eandem illam extensionem, quae corporis naturam constituit, tribuebam; vera enim corporis extensio talis est, ut omnem partium penetrabilitatem excludat; tantumdem autem gravitatis, quantum est in ligno decem pedum, putabam esse in massa auri alteriusve metalli unius pedis; quin et illam eandem omnem in punctum Mathematicum contrahi posse judicabam. Quin etiam, dum corpori gravi manebat coëxtensa, totam suam vim in qualibet ejus parte exercere posse videbam, quia ex quacunque parte corpus illud funi appenderetur, tota sua gravitate funem trahebat, eodem plane modo ac si gravitas ista in sola parte funem tangente, non etiam per reliquas, sparsa fuisset. Nec sane jam mentem alia ratione corpori coëxtensam, totamque in toto, et totam in qualibet ejus parte esse intelligo. Sed ex eo praecipue apparet illam gravitatis ideam fuisse ex parte ab illa, quam habebam mentis, desumptam, quod

442

on; and subsequently I retained the same opinions I had originally formed of these things. But at that age the mind employed the bodily organs less correctly than it now does, and was more firmly attached to them; hence it had no thoughts apart from them and perceived things only in a confused manner. Although it was aware of its own nature and had within itself an idea of thought as well as an idea of extension, it never exercised its intellect on anything without at the same time picturing something in the imagination. It therefore took thought and extension to be one and the same thing, and referred to the body all the notions which it had concerning things related to the intellect. Now I had never freed myself from these preconceived opinions in later life, and hence there was nothing that I knew with sufficient distinctness, and there was nothing I did not suppose to be corporeal; however, in the case of those very things that I supposed to be corporeal, the ideas or concepts which I formed were frequently such as to refer to minds rather than bodies.

For example, I conceived of gravity[1] as if it were some sort of real quality, which inhered in solid bodies; and although I called it a 'quality', thereby referring it to the bodies in which it inhered, by adding that it was 'real' I was in fact thinking that it was a substance. In the same way clothing, regarded in itself, is a substance, even though, when referred to the man 442 who wears it, it is a quality. Or again, the mind, even though it is in fact a substance, can nonetheless be said to be a quality of the body to which it is joined. And although I imagined gravity to be scattered throughout the whole body that is heavy, I still did not attribute to it the extension which constitutes the nature of a body. For the true extension of a body is such as to exclude any interpenetration of the parts, whereas I thought that there was the same amount of gravity in a ten-foot piece of wood as in a one-foot lump of gold or other metal – indeed I thought that the whole of the gravity could be contracted to a mathematical point. Moreover, I saw that the gravity, while remaining coextensive with the heavy body, could exercise all its force in any one part of the body; for if the body were hung from a rope attached to any part of it, it would still pull the rope down with all its force, just as if all the gravity existed in the part actually touching the rope instead of being scattered through the remaining parts. This is exactly the way in which I now understand the mind to be coextensive with the body – the whole mind in the whole body and the whole mind in any one of its parts. But what makes it especially clear that my idea of gravity was taken largely from the idea I had of the mind is the fact that I

[1] Lat. *gravitas*, literally 'heaviness'.

putarem gravitatem deferre corpora versus centrum terrae, tanquam si aliquam ejus cognitionem in se contineret. Neque enim hoc profecto sine cognitione fieri, neque ulla cognitio nisi in mente esse potest. Attamen alia etiam nonnulla gravitati tribuebam, quae non eodem modo de mente possunt intelligi: ut quod esset divisibilis, mensurabilis etc.

443   Postquam autem haec satis animadverti, et mentis ideam a corporis motusque corporei ideis accurate distinxi, omnesque alias qualitatum realium formarumve substantialium ideas, quas ante habueram, ex ipsis a me conflatas effictasve fuisse deprehendi, perfacile me omnibus dubiis, quae hic proposita sunt, exolvi. Nam primo, non dubitavi quin claram haberem ideam meae mentis, utpote cujus mihi intime conscius eram; nec quin idea illa ab aliarum rerum ideis esset plane diversa, nihilque corporeitatis haberet, quia, cum caeterarum etiam rerum veras ideas quaesivissem, ipsasque omnes in genere cognoscere mihi viderer, nihil plane in iis, quod ab idea mentis non omnino differet, inveniebam. Et longe majorem distinctionem esse videbam inter ea, quae, quamvis de utroque attente cogitarem, nihilominus distincta apparebant, qualia sunt mens et corpus, quam inter ea, quorum quidem unum possumus intelligere non cogitantes de alio, sed quorum tamen unum non videmus absque alio esse posse, cum de utroque cogitamus. Ut sane immensitas Dei potest intelligi, quamvis ad ejus justitiam non attendatur; sed plane repugnat ut, ad utramque attendentes, ipsum immensum et tamen non justum esse putemus. Potestque etiam Dei existentia recte cognosci, quamvis personae sacrosanctae Trinitatis ignorentur, utpote quae non nisi a mente per fidem illustrata percipi possunt; atqui, cum perceptae sunt, nego inter ipsas

444 distinctionem realem ratione essentiae divinae posse intelligi, quamvis ratione relationum admittatur.   [*Sextae Responsiones*]

* * *

(420) Quantumvis apud nos cogitemus, num revera mentis nostrae seu humanae Idola, hoc est cognitio atque perceptio, quidpiam corporeum in se contineat, asserere non audemus, nulli corpori, quocunque velis motu affecto, id quod vocamus cogitationem ulla ratione convenire. Cum enim cernamus quaedam corpora quae non

thought that gravity carried bodies towards the centre of the earth as if it had some knowledge of the centre within itself. For this surely could not happen without knowledge, and there can be no knowledge except in a mind. Nevertheless I continued to apply to gravity various other attributes which cannot be understood to apply to a mind in this way – for example its being divisible, measurable and so on.

But later on I made the observations which led me to make a careful 443 distinction between the idea of the mind and the ideas of body and corporeal motion; and I found that all those other ideas of 'real qualities' or 'substantial forms' which I had previously held were ones which I had put together or constructed from those basic ideas. And thus I very easily freed myself from all the doubts that my critics here put forward. First of all, I did not doubt that I 'had a clear idea of my mind', since I had a close inner awareness of it. Nor did I doubt that 'this idea was quite different from the ideas of other things', and that 'it contained nothing of a corporeal nature'. For I had also looked for true ideas of all these 'other things', and I appeared to have some general acquaintance with all of them; yet everything I found in them was completely different from my idea of the mind. Moreover, I found that the distinction between things such as mind and body, which appeared distinct even though I attentively thought about both of them, is much greater than the distinction between things which are such that when we think of both of them we do not see how one can exist apart from the other (even though we may be able to understand one without thinking of the other). For example, we can understand the immeasurable greatness of God even though we do not attend to his justice; but if we attend to both, it is quite self-contradictory to suppose that he is immeasurably great and yet not just. Again, it is possible to have true knowledge of the existence of God even though we lack knowledge of the Persons of the Holy Trinity, since the latter can be perceived only by a mind which faith has illuminated; yet when we do perceive them, I deny that it is intelligible to suppose that there is a real distinction between them, at least as far as the divine essence is concerned, although such a distinction may be admitted 444 as far as their mutual relationship is concerned.

[*Sixth Replies*: CSM II 296–9]

* * *

However much we ponder on the question of whether the idea of our mind (420) (or a human mind), i.e. our knowledge and perception, contains anything corporeal, we cannot go so far as to assert that what we call thought cannot in any way belong to a body subject to some of sort motion. For since

cogitant, et alia, utpote humana et forte brutorum, quae cogitant, numquid ipse nos sophismatis reos perages, et audaciae nimiae, si propterea concludamus nulla esse corpora quae cogitant...

(421)   Denique, quamdiu nescimus quid a corporibus et illorum motionibus fieri possit, cum et fatearis nullum omnia scire posse, quae Deus in aliquo subjecto posuit, atque ponere valet, absque ipsius Dei revelatione, qui scire potuisti hanc a Deo non fuisse positam in quibusdam corporibus vim et proprietatem ut dubitent, cogitent, etc.?

[*Objectiones Sextae*]

[N]on timui ne me... decepissem, cum ex eo quod viderem quaedam esse corpora quae non cogitant, vel potius clare intelligerem quaedam corpora sine cogitatione esse posse, malui arguere cogitationem ad naturam corporis non pertinere, quam ex eo quod viderem quaedam alia corpora, utpote humana, quae cogitant, concludere cogitationem esse corporis modum. Nam revera nunquam vidi aut percepi humana corpora cogitare, sed tantum eosdem esse homines, qui habent et cogitationem et corpus. Hocque fieri per compositionem rei cogitantis cum corporea ex eo perspexi, quod, rem cogitantem separatim examinando, nihil in illa deprehenderim, quod ad corpus pertineret, ut neque ullam cogitationem in natura corporea seorsim considerata; contra autem, examinando modos omnes tam corporis quam mentis, nullum plane animadverti, cujus conceptus a rei, cujus erat modus, conceptu non penderet. Atque ex eo quod duo quaedam simul juncta saepe videamus, non licet concludere ipsa esse unum et idem; sed ex eo quod aliquando unum ex ipsis absque alio advertamus, optime infertur esse diversa. Neque ab hac illatione potentia Dei nos debet deterrere, quia non minus conceptui repugnat ut ea, quae tanquam duo diversa

445 clare percipimus, fiant intrinsice et absque compositione unum et idem, quam ut ea, quae nullo modo distincta sunt, separentur: atque ideo, si Deus quibusdam corporibus vim cogitandi indiderit (ut revera illam humanis indidit), hanc ipsam vim potest ab iis separare, sicque nihilominus est ab ipsis realiter distincta.

[*Sextae Responsiones*]

we see that there are some bodies that do not think and others, namely human bodies, and perhaps those of the brutes, which do think, will you not yourself convict us of sophistry and of making rash judgements if we infer from this that there are no bodies that think? . . .

Lastly, since we do not know what can be done by bodies and their (421) motions, and since you confess that without a divine revelation no one can know everything which God has imparted or could impart to any object, how can you possibly have known that God has not implanted in certain bodies a power or property enabling them to doubt, think etc.?

[*Sixth Objections*: CSM II 283, 284]

I was not afraid . . . that I might have made the mistake suggested by my critics: seeing that there are 'certain bodies which do not think' (or, rather, clearly understanding that certain bodies can exist without thought), I preferred, they claim, to assert that thought does not belong to the nature of the body rather than to notice that there are certain bodies, namely human ones, which do think, and to infer that thought is a mode of the body. In fact I have never seen or perceived that human bodies think; all I have seen is that there are human beings, who possess both thought and a body. This happens as a result of a thinking thing's being combined with a corporeal thing: I perceived this from the fact that when I examined a thinking thing on its own, I discovered nothing in it which belonged to body, and similarly when I considered corporeal nature on its own I discovered no thought in it. On the contrary, when I examined all the modes of body and mind, I did not observe a single mode the concept of which did not depend on the concept of the thing of which it was a mode. Also, the fact that we often see two things joined together does not license the inference that they are one and the same; but the fact that we sometimes observe one of them apart from the other entirely justifies the inference that they are different. Nor should the power of God deter us from making this inference. For it is a conceptual contradiction to suppose that two things which we clearly perceive as different should become one and the same (that is intrinsically one and the same, as opposed to by 445 combination); this is no less a contradiction than to suppose that two things which are in no way distinct should be separated. Hence, if God has implanted the power of thought in certain bodies (as he in fact has done in the case of human bodies), then he can remove this power from them, and hence it still remains really distinct from them.

[*Sixth Replies*: CSM II 299]

Index

240

31233525R00157

Made in the USA
Middletown, DE
29 December 2018